A Church Ministering to Adults

A CHURCH *Ministering* TO ADULTS

Jerry M. Stubblefield
Editor/Compiler

BROADMAN PRESS
Nashville, Tennessee

Unless otherwise stated, all Scripture quotations are from the King James Version of the Bible.

Scripture quotations marked NASB are from the *New American Standard Bible*. Copyright © The Lockman Foundation, 1960, 1962, 1963, 1968, 1971, 1972, 1973, 1975, 1977. Used by permission.

Scripture quotations marked RSV are from the Revised Standard Version of the Bible, copyrighted 1946, 1952, © 1971, 1973.

Scripture quotations marked NIV are from the HOLY BIBLE, *New International Version*, copyright © 1978, New York Bible Society. Used by permission.

Scripture quotations marked TLB are from *The Living Bible*. Copyright © Tyndale House Publishers, Wheaton, Illinois, 1971. Used by permission.

Scripture quotations marked Williams are from *The New Testament, a Translation in the Language of the People* by Charles B. Williams. Copyright 1937 and 1966. Moody Press, Moody Bible Institute of Chicago. Used by permission.

Scripture quotations marked NKJV are from the *New King James Version*. Copyright © 1979, 1980, 1982, Thomas Nelson, Inc., Publishers.

Library of Congress Cataloging-in-Publication Data

A Church ministering to adults.

  Bibliography: p.
  Includes index.
  1. Christian education of adults. I. Stubblefield,
Jerry M., 1936-
BV1488.C48 1986   253   86-2299
ISBN 0-8054-3235-3

CONTENTS

Preface

A perusal of church papers points out that a high percentage of participants in Bible study are adults. In most churches 50 to 60 percent of Bible study attendance will be adults. Churches depend on adults to provide leadership for all age groups, to serve on church committees, to support the church financially, and to participate in the church's outreach and evangelism program.

Having worked as a minister of education, primarily responsible for the Christian education program for adults, I have been aware of the tremendous potential for effective ministry *with* and *to* adults in the church. A multitude of books are currently available about adults but not a great number dealing with their religious needs.

This book is designed to be a comprehensive volume about how a church *can* and *should* minister to adults. The book is in four major divisions—the adult life cycle, meeting the needs of adults through programs, how an adult learns, and the challenge of adult Christian education.

The book has been written by a cross section of persons who have served in churches and worked primarily with adults. The five major contributors now teach adult Christian education in theological education. The other writers are a teacher of church music and a minister to adults in a local church. Readers will recognize that each writer has a distinctive style and approach to adult ministry. We have tried to preserve the unique features of each contributor.

Readers will also find that the book can be read sequentially, or it can be consulted for major sections or an individual chapter. Each chapter stands alone and refers to other portions as appropriate. Consequently, there is some overlap, but this is inherent in the design.

The topics move from a rationale of adult Christian education, to a survey of adult development, to program planning and needs, to adult learning issues, to the challenge of adult Christian education. In addition, each chapter focuses on implications and opportunities for ministries growing out of the information presented.

Regarding the use of pronouns, we recognize the role of women as well as men in adult educational leadership. In some cases we reference both genders; at other times we use he or him in a generic sense.

Appreciation is due to our publisher, Broadman Press, for encouragement and participation throughout the process. There are many colleagues, denominational and church leaders, who provided invaluable assistance and insights in developing this product. A special appreciation must be expressed to our students who in their process of learning helped us to refine the concepts, values, and skills we share in this volume.

I would like to express my personal gratitude to the trustees and administration of Golden Gate Baptist Theological Seminary for the partial sabbatical which allowed more time to work on this project.

JERRY M. STUBBLEFIELD
STRAWBERRY POINT
MILL VALLEY, CALIFORNIA

Contributors

Lucien E. Coleman, Professor of Adult Education, Southwestern Baptist Theological Seminary, Fort Worth, Texas

R. Michael Harton, Associate Professor of Educational Administration, The Southern Baptist Theological Seminary, Louisville, Kentucky

C. Ferris Jordan, Professor of Adult Education, New Orleans Baptist Theological Seminary, New Orleans, Louisiana

Bruce P. Powers, Professor of Christian Education, Southeastern Baptist Theological Seminary, Wake Forest, North Carolina

Jerry M. Subblefield, Professor of Religious Education, Golden Gate Baptist Theological Seminary, Mill Valley, California

Jim Walter, Minister to Adults, Trinity Baptist Church, San Antonio, Texas

S. Alfred Washburn, Professor of Organ, New Orleans Baptist Theological Seminary, New Orleans, Louisiana

Introduction:

Importance of Adult Christian Education
R. Michael Harton

In excess of twenty million adults participate in planned educational activities each year.[1] That is a remarkable figure in and of itself. Perhaps even more noteworthy is the fact that nearly half (46 percent to be exact) of all courses taken by these adults were provided by nonschools— businesses, labor and professional associations, government agencies, and community organizations.[2] The latter category includes churches. However, churches were among the smallest percentage of community providers. Churches have difficulty in reaching more than 50 percent of their adult members for participation in adult religious education. In a recent study of adult Southern Baptists classified as nonparticipants, some of the reasons given for staying away from church-sponsored educational programs included:[3]

> The program topics do not meet my needs or interests.
> The educational activities I have attended in the past were boring.
> I don't like to be lectured to.
> I learned about my religion in the past.
> The ideas discussed are over my head.
> I'm afraid I'll be asked questions I can't answer.

Write-in responses in this same study clearly indicated that many adults did not consider a church a viable education provider. This alone is cause for alarm in a day when adult education is the fastest growing segment of the education field. Providers are offering an increasing variety of educational courses and activities, and adults are responding in record numbers.

The ineffectiveness of churches in reaching adults has consequences far beyond adults themselves. Children and youth are rarely more active church participants than their parents. Those who wish to reach the young must ultimately be concerned about their parents for several reasons. Parents must be the primary encouragers of participation in church activities and of interest in exploring the gospel message. They are the primary models for values and priorities. Even if children are reached for salvation and church membership, they are likely to become "dropouts" in adolescence if parents do not provide an example of the importance of worship, Bible study, and Christian nurture. Further, parents and churches must become partners if children are to be reared "in the nurture and admonition of the Lord" (see Eph. 6:4).

We must be concerned about the nurture of adults themselves. Parents must be educated, not only in nurturing their children toward faith, but in creative approaches to all aspects of child rearing. Adults need help in dealing with the insecurities and insufficiencies of life, the need for relationships, for hope. They need to develop sensitivity and skill in providing support for fellow strugglers seeking stability in a world of change and flux. More than coping, however, adults deserve help in anticipating crises and challenges so they can plan creative ways of "leaning into life."

In order to reach adults and nurture them effectively through Christian education, we must give consideration to philosophical, theological, and practical program issues. And our efforts must be informed through a knowledge of historic approaches to educating adults. In light of the current interest and proliferation of literature in adult Christian education, one might easily get the notion that it is a rather recent invention. An overview of its history clearly shows that the current concern for effectively nurturing adults in the Christian faith has roots deep in the pre-Christian era and early Christian church.

Early Concern for the Religious
Education of Adults

Sisemore asserts, "In early Hebrew history both the priest and the prophet majored on adult education."[4] This is stretching the point a bit, perhaps, because they probably were not so interested in education as in indoctrination and religious enculturation. Adults certainly were the focus of attention as parents were considered the primary teachers of children. Indeed, the entire adult community bore the responsibility for education of the young.

Most Hebrew education, and that of the early Christian era, was through what McKenzie identifies as random experiential learning.[5] The whole realm of values, norms, and beliefs were the content. Enculturation was the process as the neophyte lived in community and "absorbed" its way of life. In the first three centuries of the Christian church, this process became more formalized in the catechumenate. Though few real details are available about its functioning, it is clear that this early process of "new member training" had distinct stages.[6] Preliminary inquiry was followed by private instruction in the first stage. Then the catechumen was admitted to the first part of Christian worship. Further instruction came in group settings with other new converts. More inquiry followed in the third stage, along with intense instruction before baptism.

Not only was there concern that new converts be properly oriented, there was a recognized need for skilled apologists to defend the tenets of Christianity against its critics and to speak convincingly to educated members of the community. Thus even more formal catechetical centers, or "schools of theology," were set up by church leaders.[7] Clement of Alexandria and Origen were two prominent catechetical teachers.[8] It is to be assumed that the students of the catechumenate, both in its early form and the later schools, were adults.

The Christian church survived its early persecution to become recognized as the "state religion" of the Roman Empire. Along with its growth and eventual popularity came more formalized structures, rituals and doctrine. Among the latter was an emphasis on the ordinances as the sole means of grace. Thus infants became the focus of baptism, and adults became solely interested in partaking of communion. Many forms of instruction vanished, including the educational sermon (a primary means of teaching adults the Scriptures). It is not too farfetched to conclude that what adult Christian education did exist was elitist in that it was limited to developing teachers, intellectuals, and adult leaders of the leadership cast.[9]

The family was supposedly still responsible for whatever religious education occurred. But eventually parents, uninstructed in the Scriptures and the tenets of the faith, were unable to instruct their children. Learning, per se, degenerated to an all-time low by the early Middle Ages. About the only possible religious learning was through the liturgies, and the arts, drama, mosaics, and stained glass depictions of biblical characters and events.[10]

"Sola Scriptura" was the cry of the reformers for a refocusing on the centrality of the Scriptures after a long emphasis on the sacraments. It was important to the reformers that parents reclaim their responsibility for teaching their children. But parents themselves were largely illiterate.

Thus "reformation schools" sprang up, and the "educational sermon" was instituted. Emphasis on the educative value of drama and art continued. Luther's first catechism was for the education of priests and teachers.[11] Adult learning was restored to its former place of importance.

Adult Religious Education in America

Knowles declares from his study of the history of the adult education movement in this country that the church was the "single most universal instrument for intellectual activity" during the colonial period.[12] Education in the community was largely the province of churches. Ministers might be thought of as the first adult educators in the community, and this for several reasons. First, ministers were usually the most educated persons in the community and they often did double duty teaching school (which often met in the church house). Education for ministers was provided by such institutions as Harvard. Harvard is often celebrated as the first institution for higher education in America. What is often overlooked is that it was begun in 1636 for the training of Congregationalist ministers.

The church was often the scene of midweek lectures given by the minister, and included a variety of subjects. Also, since a book was a scare commodity, churches often had "lending libraries" especially for the use of Sunday School teachers. In the 1800s publishers started subscription plans and many ministers/schoolmasters moonlighted as publishers' salesmen. They, in effect, were responsible for encouraging reading in the community. Interestingly, in many communities adults would get together to be sure everyone bought a different book so they could share. Eventually, they began to keep the books in a central place, often the church.

If we were looking for a good example of an organized adult education effort in the early years of our country, we would perhaps have to look at the Catholic Church and its reading circles. These had as their object not only teaching Catholicism but widening the cultural and literary experiences of members as well. In 1854 the New York Catholic Library Association was established, and by 1860 this association had a historical section, a debating club, mechanics' society, and a one-thousand-volume library.[13]

Another institution hailed by adult educators as a major contributor to the adult education movement in this country actually began primarily for the purpose of religious education. Chautauqua opened with a variety of spiritual enrichment seminars and conferences for Sunday School teachers and other interested adults. The summer institutes held on the shores of Chautauque Lake, New York, drew hundreds. The curriculum was quickly expanded to include a variety of cultural subjects such as art and literature. Knowles credited Chautauqua with pioneering the development of such new forms and methods as the correspondence course, summer school, university extension, and book clubs.[14] The correspondence courses at Chautauqua were developed by William Rainey Harper for the purpose of training Sunday School teachers. Sisemore suggested that the Chautauqua movement gave birth to the leadership training programs now followed by most churches.[15]

An outgrowth of the informal summer institutes at Chautauqua was Chautauqua University—a "free university" which was largely unstructural and very unlike the more common German university model. So impressed with the concept was John D. Rockefeller that he bought Chautauqua University and moved it to Chicago where it became the University of Chicago. He hired William Rainey Harper as president, who continued training Sunday School teachers by correspondence from Chicago as he had previously at Chautauqua.

From this brief historical overview, it would be easy to conclude that adult Christian education had a profound influence on adult education in general. It would be perhaps more accurate to say that some significant religious educators who happened to be primarily involved in teaching adults influenced the development of a fledgling "learning society." They did not identify themselves as adult religious educators, per se. Nonetheless, they were deeply involved in adult education. Again witness Harper, who though a professor of Hebrew at Yale, developed correspondence Bible courses at Chautauqua and later developed an extension department as president of Chicago University.

We would, of course, be remiss if we failed to consider the influence of the Sunday School as a major factor in stimulating learning in adulthood. One may recall the huge adult classes, some numbering in the hundreds, that characterized the 1920s and 1930s. Teachers of many of these classes were paid and were expected to devote considerable time to study and preparation. No doubt, in many ways, these classes amounted to "little congregations" which would gather weekly to hear a "sermonette" on a Bible lesson from their teacher. Nonetheless, we must credit the Sunday School with stimulating interest among adults in studying the Bible and in perpetuating a significant educational institution in the community. Sunday School societies and conventions were held across the country and were for a period of time considered a major force supporting continued adult learning. These were largely ecumenical efforts which were influential in the development of the International Lesson Series and in encouraging local newspapers to publish the weekly lesson (a practice which continues to this day in some small-town newspapers).

From 1921 to 1961 Knowles notes that church-based education generally lagged behind in the expansion and differentiation of adult education.[16] Perhaps this was due in part to the institutionalized nature of many (or most) of the huge adult classes. Indeed, growth in some denominations, largely through the Sunday School, was so rapid in the 1950s that there was probably little time to be concerned about teaching methodology and expanded opportunities for learning. Still there were efforts, some national, to focus attention on the improvement of adult education in the churches. These were largely focused on how to infuse the newly developed group techniques into the planning and conducting of educational activities for adults. Most of these efforts were under the auspices of the National Council of Churches or individual churches of the council. For example, in 1956 the National Council of Churches' Department of Administration and Leadership began holding an annual Protestant Laboratory on Group Development to train church leaders to introduce these group techniques on a local level back home.[17]

One of the most elaborate plans to apply group processes to adult religious education programming was developed by Paul Bergevin and John McKinley, both professors of adult education at Indiana University. Dubbed "the Indiana Plan," it was an elaborate process of establishing planning groups, creating learning climates, and training adults to be good participants in the process. Perhaps the greatest contribution of the Indiana Plan was its emphasis upon building collaborative planning groups of the adults who would be affected by and involved in the educational activities which resulted. First published by Bergevin and McKinley under the title *Design for Adult Education in the Church*,[18] the plan was introduced in a number of Protestant and Catholic churches in the late 1950s, often under the supervision of the authors themselves. Though the plan's application to adult religious education was somewhat short-lived, the idea itself survived. After going through several revisions, the plan has become known as "Participation Training" and has been used widely by business and industry. To date it has been perpetuated by "Institutes" sponsored through the Bureau of Adult Studies at Indiana University and the publication of McKinley's *Group Development Through Participation Training.*[19]

Despite these efforts, in the 1960s and 1970s, growth had not only slowed, but many denominations experienced appreciable decline. During this period a great deal of attention was focused in the wider arena of education on the small-group movement and changing technology and methodology. Still, larger classes and the lecture method persisted in many churches.

Perhaps the difficulties churches and, consequently, adult religious education were facing is best understood from a sociological perspective. The migration to the city did not take place overnight but in perspective did occur rather rapidly. With the shift from rural to urban and, subsequently, suburban living, the church often found itself at the periphery rather than the center of community life. For example, communities no longer respected the churches' schedules as they once had and began conducting a variety of activities during traditional "church time." Thus ball games, concerts, classes, and so forth increasingly competed with Wednesday and Sunday services. It was not that society suddenly decided to ignore the church. As Orr and Nicholson suggested, "expansive man" was experimenting with new life-styles requiring more flexible discretionary time and fewer traditional loyalties.[20]

Survival became the primary concern in many religious quarters, with a narrowing of the scope of content and values, and retrenchment against the secular society. Programs were used as means to bolster the institution. Reinhart, in a book published from his dissertation, addressed the issue in 1965:

> Not only does the adult education program have to attract people to a marginal institution to begin with, the program itself is utilized to counter these secular pressures in society. This is evident in the large expenditures of energy directed to undergird the rationale and value system of the religious institution. This in part explains why the adult education program of the church has not been free to develop a broad and inclusive curriculum. The necessities of institutional security demand the focus be upon the programs that function to support this institutional mandate.[21]

Hargrove, in *Religion for a Dislocated Generation*, suggests that a major reason for the disillusionment of adults with the church in the 1960s was their perception that it was more bent on institutional survival than with meeting their needs.[22]

In the 1970s churches began to awaken to the changing demographics: the "baby boomers" were now moving into adulthood, and adults in general were living much longer. People were postponing marriage longer on the one hand while the divorce rate skyrocketed on the other. Adults in almost all age categories including older adults were better educated. Thus there were new opportunities and problems to address: How to reach this large segment of young adults experimenting with their newfound independence and affluence? What to do about this new focal group, the single adult? (Let us understand, single adults were not new, but they had largely been ignored.) How to find meaningful involvement and activity for this burgeoning gray-haired constituency that was less and less content to retire quietly to the rocking chair? How to convince all segments of adults that church-based education was of sufficient quality to be worthy of their investment of time?

Though some evidence of singles and seniors ministries can be found as early as the fifties and sixties, these began to flourish in the seventies. Accompanying the trend was an increasing number of churches which added adult ministers to their staffs. Some churches began to count a Minister to Single Adults or Minister to Senior Adults among their paid or volunteer staff. These often came from the ranks of ministers of education who had little specialized training in adult education but who had in fact spent most of their time programming for adults (whether specific adult classes or training adult leaders of younger ages).

These demographic trends and changing focus of the church on adults have continued in the 1980s. Professional organizations for adult ministers are developing, and one denomination counts more than sixty persons among its ministers specializing in some area of adult ministry. These specialists are leading varied programs of outreach, recreation, and education. In general, they are meeting with gratifying success. Denominations are holding national workshops for ministers and laypersons on how to attract and minister to special groups of adults. "Chautauquas" have become popular, attracting hundreds of older adults to varied programs of Bible study and self-enrichment largely modeled on the original Chautauqua movement.

Still, for all the effort to date, a majority of adults have not noticed or have not responded to churches' "new day for adults." Those who do respond discover that little has changed beyond intensified outreach.

Leaders are still largely untrained, teachers continue to drone on in poorly planned lectures, and there is little opportunity for stimulating and idea-generating interchange among participants. Those who attend expecting to find a worthwhile educational experience find instead that much (sometimes most) of the time is spent socializing, with a few moments reserved for moralizing. (This is not to diminish the value of "fellowship building," but adults new to the church usually have expectations *beyond* getting to know people.)

Twenty-five years ago Fry caricatured the adult Sunday School class as a place to produce "pious Protestants" by placing great emphasis on the standard evangelical-moral virtues: thrift, sobriety, doing good, salvation to the heathen, salvation to anybody, respect for the church and church work, honesty, faith believing, witnessing, and being a good disciple. "The teacher fell heir to the job of teaching these virtues, and the student was cast in the unenviable role of the taught, the never good enough, the talked at, the absorber of words."[23] In many contemporary adult classes, I suspect that the approach has changed little. On the other hand, I wonder if there is as clear a focus on the content today.

This concludes a brief review of the uneven development of what has come to be called adult religious education. A more thorough historical treatment of the growth of adult education including religious education may be found in Malcolm Knowles's *The Adult Education Movement in the United States*, a primary source for this overview. Also see John Elias's comprehensive work, *Foundations and Practice of Adult Religious Education*. The purpose of this sketch has been to show the influence of Christian education on the broad arena of adult education, yet the sporadic efforts within the church. Undoubtedly, there have been some significant developments, yet they have been so sporadic that results have not lasted.

It has been suggested that a primary factor stimulating churches to update programs and methodology today is the realization that adult members are increasingly satisfying their appetites for learning in arenas other than the church. Daffner noted that a reevaluation of their approach to the individual, and a realization that something must be done to stem the exodus, has led many churches to begin educating adults not only for "life in heaven" but also for "action on earth."[24] Such evaluation and redesign of educational efforts with adults must be based on more than current marketing strategies. They must be motivated by conviction that there is both a content and an approach that is unique to church-based education. This uniqueness is based on theological and philosophican underpinnings which guide the design and development of our adult education efforts in the church.

Theological-Philosophical Considerations

Most writers separate their discussion of theology and philosophy when writing about the foundations of Christian education. This I find very difficult, for a personal philosophy grows out of convictions about the nature and potential of humankind and the end of education. These convictions must grow out of theological presuppositions concerning God, His relationship to the crown of His creation, and humankind's response to and in that relationship. Further, it involves the purpose of our existence and the vehicles for accomplishing that purpose. I will address some of these theological issues and merge them into a philosophical structure for conducting adult Christian education.

Crucial Doctrines

Several Christian doctrines are crucial to a "theology of adult education." First we must examine what we believe about God. Some early Christian educators seemed to take the sovereignty of God to the extreme and imply that He was aloof from His creation. This was appropriate, they seemed to contend, because He had placed within His creation all the resources needed to become Godlike. There was little emphasis on the possibility of relationship with the Creator. In response to this view, it must be said that it in no way diminishes God's sovereignty to recognize Him as a God of love who desires fellowship with His creation and who actively seeks a personal relationship with humankind.

A Christian doctrine of God recognizes that He has a master plan for His creation, and He is continually working out that plan. Not only does He have a plan for creation, but He has a plan for every individual life. The Scriptures were given so that we might understand the history of God's attempt to relate to us, and might discover both God's plan for the world and our personal existence. That plan includes developing a personal relationship with Him, discovering our place in His kingdom's work, and activating that plan. God is active in that discovery process through His Spirit who interprets and directs our study of His Word and convicts us of its meaning.

A doctrine of humanity is implied in the above. Realization of God's supreme love for humankind could easily result in elevating human beings to equality with God as some early theologians did. One result of God's love was His decision to create us as beings of free choice, not as puppets or robots. Thus we are free to choose to respond to God's bidding for relationship, or to attempt to be our own "little gods." Some theologians seemed to want to minimize the tendency for us to want to "try our wings" and exercise our independence from our Creator. So one thing we must say about the crown of God's creation and object of His supreme affection is that we are rebellious. Regardless of our rebellion, however, we can never rid ourselves of the gnawing realization that we are not the prime movers of our existence. We are ever uncomfortably aware of a higher Power upon which we are dependent.

A second realization is that this is a moral-social existence. "No man is an island"; we exist in relation to others, and our behavior, even our ideas, has an affect on others. Thus come the inevitable questions: What is the purpose of my life? What is the purpose of life itself? It is our nature as beings created by God ever to seek purpose and meaning for our existence.

This leads naturally to a consideration of the doctrine of salvation. Because of man's misuse of his God-given freedom, he has rebelled against God and withdrawn from Him. Nonetheless, the love that brought persons into the world ever seeks to reunite us in fellowship to our Creator. The Bible is the story of human rebellion and God's efforts through the ages to reclaim the human race. Ultimately, He chose to live among us to accomplish what previous efforts had failed to do: to point persons to the Father, provide both salvation and an example of how to live. The divine act of God in Christ confronts us with an unavoidable decision: yes or no. Each person must ultimately choose to enter into restored fellowship with God or to continue in rebellion.

One further doctrine in a sense integrates those above. God loves people, creates us with the ability to respond to or reject that love, and provides salvation for us in our rebellion. He has a plan for each person. But each person must know about God's love and His offer of salvation. Persons must know of His plan. The vehicle God chose to make known His divine plan is the church. God called the church into being to be His means of ministry and witness to the world. He instituted His church for a twofold purpose: to carry on His ministry of reconciliation and to equip His followers for that ministry.

A warning is appropriate at this point. In organizational development circles, there is much discussion of how to balance the needs of the institution with the needs of the individual. The church corporately has a need to become what God designed: His instrument of salvation and ministry in the world. We all have a need to activate God's plan for our lives, to become all that God intends. This "becoming" takes place in the context of the corporate church. As such then, both the church and individual can actualize their potential. The needs of the corporate church are met as individuals fulfill theirs.

Any philosophical statement about the meaning of adult Christian education must be informed by such theological considerations. For philosophy considers human nature, our potential, and the meaning of our existence. A philosophy of adult education will, in addition to considering the nature of humanity, deal more specifically with the nature of the adult learner and with the goal of education. Why consider philosophy at all? Simply stated, our personal philosophies guide our personal actions and relationships.

It may seem somewhat paradoxical, in the face of world conflict and national crime, to state that human beings are inherently good. That would be, in fact, too strong a statement. And yet to reject it may imply the opposite: that humans are inherently bad or evil. Let us say that as a child, one has the potential for both good and bad but is inherently neither. One *is*, however, basically selfish, which may ultimately lead one to do evil things for self-gratification. It need not be so ultimately, however. The environment, through parents and significant others, may provide the nurture of such quality as to satisfy the inherent need for love, acceptance, a feeling of self-worth, and ultimately of personal meaning. With such nurture individuals are free to focus outside themselves on the world and their place therein.

Once again, we see the need for a theological perspective: Christian educators believe that it is through modeling Christian values, exposure to and study of the Scriptures, and ultimately through salvation that individuals achieve their true nature as co-workers with God.

The nature of the adult learner is a key component to a philosophy of adult educators also. The adult is in a constant state of becoming and is therefore potentially in a constant state of readiness to learn. Such readiness, however, occurs on several planes and a narrow focus on the spiritual, emotional, or intellectual will not recognize such readiness in its broader sense. One who has need to be directive and plan unilaterally the learning episodes of adults will frequently be frustrated with adults' seeming low motivation. Those having faith in the ability of adults to be self-directing are more likely to be in touch with this constant state of readiness.

Adults recognize some deficiencies and have needs that they see may possibly be alleviated through some learning channel. They may not recognize other needs and deficiencies, and need help in focusing on them. They may welcome such help and may even consider new interests if assisted gently by one whom they see as having their best interest at heart and who does not threaten their freedom. Not only can adults be helped to focus on what they want or need to learn, but can be helped to actively pursue learning. They may also learn to diagnose their own learning needs, to identify and secure for themselves the necessary resources.

The purpose of adult Christian education should be to help adults establish the essential saving relationship with Jesus Christ and discover their place in His divine plan. This may be done through any or all of at least three focuses: (1) to build on early nurture which contributed to helping the individual assume the natural social relationships and to enhance those relationships according to Christian principles, (2) to identify and remedy areas where early nurture failed in preparing him to be a fully functioning individual for his stage in development, and (3) to help the individual get in touch with himself, his uniqueness, the gifts he brings to his world and, further, to help him actualize those gifts so that they become identifiable contributions. Concerning the latter, adult Christian education does more than help persons cope with the world as they find it but helps them contribute toward creating a better world! Lindeman saw the purpose of adult education as putting meaning into the whole of life.[25] Indeed, this is the goal of adult Christian education as informed by the gospel of Jesus Christ.

Perhaps the best integration of the theological and philosophical may be found in Colossians 1:28: "Christ we proclaim, teaching every person and warning every person in all wisdom, that we may present every person mature in Christ Jesus" (author's paraphrase). The theological content and context are clear as is the goal toward which such proclamation and education strive. Does this mean, however, that to be *Christian* adult education, the content must be explicitly theological? And just what did Paul mean by *maturity*? A brief consideration of these two questions is in order.

Recall from the historical overview that the early Hebrews drew no sharp distinctions between the religious and the secular. If we could recapture their broad view, we could see all of life as encompassed by God's concern. This should lead to a broader view of curriculum addressing all areas of life which require thoughtful coping and the quest for meaning. McKenzie offers what is to this writer a liberating view of religious education. He suggests that our practice of religious education may be defined both by our *content* and our *intent*.[26] Thus, a study of the Gospels is religious education by virtue of the scriptural content. By the same token, however, a course that we offer internationals in English as a second language may be religious education by virtue of our intent to help them live more fully functioning and satisfying lives.

Expectations for Effective Adult Christian Education

Several writers have chastised churches for using adult programs primarily for the purpose of producing institutional loyalty.[27] Reflecting on the kinds of learning experiences provided for adults by churches, we may conclude that nearly all are directed at skill development, the end of which is keeping the organization running smoothly. Adults may legitimately ask, "Where are the resources and experiences to help me grow spiritually, mentally, emotionally, in the area of relationships, and so forth?" In a day when "lifelong learning" has become the catchword for continued development in adulthood, adults may not be too enthusiastic about spending their lives learning how to perpetuate an institution!

Besides the problem of focus on institutional loyalty, the church often has been too provincial in its curriculum. It has tended to perpetuate the Platonic separation of soul, mind, and spirit, seeking to treat only the soul. The debate is old concerning the difference between secular education and Christian education. I would not take issue with Hayes's assertion that "discovering the relationship between the inner work of the Spirit and the educative process is one of the great tasks of the Christian educator."[28] But his claim that Christian education is basically different because of the added resource of the Holy Spirit is to preclude Christian public schoolteachers from seeing their calling as spiritual in the same sense. The logical conclusion is that there is no need for this Christian teacher to pray for the Spirit to open and guide young minds that they may be developed toward their fullest as God's children through mastery of math, social studies, or language skills. What is needed is a return to the Hebrew understanding which saw all of life as being the concern of

God. This broadened theological viewpoint has implications for enabling us to address the whole realm of adult life concerns.

Christian adult education must of course be concerned with explicitly religious content. It must be concerned with evangelism, helping adults establish a vital relationship with Jesus Christ. But it must also address life concerns as Christian adults attempt to live out their sense of calling under God. This last section will identify issues and concerns which adults should expect their Christian education programs to address.

It is an outworn phrase, but nonetheless true, that we must start where people are. Where are they? It is safe to assume that all adults are in the midst of gaining or maintaining a sense of equilibrium between internal and external demands, between what they want to be, what they sense that they should be, and what they sense others want of them. The literature on adult development and life tasks is rich with implications for educational programming with adults. *Young adults* are struggling for a sense of stability and moral guidance amid the experimentation so characteristic of this age group. Many are haunted by their insufficiencies as parents, others with the dilemmas of a satisfying, singles life-style.

Fear of failure, of stagnation, and of the overwhelming challenge of teenage children concern many *middle-aged adults*. Moral guidance for professional decisions and marital enrichment are among the concerns of this age.

Fear of loss (and actual loss), despair, challenge to mentor, to broker wisdom, to creatively grandparent, to have a sense of "worthwhileness" about their contribution in their younger years—nearly all these issues face *older adults*.

John Claypool once recounted, in a faculty retreat at The Southern Baptist Theological Seminary, a conversation with an old medical doctor friend. Claypool said he remembered saying to the doctor, "I'd really like to be a doctor because you can help people so tangibly!" The doctor's response was, "What people need is someone to teach them how to live. I've got jillions of patients who are perfectly healthy but are miserable because they don't know what to do with it!"

Adults have a right to expect their church to provide spiritual insight (*not* just easy answers) to life concerns and crises. A young civil engineer, partner in his own engineering firm, once approached me for "advice." His problem concerned making the "right" political contributions in recognition that their business largely depended on government con-tracts. For this Christian adult, this presented a moral dilemma which his non-Christian partners failed to understand (and openly ridiculed). "Does Scripture offer any insight on such matters?" he wanted to know.

Christian adult educators must have not only the programming skills but the theological wisdom to bring God's Word to bear. Second Timothy 3:16-17 is pointedly appropriate for addressing adult life concerns: "All Scripture is inspired by God and profitable for teaching, for reproof, for correction, for training in righteousness; that the man of God may be adequate, equipped for every good work" (NASB).

Lewis Joseph Sherrill shared in his classic *The Struggle of the Soul* that

> the church is, above all others, the place where the Word of God is allowed to confront man, speaking its own message undiluted and unscreened. The church can then become spokesman for God to those who know their own inadequacy, who desire the healing of the self down to its deepest foundations, and who are willing to face, not merely the word of man, but the Word of God, with whatever it may promise and whatever it may require.[29]

Sherrill gave a divine realm to all human experience, challenging us to help adults see the possibility of God working in the mundane and the crisis times of life.

> By "confrontation" is simply meant that in crisis, God confronts man. That is to say, the crisis, which is a time of decision as between advancing into growth or shrinking back from its perils, is a time when God confronts the human creature.[30]

Adults need to be led to the realization that even in the traumatic, God is saying: "What will we do with this?" And He is providing the possibility for growth.

Adults should expect educational programming characterized by an atmosphere of freedom that enables exploration of ideas at a depth that does more than simply scratch the surface. Many adult Bible or discipleship classes skirt the real (excuse the colloquialism) *gut-level* issue in favor of pious "nonjudgmental" platitudes. Often such avoidance maneuvers are a function of the level of trust in the group. A part of the educator's task is to help adults probe below the surface, engaging the affective or "feeling level."

I was amused at the dynamics of my own Bible study class. On one occasion the group was attempting to analyze some brief case studies to determine if the central characters were being led by God's Spirit. The point of the studies was to prompt reflection on our ability to rely on the Spirit in our daily lives.

Several members seemed to want to avoid addressing the real issue with such comments as: "Who are we to judge another," and "It's hard to say." Without prompting, a young attorney openly admitted that, in the heat of courtroom arguments, it's not easy to know what is the "Christian" course of action. A young businesswoman followed with a difficulty she was facing professionally. Suddenly the whole tenor of the discussion was changed as ideas and testimonies were shared and challenged. No one seemed ready to leave when the bell sounded to end the period. A common point of struggle was identified, and growth through sharing took place.

Robert Bellah suggests two characteristics of the mature adult life: the passive life of contemplation and the active life of involvement in world transformation.[31] In addition to the spiritual meditative aspects of such contemplation must certainly be added the reflective observation on experience essential to real learning, as suggested by David Kolb.[32] Adults commonly report as significant to learning those approaches which allow discussion, reflection, and interaction with the materials. Leaders (traditional teachers) who are bent on "covering the lesson" or know only a didactic method of teaching may see little evidence of learning in his or her classroom because there is little opportunity for interaction or reflection. (Tough found in his research that teachers sometimes get in the way of learning!)

A theological perspective which should pervade our efforts at Christian adult education (whether adults expect it or not) is an emphasis on the dynamic nature of God's creation with all that implies, physically, emotionally, and spiritually. Specifically with regard to the spiritual, adults need to come to have a dynamic view of that relationship with Jesus Christ called salvation. For too many adults, salvation is a fire-insurance policy they took out years ago. I feel one of the reasons testimonies are so seldom a part of our gatherings is that they so often harkened back to an experience in the distant past. They rarely reflect any awareness of what God is *doing* in the present. Earl Zeigler recounts:

> I once knew an old gentleman who gave a weekly testimony in a mid-week service. He told over and over of his conversion and how because of its new power he rushed out of the house and leaped over the fence. As I think back upon it, I think his leap was the last word of his experience.[33]

A dynamic view of God's creation and His will for humankind sees us all as ever in a state of *becoming.* "To those who believed he gave the power to *become* the children of God" (see John 1:12). As we grow and change, we learn more about ourselves. Ideally, new gifts are discovered, new abilities developed. All this knowledge, the gifts, the abilities must be dedicated to God in daily commitment.

Adults should expect to discover through their Christian education program the true *nature* and *mission* of the church. They should probe the meaning of their nature as priests (1 Pet. 2:5-9) and the commensurate mission implied (2 Cor. 5; Eph. 4:12). Adults need to be challenged to realize in their own meaningful way that God never calls anyone to come and sit. One and the same with the call to salvation is a call to service. Further, adults need to understand that God never calls anyone to service whom He does not equip through spiritual gifts.

In sum, adults deserve and should come to expect from their Christian education program to be led in a discovery of God's plan, not only for His entire creation but for their individual lives. Discovering that personal plan, they need guidance in actualizing it through the development of their gifts and the implications for applying those gifts in every area of life. Such a task is consistent with the previously examined theological and philosophical presuppositions. It is the "fleshing out" of all that we believe about our calling as Christian adult educators and the potential of adults to continue to growth throughout life in Christlikeness.

Notes

1. National Center for Education Statistics, *Participation in Adult Education, 1981* (Washington, D.C. NCES, U. S. Dept. of Education, 1982).

2. Ibid.

3. R. Michael Harton, "A Factor Analytic Study of Reasons for Nonparticipation in Church-based Education Among Southern Baptist Adults," unpublished Ed.D. dissertation, Indiana University, 1984.

4. John Sisemore, "The Challenge of Adult Christian Education" *Adult Education in the Church*, ed. Roy B. Zuck and Gene A. Getz (Chicago: Moody Press, 1970), p. 10.

5. Leon McKenzie, *The Religious Education of Adults* (Birmingham, Ala.: Religious Education Press, 1982), p. 167.

6. Bruce Reinhart, *The Institutional Nature of Adult Christian Education* (Philadelphia: Westminster Press, 1962), p. 27.

7. John Elias, *Foundations and Practice of Adult Religious Education* (Malabar, Fla.: Robert E. Krieger Publishing Co., 1982), p. 122.

8. Ibid.

9. Leon McKenzie, *The Religious Education of Adults*, p. 44.

10. William Bean Kennedy, "Christian Education Through the Ages," in Marvin Taylor, ed., *An Introduction to Christian Education* (Nashville: Abingdon Press, 1966), p. 23.

11. John Elias, *Foundations and Practice of Adult Religious Education*, p. 125.

12. Malcolm Knowles, *The History of the Adult Education Movement in America* (New York: Holt, Reinhart & Winston, 1962), p. 8.

13. Ibid., p. 23.

14. Ibid., p. 38.

15. Sisemore, *Adult Education*, p. 11.

16. Knowles, *History*, p. 145.

17. Ibid., p. 147.

18. Paul Bergevin and John McKinley, *Design for Adult Education in the Church* (Greenwich, Conn.: Seabury Press, 1958).

19. John McKinley, *Group Development Through Participation Training* (New York: Paulist Press, 1980). A teacher's manual detailing leadership theory and procedures for training groups in the use of "P.T." as well as a smaller "Participant's Manual" in workbook format were still in print in 1985.

20. John Orr & Patrick Nichelson. *The Radical Suburb: Soundings in Changing American Character* (Philadelphia: Westminster Press, 1970).

21. Bruce Reinhart, *The Institutional Nature of Adult Christian Education*, p. 51.

22. Barbara Hargrove, *Religion for a Dislocated Generation* (Valley Forge, Pa.: Judson Press, 1980), p. 81.

23. John R. Fry, *A Hard Look at Adult Christian Education*. (Philadelphia: Westminster Press, 1961), p. 35.

24. Deffner in Knowles, *The Adult Education Movement*, p. 145.

25. Eduard Lindeman, *The Meaning of Adult Education* (Montreal: Harvest House, 1961), p. 5. (First published by New Republic, Inc., New York, 1926).

26. Leon McKenzie, *Adult Religious Education: The 20th Century Challenge* (West Mystic, Conn.: 1975), p. 13.

27. Compare Ray H. Ryan, *Educational Ministry with Adults*, (Nashville: Board of Education of the United Methodist Church, 1972), p. 23 and Reinhart, *The Institutional Nature of Christian Education*, p. 29.

28. Edward L. Hayes, "Theological Foundations of Adult Christian Education," *Adult Education in the Church*, p. 30.

29. Lewis Joseph Sherrill, *The Struggle of the Soul* (New York: The MacMillan Co., 1951), p. 146.

30. Ibid., p. 27.

31. Robert Bellah

32. David Kolb, *The Modern American College: Responding to the New Realities of Diverse Students and a Changing Society* ed. Arthur Chickering (San Francisco: Jossey Bass, 1981), pp. 232-255.

33. Earl F. Zeigler, *Christian Education of Adults* (Philadelphia: The Westminster Press, 1958), p. 142.

PART I:

Who are the Adults?
The Adult Life Cycle

An understanding of the adult life cycle is crucial to an awareness of the needs of adults and to effective programming. Part 1 examines the adult life cycle from several different perspectives. Seven chapters comprise this section.

Chapter 1 presents an overview of the adult life structure. It describes the various approaches to the developmental needs and tasks of adulthood. Theories of adult development are also explored.

Chapters 2, 3, and 4 examine the different developmental tasks and needs of the three major periods of adulthood—young, middle, and older. Each chapter focuses upon the demographics, characteristics, tasks, and needs of each period of adulthood. Each chapter seeks to enumerate the implications and opportunities for ministry.

Since 1970 the church has faced a new challenge: single adults, the subject of chapter 5. Single adults have been identified as: always single, widowed, divorced, and separated. Churches have been ministering to young people who are always single—college and career—but now must consider the large number of single adults in each category covering the adult life cycle.

Chapter 6 focuses upon senior adults with their expanding opportunities for ministry and service. With persons living longer, America now has an entire generation of retirees. Many churches have good ministries to senior adults and are also finding service ministries that senior adults are performing.

Adult faith development in chapter 7 concludes Part 1. Understanding where persons are in their faith development is very significant in designing programs and activities that will help adults meet their needs and also challenge them to grow.

1

Adult Life Structure

C. Ferris Jordan

Robert Browning described the adult years as the period of life "for which the first was made."[1] While this observation may appear to de-emphasize the importance of the preschool, children, and youth years, it helps overcome the lack of attention given to adulthood as a part of the life span. The quotation also negates any tendency to relegate all or most of life's excitement and dynamic to the younger years and to perceive adulthood as dull, static, and uneventful.

Most people spend most of their lives in the adult years, but this area of developmental psychology has been studied the least. Dedicated effort has been expended to explore the preschool, children, and adolescent portions of the life span. However, until recently, it was assumed that the years labeled "adulthood" did not merit special study. The assumption was based on the false premise that adults entered that phase of their lives with the personality and coping skills they had developed in their formative years adequately equipped to move satisfactorily over the plateau of adulthood. The tendency to neglect the study of adults was also enhanced by a disproportionate emphasis on staying young in a youth-oriented culture.

Recent decades have brought significant numerical growth in the adult population. Projections to the year 2030 reveal steady growth in the senior adult population in the United States.[2] These facts of life have created more awareness and curiosity about the aging process and the adult years. Adults are existentially aware that their life journeys are more like ascending a mountain, with all the adventure and risk that implies, than the falsely assumed plateau trek. They are searching for self-understanding and for insight into adult development.

The concept "adult" too often has carried with it the sense of someone who is fully developed physically and psychologically. That erroneous idea had its roots in the derivation of the word *adult*[3] and was given impetus by floundering efforts to define adulthood.[4] Fortunately, the

33

quest for enlightenment about adulthood has produced various theories about adult development, all of which point toward patterns of change, potential for continuous growth, and the need to press toward maturity. Adults have not arrived. They confront the lifelong alternatives to change and grow, or to deteriorate and die.

The purpose of this chapter is to present an overview of some theories of adult development. Three theories will be singled out for special attention. At the conclusion, a summary will be offered, and some implications will be drawn for adult ministry in the church.

Adult Development: A Biblical Concept

Before students of adult development had propounded their conclusions that the adult years are more comparable to a journey than to a destination, the writers of Scripture had described the fulfilling life as a dynamic, growing experience.

A classic illustration of the scriptural view that the satisfying life is marked by growth and change is Psalm 1. The psalmist likened the blessed man to a tree that brings forth fruit and does not wither. That life-style is contrasted with the ungodly, stagnant life that is likened to chaff which the wind drives away. A similar contrast was drawn by Jeremiah. The model adult is described in these terms:

> He shall be like a tree planted by the waters,
> Which spreads out its roots by the river,
> And will not fear when heat comes;
> But her leaf will be green,
> And will not be anxious in the year of drought,
> Nor will cease from yielding fruit (Jer. 17:8, NKJV).

The prophet pronounced a curse on persons who trust in themselves and reject God. They are likened to "a shrub in the desert" (Jer. 17:6, NKJV) and are said to inhabit "parched places in the wilderness" (Jer. 17:6, NKJV). These Old Testament references highlight the premium God places on a life marked by growth and His desire to help each person experience such vitality.

The New Testament builds upon and reinforces the Old Testament concepts of development. When Jesus called His apostles, He committed Himself to make them "becomers" (Mark 1:17).[5] He held out before adults like Zacchaeus, the Samaritan woman, Nicodemus, and the rich young ruler the possibility of a relationship with Him that would move them beyond their unfulfilled, stagnant lives toward lives potentially fruitful. Jesus proclaimed the necessity of new birth (John 3:3) and His desire to give abundant life (John 10:10). He called persons to become His disciples and commanded the church to make disciples (Matt. 28:18-20). The Greek word translated disciple in English is a word that means "learner." It implies diligent endeavor on the part of the disciple. Thus, Jesus knew humankind's potential and need for the change, adaptability, and openness that learning requires.

Building on Jesus' announced intention to help His followers be "becomers" and His expectation that they learn of Him, Paul became a model as a developing person and admonished early Christians to follow his example. Even in his latter years, Paul spoke of continued growth. With great power of concentration, diligent effort, and a goal orientation, he forgot things past that would be a hindrance and reached forth to the future (Phil. 3:13-14). Neither past achievements nor former failures would deter him from future development.

The reality of adult development is a biblical concept. Christian educators find great delight in the findings of recent researchers that corroborate the biblical record. They also are benefited by those attempts that have been made to describe patterns of development in the adult years and to formulate theories about adult life structures. The next section will present a historical sketch of adult developmental studies and an overview of the categories into which developmental theories fall.

Adult Development: A Search for Understanding

The study of life-span developmental psychology, and especially adult psychology, represents one of the most recent areas of investigation in that field. The science of life-span study began to emerge in 1838 "when Quetelet, the founder of life-span psychology, applied the cross-sectional method to the study of development."[6] Most early developmental studies focused on the child. Later, the latter periods of life were explored.

The study of adult development has claimed growing attention, and the pace of research has quickened over the past two decades. The growing interest has been stimulated by numerous factors, not the least of which have been the increasing numbers of adults, the lengthening life expectancy, and the need to know about the predictable events of adulthood in order to cope with the rapid change in highly advanced technological societies. This heightened interest in the study of adult development has resulted in numerous theories about how the adult years unfold.

A theory is simply "a system of general concepts that provides a framework for organizing and interpreting observations."[7] Theories can address the same observation from a variety of perspectives. Thus, the theories of adult life can be grouped in several categories. In the following paragraphs, some grouping will be suggested with brief attention being given to theorists and theories that are representative of each category.[8]

Psychoanalytic Theory

The first body of theory cited is psychoanalytic theory. This theory, as developed by Sigmund Freud, focuses primarily on emotional and personality development. Freud's studies about sexuality and aggression as the two primary motives underlying behavior; his concept of the unconscious; his model of the structure of personality that includes the id, ego, and superego as the components; and his ideas about identification and transference all have special interest for students of adult development.

A number of theorists have revised and expanded Freud's work. One of the early revisionists was his protegé Carl Jung. The latter's theory differed from Freud's in two significant areas. He saw personality as the result of goals and aspirations as well as needs and past experiences. The second area of difference was related to his concept of the collective unconscious. He insisted that each individual has a personal unconscious growing out of life experiences and a collective unconscious derived from previous generations. Jung's insights into the process of personal integration that brings the many elements of personality into a unified whole and produces the self have been helpful to students of adult development.

Psychosocial Theory

A second body of theory about adult development is designated psychosocial. The word includes the ideas of the person and the society, and implies interactions between tensions within the persons and societal expectations imposed upon the person. Psychosocial theory builds upon psychoanalytical theory but goes beyond it in its focus upon persons' significant roles in influencing their own development and in its emphasis upon potential for growth throughout the adult span.

Psychosocial theory is based on five organizing concepts: "(1) stages of development; (2) developmental tasks, (3) the psychosocial crisis; (4) the central process for resolving crisis; and (5) coping behavior."[9] Consider the meaning of each component.

"*Stages* refer to periods of life when behavior is dominated by a particular organization or perspective."[10] What occurs in each stage of development will impact progress in later stages. Erikson,[11] Newman and Newman,[12] Robert Peck,[13] Daniel Levinson,[14] and Roger Gould[15] are theorists who have worked within a psychosocial framework and suggested stages of adult development.

The concept of *developmental tasks* was proposed by Robert Havighurst. The tasks "refer to a set of skills and competencies that are acquired as the person gains increased mastery over the environment. . . . [They] reflect gains in physical skills, intellectual skills, social skills, and emotional skills."[16] The expectations of culture figure prominently in determining developmental tasks.

The third component in psychosocial theory is *psychosocial crisis*. This refers to persons' efforts to resolve the tension created at each stage of development when societal expectations make psychic demands upon them. Resolution must be achieved before progress can be made toward the next stage. A definite interrelationship exists between the developmental tasks and psychosocial crisis of each stage of development.

The central process for resolving crisis is the fourth component suggested by Newman and Newman. This process involves working through a polarity which is created at each stage—identity vs. isolation, generativity vs. stagnation, integrity vs. despair—so that the impact of the negative pole is minimal and can afford an opportunity for better understanding of self and one's social environment.

Coping behavior, the final component in psychosocial therapy, "refers to active efforts to resolve stress and to create new solutions to the challenges of each developmental stage."[17] Each individual develops strategies for coping with life challenges. Discovering effective strategies is an integral part of adult growth and development.

Fulfillment Theory

Many theorists take the emphasis upon adults' contributions to their development a step beyond the proponents of psychosocial theories. The latter portray adults' efforts to reduce tension and to seek equilibrium in their lives. Fulfillment theorists add to that kind of effort the very deliberate, goal-oriented struggles that mark adults as they pursue a quality of life that brings real satisfaction. The hope for achieving fulfillment and the intentionality issuing from that hope prompt psychological growth, according to fulfillment theorists. Competence, self-acceptance, and self-actualization are important concepts in this body of theory.[18] Charlotte Buhler, Carl Rogers, and Abraham Maslow are among the significant contributors to the fulfillment theory of adult development.[19]

Behavioral Learning Theory

A fourth category of adult developmental theory is behavioral learning theory. The proponents of this view hold that human behavior is learned in response to conditions in the environment. Pavlov's findings about classical conditioning, B. F. Skinner's principles about operant or instrumental conditioning with their focus upon reinforcement and punishment as factors in learning, and Albert Bandura's concepts of social-learning theory with its emphasis upon adults' tendency to imitate models who have status all have implications for understanding adult development.[20]

Cognitive Theory

Cognitive theories are another part of psychologists' efforts to understand and describe adult development. The emphasis here is upon the adult as *knower*. "The capacities to interpret meaning, to solve problems in a creative way, to synthesize information, and to critically analyze a statement are all examples of cognition."[21] The findings of Piaget about cognitive development play a prominent part in this body of adult developmental theory.[22] They reveal potential for new approaches to problem-solving in adulthood and show how adults have capability for growth through full utilization of their cognitive skills.

Social-Cultural Theory

A final category of adult developmental theory that will be mentioned here is social-cultural theory. This body of information focuses upon the impact of social roles upon adult progress. Persons become socialized and develop their personalities as they perform the increasingly diverse and complex social roles that their culture requires of them. Culture also impacts persons in terms of age-related norms and expectations. Adult responses to roles, norms, and expectations play a vital role in adult development. Berniece Neugarten is a prominent proponent of the social-cultural theory.[23]

The diversity and multiplicity of theories about adult development bespeak the complexity and dynamic character of the adult years. They also serve to warn against dogmatism about how adults develop. The student of adulthood would do well to be eclectic, drawing insights from all the theories. Whatever else the theories may communicate, they certainly represent adulthood as a period characterized by change, growth, challenge, and potential. The leader of adults in Christian education can seize the teachable moments created by the stages, developmental tasks, and psychosocial crises and can cooperate with the Holy Spirit to use those challenges to lead each person to full potential in Christ.

With this overview of adult developmental theory in mind, consider three theoretical schemes in detail. Havighurst's developmental tasks, Erikson's psychosocial stages, and Levinson's life structure view are the concepts to be considered.

Adult Development:
A Developmental Task Definition

A body of theory that has greatly aided students of life-span development in general and adult development specifically is Robert Havighurst's developmental task concept. Havighurst posited the idea that development can be studied in terms of a set of tasks that may be identified for each period of life from birth to death. He defined a developmental task as

> a task which arises at or about a certain period in the life of the individual, successful achievement of which leads to his happiness and to success with later life tasks, while failure leads to unhappiness in the individual, disapproval by the society, and difficulty with later tasks.[24]

A study of Havighurst's task statements will reveal that they are very culturally and socioeconomically determined.[25] Nevertheless, they have provided useful signposts by which an adult can study personal progress and by which adult religious educators can plan and implement learning experiences that will elicit adult participation and meet learners' needs.

According to Havighurst, adulthood includes three periods: early adulthood, middle adulthood, and later maturity. He listed the following tasks for each stage.

Early Adulthood
1. Selecting a mate (or adjusting to unmarried adult status).
2. Learning to live with a marriage partner.

3. Starting a family.
4. Rearing children (or learning to relate to the children of others).
5. Managing a home.
6. Getting started in an occupation.
7. Taking a civic responsibility.
8. Finding a congenial social group.

Middle Adulthood

1. Achieving adult civic and social responsibility.
2. Establishing and maintaining an economic standard of living.
3. Assisting teenage children to become responsible and happy adults.
4. Developing adult leisuretime activities.
5. Relating oneself to one's spouse as a person.
6. Accepting and adjusting to the physiological changes of middle age.
7. Adjusting to aging parents.

Later Maturity

1. Adjusting to decreasing physical strength and health.
2. Adjusting to retirement and reduced income.
3. Adjusting to death of spouse.
4. Establishing an explicit affiliation with one's age group.
5. Meeting social and civic obligations.
6. Establishing satisfactory physical living arrangements.[26]

Adults can chart their progress through adulthood in terms of acquiring the skills and competencies required to complete developmental tasks, according to Havighurst. Fulfillment in life is linked with successful accomplishment of each group of tasks in proper sequence. Arrested development, personal frustration, and disapproval from society are the lot of adults who fail to negotiate the tasks as they arise.

One can see how the list of tasks fits Havighurst's definition. Consider the task statements related to parenting, for example. The adult who fails to accomplish successfully the task of rearing younger children will have considerable difficulty in the middle years when confronted with the task of assisting teenage children to become responsible and happy adults. Some of the problems attendant upon that maladjustment may continue to manifest themselves in that same adult's life when he is in his senior years and must relate to his children as middle adults—those same offspring to whom he failed to relate when they were children and teenagers.

To take another example, adults who fail to develop adult leisuretime activities in their middle years may have difficulty adjusting to retirement in their senior years. Failure to complete earlier tasks does seem to have a bearing upon success with later tasks. However, students of Havighurst's theory should avoid all tendency toward determinism. The resourceful, creative adult has potential for finding ways to overcome earlier failures. Adults who are willing to avail themselves of God's resources can find ways to cope with tasks as they arise and even to deal with tasks that may present themselves out of the expected sequence.

Adult Development:
A Life Structure Approach

A second approach to the study of adult development is the life structure theory. Foremost among the researchers who have offered this proposal is Daniel J. Levinson. This psychologist worked with a team of researchers at Yale University. Their study was focused upon a group of males in the thirty-five-to-forty-five age range whom they observed and interviewed over a decade. The results of their study were published in *The Seasons of a Man's Life.*

An essential concept in Levinson's theory is his "individual life structure." Life structure is the pattern or design of a person's life at any given time. The primary components of the life structure are related to the choices a person makes. According to Levinson, the important choices in adult life have to do with work; family; friendships and love relationships of various kinds; where to live; leisure; involvement in religious, political, and community life; immediate and long-term goals.[27] Levinson concluded that two or three componets have a central place in the structure, others are important but more peripheral, and still others are marginal.[28] The components most likely to be central in a person's life structure are occupation, marriage-family, friendship and peer relationships, ethnicity and religion, and leisure.[29]

The life structure is never exactly the same for any two persons. Moreover, the life structure varies from time to time, even within a given life. The Levinson team discovered a predictable sequence in the developing life structure. The pattern "consists of a series of alternating stable (structure-building) periods and transitional (structure-changing) periods."[30] In each stable period the adult makes key choices, builds a structure around them, and pursues goals related to them. A stable period ordinarily lasts six or seven years, ten at the most. A transitional period marks the end of the existing life structure and paves the way for a new one. During the transitional period the existing structure is reappraised, possibilities for change are explored, and commitments to the crucial choices essential to a new life structure are made. Each stable and transitional period has developmental tasks that mark its unique place in the life cycle. As new developmental tasks arise and the person's values and priorities change, a component may shift from the center to the periphery and vice versa. These changes and the new commitments they require account for the new structure.

The Periods in Adult Development

The sequence of periods identified by Levinson and associates begins with the Early Adult Transition (age 17-22) which links adolescence and early adulthood. It is followed by a structure-building period, Entering the Adult World, which lasts from about 22 to 28. The Age Thirty Transition (28-33) bridges the former structure with the Settling Down Period (33 to 40), which marks the close of early adulthood. The Mid-life Transition (40-45) links early and middle adulthood. The first structure-building period in middle adulthood, Entering Middle Adulthood, lasts from age 45 to 50 and is followed by the Age 50 Transition (age 50-55). Culmination of Middle Adulthood (age 55-60) is followed by the Late Adult Transition (age 60-65).[31]

Some of the issues prominent in each of the periods included on the chart will now be presented.

Early Adult Transition. In bridging the gap between adolescence and young adulthood, a person negotiates the challenges of the early adult transition. Levinson identified twin tasks that must be accomplished. The *first task* is to begin moving out of the adolescent world. This requires that one's place in that world be questioned, that relationships be terminated or modified, and that the self formed in the adolescent world be reappraised. A significant step in performing task one is separating from parents and the family of origin. Supportive parents will prepare their older adolescents and themselves for the separation. Less-mature adults may seek to postpone the agony of the empty nest, creating a great deal of separation anxiety for their own grown offspring and for themselves. The separation may occur quite gradually as the young adult goes away to college and returns home each weekend or less frequently, or as the fledgling adult rents an apartment in the same town and comes in and out of the parental home for meals and other occasions. For the separation to be achieved, moving out of the house must be accompanied by a healthy emotional adjustment that fosters greater psychological distance from the family of origin.

The *second task* of the early adult transition is to make a successful entrance into the adult world. The young adult must test the water, so to speak. Possibilities in the new world are explored, an initial adult identity is consolidated, and some preliminary choices related to the adult world are made. This task may require educational pursuits, vocational choices, and establishing new friendships. Adults struggling with ability to achieve intimacy may have special difficulty entering the adult world because of incompetency in establishing and developing new relationships beyond the family circle.

Entering the Adult World. The chief task of the adult in this first adult life structure is to "become a novice adult with a home base of his own."[32] Meeting that challenge means finding a balance between keeping one's options open while exploring all the potential treasures of the new world and creating a stable life structure in which the young adult acts responsibly and makes something of his life. This period of life lasts from about age twenty-two to twenty-eight. During these crucial years adults must make their own living place, carve a niche for themselves in their chosen vocation, and become comfortably situated in a congenial social group.[33] Negotiating all these changes presents a challenge emotionally, socially, and spiritually. Levinson suggested that young adults who have the services of a mentor are more likely to make good adjustments.[34] The mentor is usually eight to fifteen years older than the young adult and may relate in the role of boss, more experienced co-worker, professor, Sunday School teacher, or friend.

The Age Thirty Transition. The first adult structure concludes with the Age Thirty Transition which extends from about twenty-eight to thirty-three. The Early Adult Transition, Entering the Adult World, and the Age Thirty Transition last about fifteen years (17-33) and "constitute the preparatory, "novice" phase of early adulthood."[35] The Age Thirty Transition is rather smooth for some. For them, Levinson called the transition "a time of reform, not revolution."[36] The transition is more stressful for others and may be described as "the *age thirty crisis*."[37] Whether the period is relatively uneventful or more stressful, the life structure is always different at the end of the Age Thirty Transition. Important new choices are made, and old choices are reaffirmed.

Settling Down. The second life structure falls into place after the Age Thirty Transition and extends to approximately age forty. Two major tasks claim attention during this period; namely, (1) establishing a niche in society and (2) working at making it. Levinson used *making it* "to include all efforts to build a better life for oneself and to be affirmed by the tribe."[38] During this period the person seeks to move beyond the "novice" period to become a "full-fledged adult within his own world."[39] Levinson described this period using the imagery of a ladder. He spoke of the adult's beginning this period on the bottom rung of the ladder as a junior member of the adult world and climbing the ladder to become a senior member.[40] Levinson also described a distinctive phase of the Settling Down period, between age thirty-six to forty, which he called Becoming One's Own Man.[41] During this segment of life, an adult seeks to speak with his own voice and to have a greater measure of authority.[42]

Mid-Life Transition. The mid-life transition lasts from age forty to forty-five and provides a bridge from early to middle adulthood. During this time a person reappraises, explores, and tests choices. For the great majority of men, Levinson and his fellow researchers described this period as a "period of great struggle within the self and with the external world."[43] Questions faced include: "What have I done with my life? What do I really get from and give to my wife, children, friends, work, community—and self? What is it I truly want for myself and others?"[44]

Entering Middle Adulthood. At approximately age forty-five, an adult enters middle adulthood. The move is marked by a series of changes, not a dramatic event. Most adults are aware of the change only in retrospect. The new life structure that emerges reveals varying degrees of satisfaction. For many, middle adulthood is "the fullest and most creative season in the life cycle."[45]

Age Fifty Transition. From about fifty to fifty-five adults are in the Age Fifty Transition. The life structure formed in the mid-forties may be changed. The Levinson team concluded that men seldom got through middle adulthood without at least a moderate crisis in either the Mid-life Transition or the Age Fifty Transition.[46]

Culmination of Middle Adulthood. A relatively stable period is in place from approximately age fifty-five to sixty. This structure enables an adult to complete middle adulthood and may be a time of rejuvenation and enrichment.[47] It may be comparable to Settling Down in early adulthood.

Late Adult Transition. During the years of sixty to sixty-five middle adulthood is terminated and a basis for entering late adulthood is formed. This is a major turning point in the life cycle.

The Levinson team has done a great service for students of adult development. Although the studies reported in *The Seasons of a Man's Life* were limited to males, the findings are most helpful. The descriptions of transitions and changing life structures certainly confirm the view that adulthood is dynamic and full of potential. The identified components of the life structure and the changing priorities and values related to them are quite realistic. The reappraisals and choices described certainly present fertile opportunities for religious educators.

Adult Development:
A Psychosocial Explanation

The third view of adult development to be explored is Erik Erikson's psychosocial theory. Erikson and Havighurst agreed in that the essential feature of the latter's tasks is very much like Erikson's ages: Success leads to happiness, failure breeds misery. They are dissimilar in that Erikson cautions that the psychosocial tasks are not permanently achieved while Havighurst seems to contend that successful achievement of a task normally is retained for life. Another difference is that Erikson emphasizes inner values or ego development while Havighurst sees the tasks emerging from three sources, namely, physical maturation, societal demands, and personal values.

Erikson proposed eight ages of human ego development:
(1) early infancy—birth to about one year: (2) later infancy—1 to 3 years; (3) early childhood—4 to 6 years; (4) middle childhood—6 to 11 years; (5) puberty and adolescence—12 to 20 years; (6) early adulthood; (7) middle adulthood; and (8) late adulthood. According to Erikson the crises of each stage of development is expressed as a polarity, suggesting the possibility of a successful or unsuccessful resolution of the crisis. When the resolution is successful, a specific virtue that blesses individuals and their world emerges. Polarities and desirable virtues related to

Age of Ego Development	Polarity	Virtue Emerging from Successful Resolution
Early infancy	Trust vs. Mistrust	Drive & Hope
Later infancy	Autonomy vs. Shame	Self-control & Will Power
Early childhood	Initiative vs. Guilt	Direction & Purpose
Middle childhood	Industry vs. Inferiority	Method & Competence
Puberty & adolescence	Ego Identity vs. Role Confusion	Devotion & Fidelity
Early adulthood	Intimacy vs. Isolation	Affiliation & Love
Middle adulthood	Generativity vs. Stagnation	Production & Care
Late adulthood	Integrity vs. Despair	Renunciation & Wisdom

each age are given here in chart form.[48]

Each of the adult stages of ego development will now be described in more detail.

Early Adulthood. In early adulthood, Erikson suggested that the challenge is to resolve the tension between intimacy and isolation. In Erikson's view, young adults must learn to overcome "the fear of ego loss in situations which call for self-abandon."[49] The avoidance of such experiences because of fear of ego loss "may lead to a deep sense of isolation and consequent self-absorption."[50] The young adult who is successful in the resolution of this crisis will have a healthy capacity to commit self to others in friendships, in a lasting marital relationship, and in all interpersonal exchanges. Isolation, the polarity opposite to intimacy, may be marked by character problems, promiscuous behavior, and repudiation of others. The successful negotiation of this struggle is obviously essential for good marital, social, emotional, and even vocational adjustment.

Middle Adulthood. The critical issue in middle adulthood, in Erikson's theory, is generativity vs. stagnation. The generative adult is productive and creative for himself and for others. "Generativity is primarily the interest in establishing and guiding the next generation or whatever in a given case may become the absorbing object of a parental kind of responsibility."[51] People may express their generativity, or commitment to quality of life for future generations, in many ways. Childrearing, teaching, and the creative arts are only three examples. According to the Newmans, "a sense of generativity means that a person attaches meaning to life after his or her death. People become invested in hopes for a future that may not directly benefit them."[52]

Stagnation may be marked by egocentricity, nonproductivity, excessive self-love, self-indulgence, and personal impoverishment. Adults who yield to stagnation may become so preoccupied with their own importance that they are unable to make an investment in the lives of others. They may even become so depressed that they do not believe they are capable of contributing to others.[53] Unfortunate, indeed, are the middle adults who fail to invest themselves in others. Both they and the world are losers. Moreover, they are ill prepared to face the closing years of their lives if they have to deal with a hardened selfishness and regret that they have left little or nothing that will outlive them.

Late Adulthood. In the last of the eight ages of ego development, Erikson depicted a tension between integrity and despair. The person who achieves ego integrity is one who "has taken care of things and people and has adapted himself to the triumphs and disappointments adherent to being."[54] Erikson continued his definition of ego integrity: "It is the acceptance of one's one-and-only life cycle as something that had to be and that, by necessity permitted of no substitutions."[55] The adult who lacks this ego integration is in despair. Death is feared. The one and only life cycle is not accepted. "Despair expresses the feeling that the time is short, too short for the attempt to start another life and to try out alternate roads to integrity."[56]

Integrity is achieved when persons can accept their past without intense regret and can accept death as another experience in their total life journey. Persons who experience despair cannot cope with their bitterness and disappointment about past failures. They cannot accept death because it eliminates forever all possibility of correcting past mistakes.

The challenges confronting Christian educators privileged to work with adults are obvious when Erikson's theory is reviewed. Only in

Christ can adults find the acceptance with God that is the basis for intimacy with Him, with self, and with others. As Christian leaders can assist adults in yielding their lives to Christ as Savior and Lord, they enable them to develop the capacity for the intimacy essential to successful relationships in marriage, work, and social interactions. In Middle Adulthood generativity is the issue. The caring, self-giving approach to life that contributes to the enrichment of self and others in the present and future is the outgrowth of the new birth that Christ makes possible. True generativity is seen in Paul's comment to the Corinthians,

> For Christ's love compels us, because we are convinced that one died for all, and therefore all died. And he died for all, *that those who live should no longer live for themselves* but for him who died for them and was raised again (2 Cor. 5:14-15 NIV, italics by author).

Generativity is in focus in Philippians 2:4 also, "Each of you should look not only to your own interests, but also to the interests of others" (NIV). With regard to integrity, is there any clearer statement than 2 Timothy 4:6-8?

> For I am already being poured out like a drink offering, and the time has come for my departure. I have fought the good fight, I have finished the race, I have kept the faith. Now there is in store for me the crown of righteousness. Which the Lord, the righteous Judge, will award to me on that day (NIV).

Summary and Implications

The theories about adult development are numerous and diverse. But they are marked by several common denominators. All depict change. The need for responsibility and accountability on the part of each adult is clear in almost every theory. The lifelong duration of development is clearly seen in all the theories, and so is the interdependence of the various life stages. The need and desire for a life that is vital and fulfilling to self and others is a strong implication of all these theorists.

What advantages does information about the theories of adult development offer leaders in the Christian education of adults? The theories may provide guidance for persons making grouping and grading decisions. Curriculum design may be enhanced through consideration of the issues and concerns that developmental theorists have brought into focus. Teaching may become more life centered, and teachable moments and trigger events may be used more effectively when the teacher is enlightened about adult development. Family life education may be more relevant when insight into adult development informs planners about family life cycle and family issues appropriate for various stages in the adult years.

Adult educators should make the most of the advantages cited. By the same token, they should be aware of possible pitfalls in following adult theory without discernment. The cultural limitation of many theories must be considered when working with adults in ethnic and socioeconomic circumstances that differ from the subjects studied by the theorists. All tendencies to stereotype persons along lines of theories must be avoided. Adult workers must also be sensitive to the fact that many persons to whom they minister are encountering tasks and issues that are out of sequence with the task theories. The success-failure syndrome that is a feature of some of the theories may lead adults and their leaders to a state of despair, unless proper attention is given to the transforming power of God's grace and to the totally sufficient spiritual resources that await any adult, whatever the person's past may have been.

The challenge of adult ministry in the church is to help adults build life structures that are shaped by Christian values and priorities as a result of conversion and as a continuing expression of a faith walk with Christ. To be an effective enabler in that endeavor brings personal fulfillment. It also contributes to the strengthening of the church and to the proclamation of the gospel.

Notes

1. Robert Browning, "Rabbi Ben Ezra," line 3.

2. "America in Transition: An Aging Society," *Current Population Reports*, Series P-23, No. 128, U. S. Government Printing Office, Washington, D.C.

3. The word *adult* derives from the past participle of the Latin *adolescere*, which means *to grow up*.

4. Attempts to define adulthood have proved difficult. It has been defined legally as the age at which society assumes a person is responsible for actions and entitled to certain rights and privileges. The social definition defines adulthood as the point when a person acquires social roles appropriate to adulthood.

5. Keith Miller, *The Becomers* (Waco: Word Books, 1973). For a good development of the becomer concept, consult Miller's interpretation.

6. Ledford J. Bischof, *Adult Psychology*, 2nd. ed. (New York: Harper & Row Publishers, 1976), p. 18.

7. Barbara M. Newman and Philip R. Newman, *Understanding Adulthood* (New York: Holt, Rinehart, and Winston, 1983), p. 16.

8. The six theoretical approaches introduced here are taken from Newman and New-

man, Ibid., pp. 21-52. On page 53 in that source there is a table in which the basic concepts of the approaches are summarized.

9. Ibid., p. 27.

10. Ibid.

11. Erik Erikson, *Childhood and Society*, 2nd ed. (New York: Norton, 1963).

12. Barbara Newman and Philip R. Newman, *Development through Life* (Homewood, Ill.: Dorsey, 1979).

13. Robert Peck, "Psychological Developments in the Second Half of Life," *Psychological Aspects of Aging*, ed. J. E. Anderson (Washington, D.C.: American Psychological Association, 1956). Proceedings of a conference on planning research, Bethesda, Md.: April 24-27, 1955.

14. Daniel J. Levinson, C. M. Darrow, E. B. Klein, M. H. Levinson, and B. McKee, *The Seasons of a Man's Life* (New York: Knopf, 1978).

15. R. L. Gould, "The Phases of Adult Life: A Study in Developmental Psychology," *American Journal of Psychiatry*, 1972, pp. 129, 521-531. See also R. L. Gould, *Transformations* (New York: Simon and Schuster, 1978).

16. Barbara M. Newman and Philip R. Newman, *Understanding Adulthood*, pp. 29-30.

17. Ibid., p. 32.

18. Ibid., pp. 34-36.

19. See Charlotte Buhler and F. Massarik, *The Course of Human Life: A Study of Goals in the Humanistic Perspective* (New York: Springer, 1968); C. R. Rogers, *On Becoming a Person* (Boston: Houghton Mifflin, 1961); and A. H. Maslow, *Toward a Psychology of Being*, 2nd ed. (Princeton, N. J.: Van Nostrand, 1968).

20. See I. P. Pavlov, *Conditioned Reflexes* (New York: Dover, 1960); B. F. Skinner, *About Behaviorism* (New York: Knopf, 1974); and Albert Boudura, *Social Learning Theory* (Englewood Cliffs, N.J.: Prentice-Hall, 1977).

21. Barbara M. Newman and Philip R. Newman, *Understanding Adulthood*, pp. 42-43.

22. J. Piaget, *The Psychology of Intelligence* (New York: Harcourt, Brace, 1950).

23. B. L. Newgarten, J. W. Moore, and J. C. Lowe, "Age Norms, Age Constraints, and Adult Socialization," *American Journal of Sociology*, 1965, pp. 70, 710-717.

24. Robert J. Havighurst, *Human Development and Education* (New York: David McKay Company, Inc., 1953), p. 2.

25. The task statements are middle-class American and are built on a traditional family-life model. They fail to reflect adequately the life-style of the less privileged and the developmental stages of single adults so numerous in contemporary society.

26. Havighurst, Ibid., pp. 257-83.

27. Levinson, *The Seasons of a Man's Life*, p. 43.

28. Ibid., p. 44.

29. Ibid.

30. Ibid., p. 49.

31. Ibid., p. 56.

32. Ibid., p. 57.

33. Ibid.

34. Ibid., p. 97-101.

35. Ibid., p. 59.

36. Ibid., p. 58.

37. Ibid.

38. Ibid., p. 59.

39. Ibid.

40. Ibid., p. 60.

41. Ibid.

42. Ibid.

43. Ibid.

44. Ibid.

45. Ibid., p. 62.

46. Ibid.

47. Ibid.

48. Ledford J. Bischof, *Adult Psychology*, 2nd ed. (New York: Harper and Row, 1976), pp. 13-15, 33.

49. Erik H. Erikson, *Childhood and Society* (New York: W. W. Norton & Co., Inc., 1950), p. 229.

50. Ibid.

51. Ibid., p. 231.

52. Barbara M. Newman and Philip R. Newman, *Understanding Adulthood*, p. 7.

53. Ibid.

54. Erikson, *Childhood and Society*, p. 231.

55. Ibid., p. 232.

56. Ibid.

2

Young Adult Years: Spread Your Wings and Fly
Jerry M. Stubblefield

Introduction

Life is characterized by many markers: at age six, one begins formal schooling; thirteen notes the onset of the adolescent years; sixteen means one can get a driver's license and drive a car alone; eighteen signifies one has usually completed high school, and can register to vote (males must register for the draft). Legally, at eighteen the person is treated as an adult in terms of citizenship privileges; some states use this age when one can secure credit and be responsible for personal debts; and when the criminal justice system considers one an adult.

Since 1970 many religious organizations have considered eighteen as the beginning of adulthood. Both churches and society have been heavily influenced by the developmentalists who felt that adulthood began with the completion of high school. Recently this theory has been challenged by the work of Daniel J. Levinson and his associates who concluded that seventeen to twenty-two should be considered early adult transition with early or young adulthood beginning at age twenty-two.[1]

It seems more appropriate to consider the few years immediately following high school as the transition period between adolescence and adulthood. Those from the ages of eighteen to twenty-two have many of the privileges and advantages of adulthood but do not usually carry the corresponding responsibilities. Several basic issues need to be considered: Is age an adequate determinant of whether or not a person is an adult? What place do emotional, physical, intellectual, and economic factors play in designating adulthood? How does dependency/independence influence one's being considered an adult?

I consider a person who is between the ages of eighteen and thirty-four a young adult. In this chapter I will examine the demographics of those classified as young adults. Major attention will be focused on the characteristics, tasks, and needs of young adults. The chapter will conclude with a discussion of the implications and opportunities for ministry with this group in the church.

Demographics

The purpose of a demographic study is to indicate the importance of a particular segment of society. It also reveals the potential needs and challenges presented by the young adult population both to society and to churches. Examining both the number and percentage of young adults in the various marital roles reveals that young adults are reflective of the total adult population, but they are shrinking in terms of percentage of the total adult population. All the tables are for ages eighteen to thirty-four except for those who have been married beginning at age fourteen or fifteen.

Young adults are always single, married, widowed, divorced, separated, and have been either widowed or divorced but now married. Table A shows a breakdown of young adults from 1940 to 1980. In terms of numbers, young adults have increased from 37,945,696 in 1940 to 67,-099,167 in 1980 for a numerical increase of 29,153,471. However, in terms of percentage of the adult population, there was a loss from 48 percent to 41.2 percent. Close scrutiny of the young adult figures for these forty years reveals that men have outnumbered women in each decade until 1980 when there were 254,201 more women than men—less than 1 percent. Participation in religious activities shows a much different pattern with far more women than men involved.

Always-single young adults present an even more unusual pattern. Single men outnumber single women, yet most singles ministries in the church have three to four women for each man involved. The preponderance of men can be observed for each age grouping and for each decade. Data concerning the always single can be found in Table B.

The largest number of young adults are married. Information concerning the married young adults is listed in Table C. Since 1940 there are more married women than men in each age category. Apparently, women are marrying men older than themselves. More than 50 percent of young adults are married and represent 64.5 percent of all persons married in 1980. Percentage wise, young adults were marrying less in 1980 than they did in 1940. There were 2.8 percent fewer young adults married and 1.2 percent fewer in the total adult population. Both the church and society are correct in seeking to appeal to the young married adult.

In 1940 there were slightly more widowed than divorced young adults, but by 1950 divorced young adults far outnumbered the widowed. Less than 1 percent of the young adult population has been widowed at any one time. Females far outnumber men. Only a small percentage of the widowed who have remarried are found in the years eighteen to thirty-four. Table D analyzes the widowed.

The divorce rate among young adults increased rather significantly from 1940 to 1950, 67.9 percent. For the next ten years there were 15,166 more. From 1960 to 1970 young adult divorce rose almost 80 percent, from 733,156 to 1,317,760 for an increase of 584,604. The next decade saw a drastic increase in this age group from 1,317,760 to 4,026,963, which is 205 percent. In 1980 the percent of divorced young adults was 6 percent of the young adult population and represents 6.67 percent of the divorced adult population. See Table E for specific ages, sexes, and periods. More than 8 million young married adults were identified in 1980 as having been divorced. Both the number of persons who are divorced and the divorced remarried present unique challenges to churches and to society.

A group not identified before 1980 is those who are separated from their spouses; this group numbered 1,719,654 and ranged in ages from fifteen to thirty-four. Until 1980 an adult was considered to be single, married, widowed, or divorced.

One startling fact about these statistics is the number of fourteen-, fifteen-, sixteen-, and seventeen-year-olds who have been married, widowed, or divorced, and many have remarried at these ages.

The church, home, and society must do a better job of equipping people for marital stability. It is a time for concerted action on the part of everyone to help people enter marriage more realistically and with the necessary skills for better marriages.

Characteristics, Tasks, and Needs

Characteristics

American society assumes that by age eighteen, everyone is physiologically an adult by virtue of having reached sexual maturity and the peak of physical and mental capacity. Some developmentalists have noted that young people are entering puberty at an earlier age than previous generations. However, young people take longer before assuming adult roles. They place the beginning of adulthood at age twenty-five. Many more young adults are deeply involved with political, ecological, and social issues than were their counterparts decades ago. With all these signs of maturing adulthood, the length of time spent between the last days of adolescence and full self-supporting independence of adulthood grows longer.

Viewing young adulthood as covering the years between eighteen and thirty-four, no one group of characteristics seems to provide an adequate perspective. Two transitions occur which have an impact on the young person. The first is the early adult transition, while the second is the age thirty transition.

A transitional period serves as a bridge between two eras, enabling the person to end one era so that the next can begin. A transition is a time when a person makes significant moves or decisions about the course or direction of one's life. It is a time of evaluation and review. The person must choose whether to continue with some or all of the past or to move into entirely new directions. It is a time to dream and to anticipate what one wants for the future. It may be a crisis or a smooth transition depending upon how much redirection takes place and how much of the past is left behind. It can be a very sad time or a very happy time, depending upon how the young adults have felt about the adolescent years and their attitudes about entering adulthood. It can be a very frightening time since one does not know what to anticipate in the new adult roles.[2]

Tasks and Needs

The early adult transition covers the ages of eighteen to twenty-two, or commences with the completion of high school. Two tasks must be completed: to terminate the latter part of adolescence and begin adulthood. As the individual leaves adolescence, the young adult must establish a self-identity separate from that of parents, select a way of life, and develop a solid intimate relationship.[3]

Moving through the young adult transition seems to provoke a common experience—disillusionment. Young people begin to experience new perceptions of their parents, peers, and their own status as individuals. Parents and persons in authority lose their influence over young people. Moral values become more complex in the areas of sex and personal security. Young people find it difficult to meet the challenges intrinsic to growth during this period and still maintain simple faith in prior notions.[4]

Bruce Powers found this to be true in his spiritual life. In describing his own experience he wrote:

> I found that every dimension of my life came under scrutiny. So much of my religion, work habits, patterns of living, and even personal life-style previously had been community-oriented, first in my family and then in my peer group. Gradually, I came to feel that whatever I was knowing, feeling, or doing had to be *mine*. That which I packed and carried with me from earlier years was my parents, my church's, my group's, or my culture's, and I became disillusioned as I saw parts of my past were inconsistent with present experience.[5]

Levinson saw this as the first task of moving out of the preadult world during the early adult transition. One may either change or even terminate present relationships with persons, groups, or institutions deemed important.[6]

Many illusions are lost or gradually changed. Individual growth brings cumulative changes which may be suddenly recognized as a new insight. This is what happens to many college students who realize after having been away in college that their parents have suddenly gotten smarter or wiser.

A crucial task and need of *all* young adults is the development of a healthy or strong self-image or identity apart from one's family. Persons must know who they are in order to relate to other persons on a significant level. This is an important part of young adult development involving every aspect of the individual. During the early adult transition, all persons must have a clear concept of who they are as sexual beings, as social beings, as independent, unique persons, and as individuals with places in society.[7]

It is important for young adults to have a relatively strong sense of identity as a prerequisite for the beginning of intimacy. Erikson feels that a sense of identity should be achieved during the latter teen years so that individuals will seek to merge their identity with that of others.[8] Assuming that the task of identity has been accomplished, the individual should be prepared for intimacy. The opposite of intimacy is isolation or distantiation—the desire to isolate or be apart from others. The person who moves in this direction will go to almost any extreme to eliminate anyone or anything seen as a threat to him or her.[9]

Erikson has defined intimacy as, "The capacity to commit himself to concrete affiliations and partnerships and to develop the ethical strength to abide by such commitments, even though they may call for significant sacrifice and compromises."[10] If intimacy is to be achieved, each person must have a strong, positive, and wholesome self-image. When a person's self-image is weak, negative, and poor, he will avoid or be unable to create intimacy. Personality traits that can help in establishing intimacy include a feeling of inner security, self-confidence, and a clear conscience. A strong self-image is needed to handle the intensity of intimacy.[11]

Webster's New Ninth Collegiate Dictionary defines intimate as "belonging to or characterizing one's deepest nature; marked by very close association, contact, or familiarity; marked by a warm friendship developing through long association; suggesting informal warmth or privacy; of a personal or private nature."[12] Neither Erikson nor this definition have any sexual connotations. However, we usually identify intimacy with marriage or a sexual relationship. The marital relationship does not automatically bring with it intimacy, though the oneness of marriage should provide fertile soil for the growth of intimacy. It is also possible to achieve intimacy with persons other than one's spouse; even with persons of the same sex or of the opposite sex; in these relationships sex has nothing to do with closeness.[13]

Erikson may have provided us with a partial explanation of the reason for so much marital breakup or the desire for singleness. Many persons are not willing to make deep, abiding commitments to another. He feels that such relationships may require, even necessitate, making significant sacrifices or compromises. One cannot have one's way and have this kind of depth relationship. Commitment must be as selfless as possible.

Levinson noted that as one enters the adult world, one makes and tests a variety of initial choices which include occupation, love relationships, peer relationships, values, and life-style.[14] A young adult would not be expected to have every aspect of one's life worked out. It seems that many young adults do not take these important decisions seriously. Instead of viewing these as initial choices, the young adult would do well to enter each of these areas as if these choices were lifelong decisions.

During the "Entering the Adult World" phase, the first task is to explore the possibilities for adult living; the person will keep options open, avoid strong commitments, and maximize alternatives.[15] The avoidance of strong commitments is contradictory to Erikson's concept of intimacy. This epitomizes the negative side of isolation. Verification of Levinson's observation may be seen in an article which quoted the feelings of a man in his late twenties. He said: "It was a year marked by a continuous flouting of commitment. . . . We had freedom to come and go as we chose, freedom to date whom we wanted when we wanted. No explanations, no permission, no guilt. No commitment."[16]

Patterns for the early adult transition may be different for those who join the armed forces, go to work after high school and postpone marriage and parenthood, or who cannot find jobs. All of these may experience an extended period of transition when they are not adolescents but have not fully assumed the typical adult roles in society.[17]

Potentially, six of Havighurst's eight developmental tasks of early adulthood may be occurring during early adulthood in various degrees. Selecting a mate often occurs between the ages of eighteen and twenty-two. Determining whom to marry has been described as one of the most interesting and most disturbing tasks of early adulthood. After the marriage, the couple must learn how to live successfully with each other. Each must learn to communicate and control feelings of love, joy, anger, and disgust so that the two can live intimately and happily together. Sexual relations make this task easier; it is made more difficult by emotional dependence upon parents. The young woman often finds herself in conflicting roles of being a wife and of having a career.[18]

Finding suitable housing can be a major hurdle for young adults as they want to start out at the same level which they were accustomed to in their parents' home. The couple must choose between a house and an apartment. One young couple wanted a house but found it too expensive. They definitely did not want an apartment, so they compromised on a duplex. Basically it is a matter of economics: "What we can afford!"

Starting a family and rearing children are choices about which couples now have many options that were not available a few years ago. With modern birth control techniques, couples may choose when or if they want to have children. Many two-career families are waiting until age thirty to decide whether or not to have children. When the first child is born, it has a profound effect upon the couple's relationship. It requires major physical and emotional energy. If the wife has been working, she will need to reassess her role as a person and will have to decide whether or not to continue working or to stay at home with the child.

Getting established in the work world is a major task of young adulthood. This is a task faced by men and women. Work is both time- and energy-consuming. Traditionally, the man has been the major wage earner in the family. Many wives now earn significantly more than the husband. A term that has become popular is "househusband"—the husband manages the house and children while the wife supports the family. These role reversals have created ego or self-image problems for many men.

During the "Entering the Adult World" phase which begins around age twenty-two and continues until age twenty-eight, the young adult must deal with two primary but antithetical tasks. First, one should explore the possibilities for adult living. The person will keep options open, avoid strong commitments, and maximize alternatives.[19] The second task is to establish a stable life structure in which one would become more responsible or make something out of life. The young adult who follows the first task would have a very transient, rootless type of life. The danger of the second would be that one has prematurely committed oneself without adequately exploring the alternatives.

The third phase of young adulthood is the Age Thirty Transition. It usually begins around twenty-eight and ends at thirty-three. This gives the person a chance to alter areas that were weak or problematic during the earlier period. It is also a time to develop a foundational base on which to complete early adulthood.[20]

Whether it is a smooth transition or a crisis depends upon the individual's attitude and the attitude of society. Beginning with the thirtieth birthday, many people have fear and anxiety about decadal ones—forty, fifty, sixty. Ambiguous feelings about the thirtieth birthday may be a carry over from the 1960s when it was stated, "You cannot trust anyone over thirty." It may be a sign that youth is over. Personal attitudes could be influenced by the idea that if people have not married by thirty, they never will. I have observed both single and married persons of both sexes become depressed and very anxious about reaching this milestone.

The Age Thirty Transition is a period of life to chart one's course, to begin to make those decisions about one's occupation, marriage, and life-style. During this period many couples decide either to have children or not to have them. Much has been written concerning the risk factors involved. This is a significant stage in adult development. It is a time when momentous new directions are chosen, or old choices are reaffirmed. These decisions must be in harmony with one's ambitions and abilities and be personally achievable. If so, they will provide for a relatively satisfactory life structure. If not, then the Settling Down phase of young adulthood probably will be chaotic and filled with frustrations.[21] The Settling Down phase will be discussed in the next chapter on Middle Adulthood since it covers the years between thirty-three and forty.

Central concerns of young adults include seeking an identity in terms of a career and of social participation in adult roles, seeking a mate or choosing a single life-style (at least for the present), searching for and selecting a meaningful life-style and a circle of friends who support their life-styles. It involves broadening social contacts and being vulnerable to social pressure, feelings of potential loss of freedom, and increased responsibility when jobs and marriage are begun. It means that one must accept the future consequences of one's actions and choices in a way never before realized. Being a young adult means that other people react to one as an adult, and one reacts to oneself as an adult.[22]

Doing all that needs to be done in young adulthood is not an easy task. It is difficult to engage in meaningful, intimate relations with someone of the opposite sex and maintain primary loyalty to parents and peer groups. Earlier ties cannot be kept intact while one puts oneself completely into the struggle to find a meaningful career. There is a high probability that either the choice of a mate, or a career, or both, will run counter to general expectations held by family or friends. It seems as if young adults must choose whether to live their own lives or be dominated by others.[23]

Havighurst has two additional tasks for young adults which are taking on civic responsibility and finding a congenial social group. When young adults take on civic responsibility, they must assume responsibility for the welfare of a group outside of the family. This would be evident by involvement in neighborhood, community, social, political, or religious groups. Young adults are active in a variety of organizations outside the family. Having children and owning property usually makes one more participative in religious, community, and civic activities. Young adults become active in these areas as early as age eighteen when they have the right to vote.

Young adult mobility and marriage cause young people to need to discover new congenial social groups. Persons tend to look for new friends who are similar in age, interests, and with whom they can develop a new kind of social life. These new friends provide a support base for young adults in terms of occupation but primarily for the life-style chosen.[24]

Implications and Opportunities for Ministry

While young adults comprise more than 40 percent of the adult population in America, that same ratio is not found in churches. These are the children of the young adults who dropped out of churches in the 1960s. In 1983 in the Southern Baptist Convention, the number of young adults enrolled in Bible study was 28 percent of the total adults reported. In the same year young adults accounted for more than 51 percent of the adults baptized.[25] This points out the need to provide Bible study opportunities for young adults. It highlights the fact that young adults can be reached for Christ and church membership. A church needs to have Bible study groups for the various ages of young adulthood as well as the different categories of young adults: always single, married, divorced, and possibly for the widowed. Where possible, groups should be organized for men and women. Many churches have been effective in reaching a large number of young adults through coed classes. The Bible teaching program should be the foundation out of which the religious needs of young adults can be met.

Not all of the religious needs of young adults can be met in the Bible teaching program. They need to be involved in discipleship training, mission education, and music. Music in particular might be effective in reaching young adults. Many persons cease to use musical talent and training once formal schooling has ended. Special musical ensembles may involve young adults in the life and work of the church. Bands, orchestras, and choral groups may challenge and utilize the musical skills as they lead in worship and special activities of the church. Through mission education and mission activities, young adults can make significant contributions that would meet the needs of many persons in the church and in the community.

If Levinson and current studies of young adults concerning the unwillingness to make commitments are accurate, then the church must endeavor to minister to and reach the always-single and the increasing number of divorced persons. Opportunities for ministry will be not only to the young adults but to their children. Churches will be able to have special classes for them but also must provide programs that will assist these persons to live effective lives. Churches must minister *unto* them but must also give them an opportunity *to* minister to others in the church and the community in the name of Christ. This group will continue to increase, so churches must be alert to persons whose needs are not now being met and expand their programs and organizations to effectively minister to and reach these persons for Christ and church membership.

The task of more adequately preparing persons for more effective marriages must be accepted by the church. This means that the church must begin this process much earlier than adulthood. Not only must persons leading Christian educational activities be equipped to help persons make better preparation for marriage, but parents must develop skills so that they can have better marriages and be able to communicate and demonstrate these skills to their children. Churches would be wise to spend time and money on helping couples be better "spouses" as well as planning "parenting workshops." Children need to see good family and marriage models in the home.

With divorce increasing, the number of divorced persons who remarry will also increase. Churches must find redemptive ways to minister to these persons and assimilate them into the life and work of a church. This will necessitate some changed attitudes and forgiving spirits if the remarried divorced are to feel comfortable in a church. Consideration will have to be given to the nuclear family but also to the family where children may have come from two or more marriages. Her children, his children, and their children might be involved. Spiritual insight and creative programming will be required to meet the multitude of needs generated by these unusual mixtures of families.

Young adults have been reached in large numbers by many churches. A church should endeavor to assist young adults in meeting the variety of life needs and tasks that they confront. Interestingly, the young adult may be one of the most difficult tasks facing a church. If church programs will be structured and organized to help young adults live effectively as adults, the task of continued enlistment will be greatly lessened. This group has unlimited possibilities for evangelism and church growth. Many in this group can provide the leadership for a growing church. Churches should focus on the needs and characteristics of young adults. Special activities should be designed to meet the genuine, expressed needs of young adults.

Church buildings must be attractive to young adults. Young families with young children want clean, bright, well-kept rooms for their preschool and school-age children. Churches must give careful attention to workers in these age groups. Persons working with preschoolers must help the children be happy and feel that they are loved. I know a man who has three married children whom he brought to the church where he belongs. The preschool area is in need of fresh paint and brightening up. As a result, two of his three children and their families have gone to other churches where the facilities are in good repair.

In organizing and structuring young adults, care should be taken to group them in compatible, congenial groups. They should not be divided at transitional times since they are already under stress in other areas of their lives. Some churches let the age of either of the spouses determine the class to which they are assigned. Grouping of young adults should take into account where they are in the adult life span. A good rule would be to use a point other than the decade, twenty or thirty, as the dividing line.

Possibilities in terms of numbers and variety of programs are unlimited in the young adult years. Being successful in reaching young adults will require creativity, sensitivity to the needs of young adults, mature, loving, caring persons who will lead and guide them into the discovery of biblical truths applicable to their everyday life, and a great deal of hard work.

Notes

1. Daniel J. Levinson, D. M. Darrow, E. B. Klein, M. H. Levinson, and B. McKee, *The Season's of a Man's Life* (New York: Ballantine Books, 1978), p. 56.

2. Ibid., pp. 49-51.

3. Douglas C. Kimmel, *Adulthood and Aging: An Interdisciplinary Developmental View* (New York: John Wiley and Sons, Inc., 1974), p. 84.

4. Leon Rappoport, *Personality Development: The Chronology of Experience* (Glenview, Ill.: Scott, Foresman, and Company, 1972), p. 338.

5. Bruce P. Powers, *Growing Faith* (Nashville: Broadman Press, 1982), pp. 17-18.

6. Levinson, p. 56.

7. Kimmel, p. 108.

8. Erik H. Erikson, *Childhood and Society* (New York: Norton, 1963), pp. 261-263.

9. Ibid., p. 264.

10. Ibid., p. 263.

11. Guy Greenfield, *We Need Each Other* (Grand Rapids, Mich.: Baker Book House, 1984), pp. 156-157.

12. *Webster's Ninth New Collegiate Dictionary* (Springfield, Mass.: Merriam-Webster Inc., 1983), p. 634.

13. Greenfield, p. 151.

14. Levinson, p. 57.

15. Ibid., p. 58.

16. "The New Male," *The Oregonian* 2 Apr. 1985, p. C1.

17. Kimmel, p. 78.

18. Robert J. Havighurst, *Human Development and Education* (New York: Longmans, Green, and Co., 1953), p. 259.

19. Levinson, p. 58.

20. Ibid.

21. Ibid., pp. 58-59.

22. Kimmel, pp. 94-95.

23. Rappoport, p. 331.

24. Havighurst, pp. 263-267.

25. *The Quarterly Review*, The Sunday School Board of the Southern Baptist Convention, July-Sept. 1984, 44, No. 4, pp. 32,21.

TABLE A

Young Adult Profile 18-34
1940-1980

Ages	1940		1950		1960		1970[1]		1980[2]	
	Males	Females	Males	Females	Males	Females	Males	Females	Males	Females
18-19	2,495,373	2,523,461	2,135,960	2,205,525	2,357,202	2,417,335	3,646,704	3,660,096	4,349,036	4,274,943
20-24	5,692,392	5,895,443	5,559,265	5,878,040	5,283,228	5,519,937	7,761,704	8,354,509	10,639,312	10,654,502
25-29	5,450,662	5,645,976	5,904,975	6,277,480	5,333,282	5,537,104	6,569,934	6,810,076	9,678,198	9,793,296
30-34	5,070,312	5,172,076	5,562,315	5,896,625	5,840,287	6,111,422	5,607,593	5,868,858	8,755,937	8,953,943
Totals	18,708,739	19,236,957	19,161,515	20,257,905	18,813,999	19,583,798	23,585,935	24,693,539	33,422,483	33,676,684
Combined Totals	37,945,696		39,419,420		38,397,797		48,279,474		67,099,167	

1. Source: U. S. Department of Commerce, Bureau of the Census, Historical Statistics of the United States Colonial Times to 1970, Part I, Series A 160-171, Marital Status of the Population by Age and Sex: 1890-1970. U. S. Government Printing Office, Washington, D.C., 1975, p. 20.

2. Source: U. S. Department of Commerce, Bureau of the Census, 1980 Census of Population, Volume I, Characteristics of the Population, Chapter D, Detailed Population Characteristics, Table 264, Marital Status, Presence of Spouse, and Marital History for Persons 15 Years and Over.

TABLE B

Single Young Adults 18-34
1940-1980

Ages	1940 Males	1940 Females	1950 Males	1950 Females	1960 Males	1960 Females	1970[1] Males	1970[1] Females	1980[2] Males	1980[2] Females
18-19	2,402,878	1,962,777	1,995,250	1,519,215	2,146,876	1,642,135	3,328,546	2,804,666	4,101,040	3,557,993
20-24	4,109,304	2,728,001	3,281,540	1,898,910	2,807,784	1,567,622	4,307,592	3,030,876	7,255,520	5,450,056
25-29	1,964,118	1,288,092	1,404,860	833,040	1,111,768	582,114	1,288,594	827,906	3,106,296	2,111,744
30-34	1,050,199	761,698	734,195	546,245	694,924	422,915	601,868	435,897	1,303,972	951,028
Totals	9,526,499	6,790,068	7,415,845	4,797,410	6,761,352	4,214,786	9,526,600	7,099,345	15,766,828	12,070,821
Combined Totals	16,316,567		12,213,255		10,976,138		16,625,945		27,837,649	

1. Source: U. S. Department of Commerce, Bureau of the Census, Historical Statistics of the United States Colonial Times to 1970, Part I, Series A 160-171, Marital Status of the Population by Age and Sex: 1890-1970. U. S. Government Printing Office, Washington, D.C., 1975, p. 20.

2. Source: U. S. Department of Commerce, Bureau of the Census, 1980 Census of Population, Volume I, Characteristics of the Population, Chapter D, Detailed Population Characteristics, Table 264, Marital Status, Presence of Spouse, and Marital History for Persons 15 Years and Over.

TABLE C

Married Young Adults 18-34
1940-1980

Ages	1940		1950		1960		1970[1]		1980[2]	
	Males	Females	Males	Females	Males	Females	Males	Females	Males	Females
18-19	90,933	548,809	136,545	670,290	205,527	756,653	306,760	822,618	237,709	679,507
20-24	1,557,104	3,025,923	2,217,810	3,856,760	2,417,552	3,833,956	3,329,772	5,054,321	3,140,110	4,732,727
25-29	3,417,046	4,185,325	4,381,375	5,227,960	4,117,072	4,772,006	5,066,314	5,616,300	5,915,237	6,739,235
30-34	3,912,820	4,155,872	4,690,995	5,082,260	5,000,763	5,432,915	4,803,203	5,055,678	6,677,112	6,917,901
Totals	8,977,903	11,915,929	11,426,725	14,837,270	11,740,914	14,786,530	13,506,049	16,548,917	15,970,167	19,069,370
Combined Totals	20,893,832		26,263,995		26,527,444		30,054,966		35,039,537	

1. Source: U. S. Department of Commerce, Bureau of the Census, Historical Statistics of the United States Colonial Times to 1970, Part I, Series A 160-171, Marital Status of the Population by Age and Sex: 1890-1970. U. S. Government Printing Office, Washington, D.C., 1975, p. 20.

2. Source: U. S. Department of Commerce, Bureau of the Census, 1980 Census of Population, Volume I, Characteristics of the Population, Chapter D, Detailed Population Characteristics, Table 264, Marital Status, Presence of Spouse, and Marital History for Persons 15 Years and Over.

TABLE D

Widowed Young Adults 18-34
1940-1980

Ages	1940		1950		1960		1970[1]		1980[2]	
	Males	Females	Males	Females	Males	Females	Males	Females	Males	Females
18-19	1,232	9,053	720	4,694	887	2,877	3,472	10,656	1,089	3,691
20-24	17,657	56,375	8,394	32,751	4,780	17,252	12,878	56,508	5,970	24,746
25-29	39,013	102,041	20,973	71,878	9,548	37,047	19,196	71,530	11,759	51,751
30-34	59,493	148,571	36,714	128,256	17,246	74,109	19,574	86,494	16,531	79,480
Totals	117,395	316,040	66,801	237,579	32,461	131,285	55,120	225,188	35,349	159,668
Combined Totals	433,435		304,380		163,746		280,308		195,017	

1. Source: U. S. Department of Commerce, Bureau of the Census, Historical Statistics of the United States Colonial Times to 1970, Part I, Series A 160-171, Marital Status of the Population by Age and Sex: 1890-1970. U. S. Government Printing Office, Washington, D.C., 1975, p. 20.

2. Source: U. S. Department of Commerce, Bureau of the Census, 1980 Census of Population, Volume I, Characteristics of the Population, Chapter D, Detailed Population Characteristics, Table 264, Marital Status, Presence of Spouse, and Marital History for Persons 15 Years and Over.

TABLE E

Divorced Young Adults 18-34
1940-1980

Ages	1940		1950		1960		1970[1]		1980[2]	
	Males	Females	Males	Females	Males	Females	Males	Females	Males	Females
18-19	842	7,181	2,630	12,815	3,912	15,670	7,926	22,156	9,190	33,752
20-24	17,590	55,768	50,855	87,090	53,112	101,107	110,967	212,804	237,712	446,973
25-29	48,525	100,681	103,255	158,990	94,894	145,937	195,830	294,340	644,906	890,566
30-34	70,579	126,250	116,180	176,175	127,354	191,170	182,948	290,789	758,322	1,005,534
Totals	137,536	289,880	272,920	445,070	279,272	453,884	497,671	820,089	650,130	2,376,825
Combined Totals	427,416		717,990		733,156		1,317,760		3,026,955	

1. Source: U. S. Department of Commerce, Bureau of the Census, Historical Statistics of the United States Colonial Times to 1970, Part I, Series A 160-171, Marital Status of the Population by Age and Sex: 1890-1970. U. S. Government Printing Office, Washington, D.C., 1975, p. 20.

2. Source: U. S. Department of Commerce, Bureau of the Census, 1980 Census of Population, Volume I, Characteristics of the Population, Chapter D, Detailed Population Characteristics, Table 264, Marital Status, Presence of Spouse, and Marital History for Persons 15 Years and Over.

3

Middle Adult Years

Jerry M. Stubblefield

Introduction

The middle adult years have been described in many ways. They have been noted by the five *Bs*—bunions, bulges, bifocals, baldness, and bridges. A professional friend observed that in his work one could expect to take ten years to build a practice, ten years to enjoy it, and ten years to watch it leave. Middle adulthood has been compared to riding an elevator in that during this time one usually ascends to the top of the work world, then descends to the bottom.

Middle adulthood is a period of great contrasts. It is a time when one usually reaches the peak of earning power, yet often has the greatest expenses. Society has highlighted the major developmental task for men as "the mid-life crisis," ignoring two significant transitional periods that occur earlier in a man's life—the Early Adult Transition and the Age Thirty Transition.

It is difficult to get the developmentalists and society to agree on the age boundaries for middle adulthood. Some start as young as twenty-six and others as late as forty. It is a period of tremendous contrasts—a time when adults may experience both joy and grief, a sense of accomplishment and a sense of loss. It requires a great deal of flexibility and adaptability to cope with such sweeping changes and challenges experienced during these thirty-plus years.

We probably know less about middle adulthood than any other phase of human life as there has been a scarcity of research covering those years. This is due in part to the fact that many social scientists who could do this research are themselves in the middle adult years and thus are not inclined to investigate themselves. Physiologically, much knowledge has been gained through studies interested in the physical changes that occur in the human body, particularly as it affects women during menopause and whether a similar change occurs in men.

70

Recently, studies have been conducted to see if there are peculiar or unique aspects in the area of faith development. A number of insights have been gained through several studies.[1]

This chapter will examine the demographics of middle adulthood, noting any unique or special characteristics evidenced. Major attention will focus on the characteristics, needs, and tasks of middle adulthood. Implications and opportunities for ministry will be described.

Demographics

Since 1940 there have been significant changes in the profile of middle adulthood. Table A examines the middle adult marital profile. Most noticeable of the demographic changes has been the steady decline in the number of always single. Numerically, the always single have lost 770,590 with a percentage decrease of almost 18 percent over the forty-year period as a part of the total middle-adult population. Widowed middle adults also reflect a decrease. There are 542,042 fewer widowed persons in 1980 than there were in 1940, a decline of almost 19 percent.

The greatest change has occurred among the divorced middle adults. Beginning with 854,105 in 1940, those divorced increased to 5,231,672 in 1980, a gain of 4,377,567 or a percentage growth of 612.53 percent. A group not identified prior to 1960 were those who were separated from their spouse. Numerically, the separated have not greatly increased, however, over the past twenty years; the percent of separated in the total middle-adult population has moved from 2 percent to 2.9 percent.

The always-single profile shows less in the middle adult years than the rest of the adult population as shown in Table B. Their highest percentage was in 1940 when 10.95 percent of middle adults were always single. Men outnumber women in each of the decades from as low as 2 percent to as high as 7.4 percent. Churches would be wise to seek to reach this large number of always-single middle adults. Strong efforts should be made to reach men as well as women. Though women are a numerical minority, they are in the majority with reference to participation in religious activities and programs.

Eighty-plus percent of middle adults are married. This is ten to fifteen percentage points more than the overall adult population. Surprising is the fact that there are more married men than married women for each of the decades since 1940 (see Table C). This high percentage of married middle adults signifies that this age group strongly believes in marriage.

Married middle adulthood provides a great opportunity and challenge for the church to effectively minister to and involve this group in the life and work of the church. From their ranks come many of the leaders to serve churches in teaching and ministering to persons of all ages. Middle adults have provided a base of leadership for the functioning church, and have enlisted unnumbered participants for the various activities and programs of the church.

The middle-adult widowed have been declining in numbers since 1940. As expected, there are more widowed women than widowed men. An examination of Tables D and G cause us to rethink what sociologists have said about men needing marriage more than women. There are fewer widowed men because they have a shorter life span than women, or they remarry soon after a wife's death. Table G shows that three times as many widows remarry as widowers.

Both men and women widowed in middle adulthood will have children still at home. This places heavy responsibility on each parent who tries to be both father and mother to the children. Parenting is not a one-parent task. Opportunities for ministering to the person remaining are great, but surviving children should not be ignored in the process. The surviving spouse may feel that emotions should not be shown in front of the children, thus blocking the natural process of grief being experienced by both.

The skyrocketing divorce rate should cause great alarm on the part of the church, community, school, and society. Not long ago, sociologists predicted that one out of every five marriages would end in divorce. Currently, the prediction is that one out of every two marriages will end in divorce. Divorce among middle adults has doubled from 1960 to 1970, and then it has doubled again from 1970 to 1980. Table E lists the numbers and sexes of divorced middle adults.

Divorced women outnumber divorced men for each age group except for a few in 1940 and 1950. In 1980 there were more than 31 percent more women than men identified. Table G shows that 8.9 percent more divorced women remarry than divorced men. Churches have not known how to deal with the increasing number of divorces affecting church members. The issue has been compounded by the fact that 13.5 million divorced persons were listed as remarried in 1980, representing 27.6 percent of the total number of the married middle-aged population.

Those who are divorced and the remarried divorced present many challenges and opportunities for churches to meet not only individual needs, but also to minister to their families. Sometimes as many as three different family components may be living in the same home. Each of the adults may have children from a previous marriage plus children from the current marriage. This has created many problems. One problem is the role and function of a stepparent—how to discipline or work with the child and in what ways.

Persons who are separated from their spouses create several interesting questions. Are these persons to be considered married or single? With which group will those separated be more compatible? Should churches try to have a special ministry to the separated? Where do the separated middle adults fit into the organizational life of the church? Who can best meet the needs of the separated: the marrieds or the singles? There is no easy or simple answer to these questions.

Table F shows patterns for separated middle adults from 1960 to 1980. The census data lists the separated as part of the married but shows them in a special column where the spouse is absent. Separated women outnumber the men in each age category during the twenty-four-year period. Numerically, the separated population has grown about six-hundred thousand but has increased by almost 1 percent of the total adult population. Issues related to ministering to the separated can be found in chapter 5.

Characteristics, Tasks, and Needs

Characteristics

There is disagreement concerning the boundaries of middle adulthood, particularly as to when middle adulthood commences. Some suggest as early as age twenty-six, others age thirty, some age thirty-five, or even as late as age forty. The ending age for middle adulthood is not so confusing. It is seen as being either age fifty-five or age sixty or with the beginning of retirement. The only problem with making retirement the same as the ending of middle adulthood is that many persons retire from military or civil service and begin a second career, sometimes as early as age forty-five.

A characteristic that describes the transition into middle adulthood is that the individual learns to live without many previously held illusions. While the young adult had a great deal of freedom to move in many directions, the mature middle adult is committed to relatively fixed lines with fewer available options. Middle adults do not perceive that changes can be made as easily as in young adulthood. This partly arises from a sense of fixed responsibilities with many people dependent upon them.[2]

A word that seems to characterize middle adulthood is *attrition* which has the meaning of "wearing down or away, weakening, depreciation, gradual disintegration." Loss is an issue that is a feature of middle adulthood. One issue is that scores made on intelligence tests have reached their highest when one is between the ages of twenty-five and thirty. There are differences of opinions as to why the scores drop, but the evidence shows a decline.

Another area of noticeable loss is in the physical realm. Attrition sets in on the human body in a significant way by age forty. Studies indicate an increasing loss of ability to hear high-pitched tones, a sharp drop in visual acuity, and a slowdown of physical metabolism which causes weight problems. After age forty such vital organs as the heart, lungs, kidneys, and liver are more prone to start malfunctioning.

While the adult at age thirty-five, or forty may not be as good at taking intelligence tests or learning new skills, these things usually are not required. Various work roles do demand new learning; however, the skills, tricks, techniques, or other devices acquired from years of relevant experience often easily make up for losses in native ability.

Psychologically, attrition has an impact. It produces a demand for personal meaning. Middle adults cannot help but ask themselves: Why? What is its purpose, function? What contribution has my life made? This may be seen in how one views one's work. Work has a lot of ego-involvement. There is a commitment of one's self to an activity which one sees to be intrinsically worthwhile. It is not something one does as an act of expediency for the sake of money, prestige, or any other venial consideration.[3]

Another characteristic of middle adulthood is the perception men and women have of themselves and each other. Identity comes as a result of at least three interrelated processes—one's physiological (inner) environment, one's social-cultural environment, and one's psychological development from birth on. Whether one perceives oneself as male or female results from the interaction of the inner and outer experience of being a male or a female in family and society from birth until death.[4]

The personality differences between men and women have borne the brunt of many jokes and stereotypes. Research has verified that there have been clearly defined sex-role stereotypes for men and women. Women have been seen as being less competent, less independent, less objective, and less logical than men. Men have been viewed as lacking interpersonal sensitivity, warmth, and expressiveness as compared to women. The ideal woman has been portrayed as less competent than the ideal man. The mature, healthy women has been seen as more submissive, less independent than either mature, healthy men or adults in general. This places women in a bind because different standards exist for women than for other adults.[5]

Three areas of sex differences in personality provide a basis for understanding middle adult men and women: self-esteem, fear of success, and motivation. In the area of self-esteem, men have functioned as *subjects* —they are active, manipulative, controlling, and generally take an active stance toward the world of objects which includes women. Women are seen more like *objects*—they are looked at, manipulated, controlled, and generally passive. The source of self-esteem for women is that they tend to be prized for how they appear to others, as *objects*, while men are valued for what they accomplish, as *subjects*.

A woman's self-esteem is reinforced as she feels esteemed by those she loves and respects while a man is considered successful through occupational achievements. A woman is not generally considered successful by her achievements unless she has a husband and children. Women perceive men significantly more favorably than they perceive other women. It appears that women have lower levels of self-esteem and self-confidence than men partly because their sources of esteem differ and in part because a man's sources of esteem and being a man are more highly valued by society in general.[6]

The woman who has potential for excellence in the work world also has been characterized by some negative qualities. Women have not felt that they could be successful or achieve and maintain their feminine identity. Women fear the loss of femininity, social rejection, personal or societal destruction, or a combination of the three. Many women have a high motivation to avoid success. They explore their intellectual potential fully only when they are in a noncompetitive setting and when not competing against men. The research data suggests that striving for socially valued types of esteem—success and achievement—may be threatening for many young women because it may interfere with winning affection, approval, and social success. Women tend to be more socially conscious or more dependent on receiving esteem from others than is true for men.[7]

Two kinds of achievement motivation have been identified—internal and affiliative. Achievement motivation is a desire to compete in situations where there are standards of excellence. Internal achievement motivation is based on a person's internal standard of excellence which brings satisfaction by producing a successful accomplishment. Affiliative achievement motivation strives to accomplish a goal to receive esteem from others. Women have proven to be characteristically higher on affiliative motives than men. A woman's achievement behavior has been motivated more by a desire to please than has that of men. When achievement behavior comes into conflict with affiliation, then achievement has been sacrificed. Men seem to be motivated by internal standards of excellence and competition and are reinforced by the social role for men and our highly achievement-oriented society. Women seem to strive for affiliative achievement and are motivated to achieve success in interpersonal relationships and in the affiliative role with husband and children.[8]

The differences between men and women may be positive qualities related to satisfaction and morale. For example, personality traits on which women may excel need not be considered negative. They may be "healthy" and competent personality styles such as passivity or dependency. In women, a healthy dependence means a sensitivity to the needs of persons who are important to them, allowing appropriate nurturant or supportive behavior. Passivity in the sense of indrawing, of elaborating and evolving a rich empathic, intuitive inner life may be a necessary part of the personality equipment of healthy women. This may be a preferred coping technique at particular times such as during pregnancy or when one is nurturing young children.

Obviously, not all women are passive, and not all men are aggressive. However, in our society these characteristics seem to stand out as differential aspects of femininity and masculinity.[9]

Tasks and Needs

The family cycle offers insight into the tasks and needs of middle adulthood. Two phases have particular relevance. First, parents have helped their adolescent children become responsible, functioning adults. The family acts as a launching center as their children establish families of their own at marriage or move into separate living arrangements. For there to be a successful launch, parents must "let go" of their children while the children increase in the exercise of independence and autonomy.

This can be a crisis time for the parents, for when the nest empties, the woman, in particular, has to refocus her energy and attention. This may occur while she is going through menopause. This can be a potential crisis point in the family cycle for women. Often the man is heavily involved in his own career and thus more distant and preoccupied.

The second phase is the postparental family. With the departure of the last child, the family finds itself at a time of high economic productivity, more independence and freedom, and a high degree of marital happiness. Often the couple must begin to face the need to provide some form of care for aging parents. Eventually, they must deal with their feelings of mourning upon the death of their own parents. During this time, they themselves might become grandparents. This in itself brings a great deal of pride and enjoyment. It also brings about a shift in roles and may bring about the realization of one's own advancing age.[10]

A new phenomena is that the nest empties but may fill up again. This time it may be the return of the child, or it may also include grandchildren, and the child's spouse. This puts a great deal of strain upon both the parents and those who move in. There may be significant periods of time when the nest is empty, but there is no guarantee that it will stay empty.

The work cycle and the family cycle go hand in hand. A new pattern is for women to enter the work force earlier and to work more years. Men tend to enter the work force later and retire sooner. For men and an increasing number of women, work involves a great investment of time, emotional energy, and commitment. Success and satisfaction in work and family reaffirm an individual's sense of identity. A person's work is an important part of personal identity. Success and a sense of satisfaction in one's work, in raising children, and in managing a home brings resolution to the issue of identity and leads to a sense of generativity.[11]

Erikson identified generativity vs. stagnation as the seventh stage of man. By generativity, Erikson meant concern for establishing and guiding the next generation. It means productivity and creativity. Emphasis is on the need for institutions that provide generative succession. The opposite of generativity is stagnation where one does not feel satisfaction or fulfillment from an occupational role—including that of homemaker.[12] Both family and work compete for the individual's time and loyalty.

The middle years of an occupation involve readjusting one's goals and idealistic hopes to what one perceives as realistic future possibilities. Also during the middle years, a person usually becomes aware of the years left before retirement and how quickly one must move to attain goals.[13]

During early middle adulthood, a person tries to realize earlier dreams and ambitions. The person expends major energy in work, friendships, leisure, and community. Levinson describes this as Settling Down, the second adult life structure. Two tasks are very significant in this phase of life. The person wants to establish his place in society. This task can be achieved by building on what the person feels is significant, by developing skills in one's chosen vocation, and by becoming a worthwhile member in the person's valued world. The second task is to strive to achieve a place in society. The individual devotes much time and energy at this task in order to build a better life for oneself and also to be affirmed by those he feels are important.

During this phase of middle adulthood, the person is recognized as a full-fledged adult, no longer is she considered a "novice." One strives to move up the "ladder" in every dimension of life: social rank, influence, wealth, fame, creativity, ingenuity, improved family life, social life, or whatever is important to the person. She wants recognition from her world but also is moving up the ladder by what she values and has committed to. While the person receives various rewards for her efforts, this new position has greater responsibilities and pressures.[14]

The Settling Down phase of early middle adulthood corresponds with several developmental tasks identified by Havighurst. This is when one achieves adult civic and social responsibility, establishes and maintains an economic standard of living, and develops adult leisuretime activities. The adult is heavily involved in the civic and social life of the community. A man frequently belongs to a civic club and takes a great deal of interest in community events and activities. The woman usually is more involved with the PTA, garden clubs, and so forth. It is not unusual for a family to buy a house other than the one in which they began. It will be larger and in a "better" or more prestigious neighborhood. Leisuretime activities may include those for the entire family—boating, skiing, and so forth. The adults will begin participating in less-strenuous activities.[15] This would be a good time to begin developing some leisuretime hobbies or activities that one would enjoy during retirement. This task is more crucial for men than women since women usually stay more active around the home.

Mid-life transition is the next phase of middle adulthood for the man. Levinson saw this as the bridge between early and middle adulthood.

This seems to make middle adulthood begin rather late as mid-life transition runs between the ages of forty and forty-five. I prefer Levinson's term *transition* to that of *crisis*. This period has also been labeled "middlesence" since much of the behavior may be similar to that of adolescence. Much life review or reflection begins to take place. To some extent it is the time to examine the meaning of one's family, work, community, self, and values. Jim Conway has described his feeling and actions during this period of his life as a crisis event.[16]

While it is a crisis for some, others seem to handle this period as a manageable transition. Many men begin to make corrections in their life structures which are seen as a reordering of priorities in order to achieve what the man feels to be more important.[17] Havighurst added insight to events that may be occurring during the mid-life transition. With children assuming adult roles or leaving home, a couple must begin to relate to each other as persons.[18] During childbearing and child rearing, the couple have been involved in fulfilling functional roles—mother, father, worker, and so forth. Each one has been engaged in tasks other than the special relationship with which they began the marriage. Often, this is the time when the marriage breaks up.

Physiological changes occur during middle age. The man begins to feel that his youth is slipping or fading away. Some of his behavior during the mid-life transition is an attempt to prove that he is still as vigorous as ever. The woman experiences physiological change when she experiences menopause. When this has occurred, she can no longer conceive children. Her self-image is involved. Some women feel that they are now less a woman and thus not as attractive sexually to their spouses. Other feel the freedom of not fearing pregnancy and enjoy sex more. Women experience some physiological effects but do not usually engage in behavioral actions to prove their virility. Both men and women experience some identity and/or ego adjustment due to these changes.

From about age forty-five to fifty the person is trying to build a new life structure. Some move into this period of life wihout evidence of any major changes or disruptions. Some changes have been made as one has sought to improve in one's work, marriage, and so forth. Others make drastic changes in work; a divorce or a love affair happens; there may be serious illness (such as a heart attack), death of a loved one, or a move to a new locale. Some feel that changes cannot be made satisfactorily, so the person begins to mark time until retirement. Other aspects of life are devoid of inner excitement and meaning. For others, this period of life can often be the fullest and most creative period of adulthood as ambitions, desires, and illusions of young adulthood are left behind.[19]

The age fifty transition occurs between the ages of fifty to fifty-five. Little is known about what happens during this period of life. It is a time similar to the age thirty transition in that one seeks to modify or make corrections in the life structure formed in the mid-life transition. Many persons seek to make one last change of jobs as they feel it would be impossible after this time. Levinson feels that it is not possible to get through middle adulthood without having a moderate crisis during either the mid-life or age fifty transition.

The last phase of middle adulthood covers ages fifty-five to sixty. For those who have been able to rejuvenate themselves and enhance their lives, this can be a time of great fulfillment. This period is reflective of the Settling Down phase which began middle adulthood. It can be a very productive period of one's life.[20]

Implications and Opportunities for Ministry

The greatest opportunity for ministry is with married middle adults since more than 80 percent are married. The church has been wise to emphasize the family and should continue to do so. Ministry to middle adults should seek to strengthen, enhance, and equip them for more effective family life. Family-life education should not take the place of Bible study, but family life ought to have a prominent place in the activities and programs in the church.

A majority of family needs can be met through seminars, workshops, and retreats. While parenting workshops are needed and valuable, strong efforts must be expended to strengthen the relationships between the couple. Many denominations are encouraging and sponsoring marriage enrichment activities. These usually are done over a weekend so the couple can have adequate time to work on identifiable need areas.

Personal growth should be a priority area for programming with so many middle adults who experience divorce. Divorce leaves many scars on all persons involved. Counseling and support groups can be beneficial to the divorced persons and their families, including children.

Single parents need help in providing role models. Church families can adopt single-parent families, assisting with tasks and activities the person cannot do.

A church can assist middle adults in developing leisure activities both for now and potentially for retirement. This may be in recreational and hobby areas. Family recreational programs provide quality family time which should carry over into routine activities.

A crucial need for families, especially families in middle adulthood, is family money management. With inflation and the added expense as families get older, the need to practice good stewardship becomes even more apparent. Periodic seminars and programs for the entire family have proven to be very helpful not only for parents but for teenage children.

A group that must receive some special attention of the church is the singles. Retreats and special seminars help singles feel that the church cares for them and that they are important to the church. Provisions for singles need to be throughout the church program organizations, especially the Bible teaching program. Child-care and activities need to be provided at times other than regular church activities.

Middle adults are prime prospects for evangelism and church membership. Many middle adults are church members but do not regularly participate in the church's Bible teaching program. They should be assigned to existing Sunday School classes for visitation, cultivation, and enlistment for Bible study. Enrollment in Bible study has often been the first step in accepting Christ as Savior and Lord of one's life.

Notes

1. James F. Fowler, *Stages of Faith* (San Francisco: Harper and Row, 1981). Bruce P. Powers, *Growing Faith* (Nashville: Broadman Press, 1982). John H. Westerhoff, *Will Our Children Have Faith?* (New York: Seabury Press, 1976).

2. Leon Rappoport, *Personality Development: The Chronology of Experience* (Glenview, Ill.: Scott, Foresman and Company, 1972), p. 373.

3. Ibid., p. 380.

4. Douglas C. Kimmel, *Adulthood and Aging: An Interdisciplinary Developmental View* (New York: John Wiley and Sons, 1974), p. 152.

5. Ibid., p. 156.

6. Ibid., pp. 158-159.

7. Ibid., p. 161.

8. Ibid., pp. 161-162.

9. Ibid., pp. 163-164.

10. Ibid., pp. 199-215.

11. Ibid., pp. 243-245.

12. Erik H. Erikson, *Childhood and Society* (New York: Norton, 1963), pp. 266-268.

13. Kimmel, pp. 253-254.

14. Daniel J. Levinson, D. M. Darrow, E. B. Klein, M. H. Levinson, and B. McKee, *The Season's of a Man's Life* (New York: Ballantine Books, 1978), pp. 60-61.

15. Robert J. Havighurst, *Human Development and Education* (New York: Longmans, Green and Co., 1953), pp. 270-272.

16. Jim Conway, *Men in Mid-Life Crisis* (Elgin, Ill.: David C. Cook Publishing Co., 1978).

17. Levinson, pp. 60-61.

18. Havighurst, p. 272.

19. Levinson, pp. 61-62.

20. Ibid., p. 62.

TABLE A

Middle Adult Marital Profile (35-59) 1940-1980

	Single	Married	Widowed	Divorced	Separated	Total
1940	4,345,505	31,619,845	2,869,701	854,105		39,680,156
1950[1]	3,875,275	37,638,885	2,660,775	1,399,095		45,574,030
1960[2]	3,894,454	45,059,412	2,506,139	1,836,854	1,132,748	53,296,859
1970[3]	2,574,705	47,558,465	2,553,011	2,598,864	1,340,840	56,285,045
1980[4]	3,574,915	48,886,877	2,327,659	5,231,672	1,729,903	60,021,123

1. Source: U. S. Department of Commerce, Bureau of Census, Census of Population, 1950, Volume II, Part I, Table 102, Marital Status by Age and Sex.

2. Source: U. S. Department of Commerce, Bureau of the Census, Census of Population, 1960, Volume I, Part I, Characteristics of the Population, Table 176, Marital Status.

3. Source: U. S. Department of Commerce, Bureau of the Census, 1970 Census of Population, Volume I, Part I, Characteristics of the Population, Table 203, Marital Status.

4. Source: U. S. Department of Commerce, Bureau of the Census, 1980 Census of Population, Volume I, Characteristics of the Population, Chapter D, Detailed Population Characteristics, Table 264; Marital Status.

TABLE B

Single Middle Adults (35-59) 1940-1980

Ages	1940		1950[1]		1960[2]		1970[3]		1980[4]	
	Males	Females	Males	Females	Males	Females	Males	Females	Males	Females
35-39	725,987	536,205	549,180	477,035	534,350	389,524	447,460	337,144	595,951	479,202
40-44	558,007	414,671	447,390	423,445	414,434	359,242	436,912	335,111	383,571	314,845
45-49	471,982	349,238	388,205	360,110	385,408	362,948	381,353	334,549	319,592	265,239
50-54	413,022	305,074	337,150	320,500	363,982	375,318	329,746	327,957	338,030	282,463
55-59	325,220	246,099	294,220	278,500	346,176	363,072	305,561	338,912	307,557	288,465
Totals	2,494,218	1,851,287	2,016,145	1,859,130	2,044,350	1,850,104	1,901,032	1,673,673	1,944,701	1,630,214
Combined Totals	4,345,505		3,875,275		3,894,454		3,574,705		3,574,195	

1. Source: U. S. Department of Commerce, Bureau of Census, Census of Population, 1950, Volume II, Part I, Table 102, Marital Status by Age and Sex.

2. Source: U. S. Department of Commerce, Bureau of the Census, Census of Population, 1960, Volume I, Part I, Characteristics of the Population, Table 176, Marital Status.

3. Source: U. S. Department of Commerce, Bureau of the Census, 1970 Census of Population, Volume I, Part I, Characteristics of the Population, Table 203, Marital Status.

4. Source: U. S. Department of Commerce, Bureau of the Census, 1980 Census of Population, Volume I, Characteristics of the Population. Chapter D, Detailed Population Characteristics, Table 264; Marital Status.

TABLE C

Married Middle Adults (35-59) 1940-1980

Ages	1940 Males	1940 Females	1950[1] Males	1950[1] Females	1960[2] Males	1960[2] Females	1970[3] Males	1970[3] Females	1980[4] Males	1980[4] Females
35-39	3,874,210	3,911,529	4,717,260	4,882,565	5,376,707	5,658,013	4,772,338	4,944,969	5,656,541	5,691,415
40-44	3,677,764	3,519,262	4,329,415	4,257,490	5,033,384	5,083,593	5,123,593	5,242,784	4,834,421	4,812,272
45-49	3,517,891	3,167,650	3,832,980	3,635,340	4,754,204	4,579,971	5,131,288	5,207,386	4,574,853	4,553,757
50-54	3,073,063	2,568,964	3,434,635	3,102,335	4,142,564	3,799,854	4,682,225	4,520,709	4,793,715	4,737,284
55-59	2,407,253	1,902,259	2,955,480	2,491,385	3,546,065	3,085,057	4,156,178	3,776,995	4,716,683	4,515,936
Totals	16,550,181	15,069,664	19,269,770	18,369,115	22,852,924	22,206,488	23,865,622	23,692,843	24,576,213	24,310,664
Combined Totals	31,619,845		37,638,885		45,059,412		47,558,465		48,886,877	

1. Source: U. S. Department of Commerce, Bureau of Census, Census of Population, 1950, Volume II, Part I, Table 102, Marital Status by Age and Sex.

2. Source: U. S. Department of Commerce, Bureau of the Census, Census of Population, 1960, Volume I, Part I, Characteristics of the Population, Table 176, Marital Status.

3. Source: U. S. Department of Commerce, Bureau of the Census, 1970 Census of Population, Volume I, Part I, Characteristics of the Population, Table 203, Marital Status.

4. Source: U. S. Department of Commerce, Bureau of the Census, 1980 Census of Population, Volume I, Characteristics of the Population, Chapter D, Detailed Population Characteristics, Table 264; Marital Status.

TABLE D

Widowed Middle Adults (35-59) 1940-1980

Ages	1940		1950[1]		1960[2]		1970[3]		1980[4]	
	Males	Females	Males	Females	Males	Females	Males	Females	Males	Females
35-39	60,759	219,608	36,215	155,500	29,446	138,383	27,586	124,615	22,337	111,579
40-44	94,646	317,976	58,650	253,750	46,990	235,833	47,960	229,145	31,037	167,725
45-49	135,957	432,856	92,070	391,825	73,981	372,811	74,526	366,406	52,711	285,345
50-54	192,173	558,592	148,685	575,770	108,279	548,447	111,618	576,390	99,713	530,289
55-59	222,202	634,932	210,065	738,245	160,729	791,240	153,163	841,602	153,611	873,312
Totals	705,737	2,163,964	545,685	2,115,090	419,425	2,086,714	414,853	2,138,158	359,409	1,968,250
Combined Totals	2,869,701		2,660,775		2,506,139		2,553,011		2,327,659	

1. Source: U. S. Department of Commerce, Bureau of Census, Census of Population, 1950, Volume II, Part I, Table 102, Marital Status by Age and Sex.

2. Source: U. S. Department of Commerce, Bureau of the Census, Census of Population, 1960, Volume I, Part I, Characteristics of the Population, Table 176, Marital Status.

3. Source: U. S. Department of Commerce, Bureau of the Census, 1970 Census of Population, Volume I, Part I, Characteristics of the Population, Table 203, Marital Status.

4. Source: U. S. Department of Commerce, Bureau of the Census, 1980 Census of Population, Volume I, Characteristics of the Population, Chapter D, Detailed Population Characteristics, Table 264; Marital Status.

TABLE E

Divorced Middle Adults (35-59) 1940-1980

Ages	1940 Males	1940 Females	1950[1] Males	1950[1] Females	1960[2] Males	1960[2] Females	1970[3] Males	1970[3] Females	1980[4] Males	1980[4] Females
35-39	84,703	132,376	129,975	197,455	149,277	232,616	184,425	303,895	587,739	827,463
40-44	88,718	116,799	134,110	190,410	154,603	239,137	221,457	342,652	458,610	662,847
45-49	83,439	96,212	130,940	165,980	161,342	238,213	221,616	346,837	398,752	574,676
50-54	74,492	71,466	119,850	136,205	149,911	208,147	205,809	316,174	379,782	546,100
55-59	56,689	49,211	97,790	96,830	131,687	171,921	185,483	270,516	319,824	475,879
Totals	388,039	466,064	612,665	786,880	746,820	1,190,034	1,018,790	1,580,074	2,144,707	3,086,965
Combined Totals	854,105		1,399,545		1,836,854		2,598,864		5,231,674	

1. Source: U. S. Department of Commerce, Bureau of Census, Census of Population, 1950, Volume II, Part I, Table 102, Marital Status by Age and Sex.

2. Source: U. S. Department of Commerce, Bureau of the Census, Census of Population, 1960, Volume I, Part I, Characteristics of the Population, Table 176, Marital Status.

3. Source: U. S. Department of Commerce, Bureau of the Census, 1970 Census of Population, Volume I, Part I, Characteristics of the Population, Table 203, Marital Status.

4. Source: U. S. Department of Commerce, Bureau of the Census, 1980 Census of Population, Volume I, Characteristics of the Population, Chapter D, Detailed Population Characteristics, Table 264; Marital Status.

TABLE F

Separated Middle Adults (35-59) 1960-1980

Ages	1960[1] Males	Females	1970[2] Males	Females	1980[3] Males	Females
35-39	103,859	175,349	100,815	194,021	182,561	283,669
40-44	98,383	156,025	112,310	199,552	151,594	230,623
45-49	98,014	139,178	110,904	178,032	129,739	193,125
50-54	84,602	112,444	98,502	146,005	126,693	179,197
55-59	76,030	88,864	86,451	114,248	106,794	145,908
Totals	460,888	671,860	508,982	831,858	697,381	1,032,522
Combined Totals	1,132,748		1,340,840		1,729,903	

1. Source: U. S. Department of Commerce, Bureau of the Census, Census of Population, 1960, Volume I, Part I, Characteristics of the Population, Table 176, Marital Status.

2. Source: U. S. Department of Commerce, Bureau of the Census, 1970 Census of Population, Volume I, Part I, Characteristics of the Population, Table 203, Marital Status.

3. Source: U. S. Department of Commerce, Bureau of the Census, 1980 Census of Population, Volume I, Characteristics of the Population, Chapter D, Detailed Population Characteristics, Table 264; Marital Status.

TABLE G[1]

Remarried Widowed/Divorced Middle Adults (35-59) 1980

Ages	Widowed		Divorced	
	Males	Females	Males	Females
35-39	58,988	196,351	1,637,496	1,820,033
40-44	80,820	270,777	1,367,358	1,479,571
45-49	124,483	424,572	1,208,255	1,300,497
50-54	220,747	736,073	1,180,559	1,283,074
55-59	325,306	1,151,623	1,052,321	1,170,240
Totals	810,344	2,779,396	6,445,989	7,053,415
Combined Totals	3,589,740		13,499,404	

1. Source: U. S. Department of Commerce, Bureau of the Census, 1980 Census of Population, Volume I, Characteristics of the Population, Chapter D. Detailed Population Characteristics, Table 264; Marital Status.

4

Later Adult Years
Lucien E. Coleman

My wife and I had just finished an evening meal in a Florida restaurant. As the waitress wrote the check, she eyed my graying hair and asked, "Do you get a senior citizen's discount, sir?"

Since it should have been obvious to anyone that I was still in the prime of life at fifty-two, the question seemed unnecessary. But, to satisfy my curiosity, I inquired, "How old does one have to be to qualify for a senior citizen's discount?" "Fifty-five," she said. "That's when you start being a senior citizen around here."

That might be true in Florida restaurants, but, in other sectors, one starts being a senior citizen somewhat later. Since 1970, for instance, Southern Baptists have designated sixty as the dividing line between middle and later adulthood. And the U. S. Census Bureau marks the beginning of older adulthood at sixty-five, the traditional age of retirement. (Retiring before sixty-five is universally referred to as "taking early retirement.") However, this could change in the not-to-distant future if forces already at work in our society push the age of retirement further up the age ladder.

For example, in 1978, Congress eliminated mandatory retirement for federal employees and raised the compulsory retirement age from sixty-five to seventy in the private sector. One of the priority recommendations coming out of the 1981 White House Conference on Aging was a proposal to prohibit mandatory retirement at any age. And in March, 1982, President Reagan announced that he favored such legislation. If the laws regulating retirement were to change, and if significant numbers of adults were to exercise the option to continue working even beyond age seventy, the present parameters of later adulthood could undergo significant redefinition.

The Scope of Later Adulthood

Whether it begins at fifty-five, sixty, or sixty-five, "later adulthood" covers a good portion of the life span. This category includes the eighty-one-year-old Texan who drove one-hundred miles to be present at his mother's birthday party—and with his one-hundred-three-year-old mother. It also includes a sixty-five-year-old surgeon who is still at the peak of his career and a Sunday School teacher who, though blind since birth, launched a productive writing career at age sixty-four.

Increasing longevity has dramatically expanded the horizons of older adulthood in this century. In 1900, life expectancy was forty-six for males and forty-eight for females. Today, life expectancy at birth is seventy years for men and seventy-eight years for women. In other words, today's children can expect to live a quarter of a century longer than their great-grandparents.

Stimulated by advances in medical science, sanitation, nutrition, and generally better living conditions, the trend toward longer life is creating a new class of elderly adults. At the turn of the century, fewer than one million Americans had reached their seventy-fifth birthday. Today, some nine million persons, one fourth of the older adult population, have lived past seventy-five. At present, one of every sixteen elderly persons is eighty-five or older; by the year 2000, one of every eleven older adults will be in this "oldest-of-the-old" category.

This lengthening of life may require us to rethink present age-group classifications in church programs. "Sixty-and-up" now covers a broad chronological spectrum. At ages twenty-five, forty-five, and sixty-five, men and women are thought of as being "young," "middle," and "older" adults, respectively. But "older adulthood," as presently defined, lumps sixty-five-year-olds and eighty-five-year-olds into a single category even though they are separated by precisely the same twenty-year span.

The "Graying" of the Population

The size of the sixty-five-and-over population grew from 3,084,000 in 1900 to 25,544,000 in 1980, a sevenfold increase. And, by the year 2020, the 1980 figure will have doubled to 51,386,000. Today, one of every nine persons in our country is an older adult, and, by 2020, one of every six will be sixty-five or older.[1]

Obviously, America is aging. And this trend will continue well into the twenty-first century. Between 1980 and 2050, the proportion of the population in the older adult category will have nearly doubled, from 11.3 to 21.7 percent.

In 1970, there were one third more youth than older adults in the United States. In November 1984, the older adult population equaled the number of youth. And by 1995, it is estimated, there will be one third more older adults than youth.

The impact of this accelerating growth of the aging population will be felt in almost every sector of public life. There will be increasing pressure to reformulate public policy to better meet the needs of older adults as senior citizens become an increasingly formidable lobbying group. Already, the American Association of Retired Persons (AARP), with its 13 million members, is a force to be reckoned with in the legislative arena.

Changes in the educational system, already visible, will become more pronounced in the years ahead. While the pool of eighteen to twenty-two-year-old college students is steadily diminishing, large numbers of older adults are claiming opportunities for study which they had forfeited in earlier years. And institutions of higher learning are actively seeking the older learner in student recruitment programs. No longer is the college classroom the exclusive province of younger adults.

As the elderly become more numerous and relatively more affluent, marketing and advertising will reflect the economic importance of older consumers. This is not to say that older Americans will constitute a monolithic "consumer class" since research shows that buying habits and product preferences are as diversified among the aging as they are among younger adults. But as business and industry recognize the increasing significance of older consumers, marketing efforts will be focused less exclusively on "the now generation."

The "graying of society" will inevitably effect the makeup of church congregations, and this will have a corresponding impact upon church programs. With a proliferation of older adults in prospect files, churches will be challenged to work out evangelistic strategies specifically designed to reach the elderly. And older adults themselves should become an important element in planning and implementing such strategies.

Leaders of church recreation programs will find it increasingly important to seek specialized training in the area of gerontology. Physical-conditioning classes for the aging and specialized medical seminars (for example, stroke recovery groups) will be added to more traditional activities for senior adults (for example, arts and crafts). And the best church activities programs will make creative use of the leadership skills of older adults themselves. Picture, for example, a Saturday morning bicycle clinic for youngsters conducted by a retired mechanic, or a baby-care course for expectant mothers taught by a seasoned nurse.

The Mythology of Aging

Mrs. Nan Cantrell, longtime citizen of a small Texas town, was honored by her church for her many years of Christian service. The local newspaper carried the story along with a nice photograph under the headline: "93 YEARS YOUNG." The headline was intended to be complimentary, but it subtly reflected the negative bias toward old age so ingrained in our culture. Why "ninety-three years *young?*" Why not "ninety-three years *old?*" Because, in our society, everyone knows that young is better than old. Americans tend to regard old age as a disease to be postponed as long as possible.

In our culture, those who wish to learn about older adults must begin by unlearning what society has taught them about the aged. It is widely believed that most old people are sick, poor, grouchy, forgetful, lonely, senile, sexless, rigid, incapable of learning, and useless to society. Yet, not one of these traits is characteristic of most older adults. They are products of our mythology of aging.

Are most old people sickly? The truth is, although chronic maladies like arthritis, rheumatism, high blood pressure, and depression are more common among older adults, the vast majority of elderly people in this country are well enough to live quite normally. Only 5 percent of all older adults live in nursing homes. (Beyond age eighty-five, this figure goes up to 19 percent.) Nine out of ten men and women over sixty-five live active, independent lives. Sickness keeps them in bed only fourteen days a year, on the average.[2]

Are the elderly poor? Not as poor as the average American pictures them. Between 1959 and 1979, the number of older people who were officially counted as "poor" dropped from 5.5 million to 3.6 million or from 35.2 percent of the elderly population to 15.1 percent. In 1970, older adults accounted for about one fourth of the people living below the poverty level. By 1977, however, only one in seven older adults had incomes below the poverty level. From the mid-1960s to 1977, median family income for the elderly rose from 50 percent of the national average to 57 percent; and income for single adults in this older age group was 65 percent of the national average in that same year.[3]

Even though the majority of senior adults live in older homes, purchased some thirty or more years before retirement, this does not mean that they live in rundown housing. The nationwide *Annual Housing Survey* shows each year that the elderly are almost as well-housed as the population at large.[4]

These observations should not be allowed to obscure the fact that substantial numbers of elderly people live in abject poverty. But, thanks to the Social Security system and the growth of private pension plans, the economic situation of retired adults has improved substantially in recent years.

Does advancing age make people irritable, critical, and demanding? Not really. There are plenty of unpleasant people in older age brackets, but most of them were like that in earlier years. Research shows that personality traits remain consistent throughout adult life. Persons who are loving, warm, and open as young adults tend to remain that way in old age. Persons who are abrasive in their later years usually learned to be like that in early and middle adulthood.

Some personality changes are attributable to organic causes. Physical events such as strokes, reactions to medications, infection, brain tumors, and other diseases can cause persons to become suspicious, depressive, irritable, and anxious. But these symptoms are not the direct result of aging. Although it happens that older persons are more susceptible to such maladies, younger people are affected by them in much the same ways when they are similarly afflicted.

Are older people senile? The phenomenon of senility is widely misunderstood. It is often associated with feebleness, forgetfulness, and mental decline; all of which are assumed to be the inevitable result of chronological aging. In actual fact, true senility is caused by chronic brain damage brought on by hardening of the arteries in the brain or by a catastrophic ailment like Alzheimer's disease. Only 4 percent of older people are affected by either of these problems. Research shows that older people do not typically suffer loss of memory or other forms of mental decline usually attributed to "senility."

Does intellectual capacity decline with age? A friend told me of hosting Dr. Gaines S. Dobbins, a pioneering Southern Baptist educator, at a church-sponsored religious education conference. He was ninety at the time, physically frail but strong in mind and spirit. At the motel where Dr. Dobbins was to stay, the desk clerk, without saying a word to the elderly man, asked his younger companion to fill out the registration card. Irritated by the clerk's callous treatment of her distinguished guest, she said, "Young man, this gentleman has written more books than you probably will ever read; he most certainly is capable of signing his name." And, indeed, Dobbins had added two more titles to his growing list of publications that very year.

In 1974, Paul Baltes and Warner Schaie published an article entitled "The Myth of the Twilight Years."[5] Summing up ten years of research on intelligence in the aged, they reported: "In our opinion, general intellectual decline in old age is largely a myth." They went on to say: "On at least some dimensions of intelligence, particularly the crystallized type, people of average health can expect to maintain or even increase their level of performance into old age."

Other research has shown that the mental habits of people in their later years tend to perpetuate patterns formed earlier. Individuals who put their minds to work through early and middle adulthood are likely to maintain intellectual ability as they grow older.

What about sexual capacity? It is true that older men and women undergo a gradual decline in sexual powers even as they experience changes in other bodily functions. But there is evidence that changes in sexual behavior in old age are more attributable to psychological than to physiological factors. In our society, sexuality is invariably associated with youthful beauty. In such a climate, sexual desire in older adults is regarded as being more pathological than normal. And this makes it increasingly difficult for the elderly to acknowledge their sexual needs.

However, research consistently shows that people who have been sexually active during the earlier years of marriage are likely to continue sexual activity as they grow older. A recent Consumer's Union survey of more than four thousand men and women, ages fifty to ninety-three, found two thirds of the women and four fifths of the men over seventy to be sexually active.[6]

Are the elderly lonely? Loneliness is one of the problems frequently reported by older people, particularly by those who have suffered the loss of spouses. And in virtually every community, one can find aging women and men whose families have abandoned them. But loneliness is not nearly so universal among the elderly as was once thought. A 1974 Harris Survey found that 80 percent of the older respondents with living children had seen them within the past week, and more than half within the last day. Other studies indicate that most older people prefer a measure of separation from their children, even if they have enjoyed a lifetime of close ties.[7]

Are older people alike? One of the myths of aging in our society is that the elderly tend to lose their individuality in the process of aging, becoming pretty much alike in their ideas, attitudes, and ways of living. But, in recent years, psychologists have discovered that older persons become quite diverse with advancing years.

In 1976 a team of researchers conducted an extensive study of the life-styles and consumer behaviors of older Americans. Contrary to the popular notion that elderly persons develop a sameness in their thinking, these investigators found that no single life-style was typical of elderly persons and that consumer behavior (for example, buying style, store choice, selection of food, housing, clothing) remains stable in individuals throughout the adult years. Older adults are just as diversified in tastes, preferences, and life-styles as younger adults.[8]

The Problems and Promises of Retirement

The meaning of retirement cannot be properly assessed apart from the significance of work in the lives of most adults. A person's work has a great deal to do with self-esteem, role in society, economic status, and the whole personal identity. The abrupt termination of work can call for major adjustments in a person's life-style, everyday routines, social contacts, and family relations.

One of the more formidable problems presented by retirement is the loss of automatic job-defined roles. The ex-president of a corporation, a former military officer, or a school administrator may find it difficult to operate outside the system which supported his personal authority and fall back upon his self-perceived old status rather than to redefine relationships with others.

Some researchers have observed a similar problem within family life. A man may be looked upon as the primary breadwinner for the family throughout his working years, deriving respect and authority from that role. When he suddenly relinquishes the role of income earner, he and other members of the family may wonder where he now fits into the scheme of things.

Another potential problem in the experience of retirement is the loss of life structure. Prior to retirement, a person's schedule is set by his job. Five working days followed by a two-day weekend is the normal pattern. Then retirement comes, and soon the days take on a kind of sameness.

Saturday becomes no different from Tuesday. The rhythm of life is broken.

Perhaps the greatest problem posed by retirement is rooted in our culture's "work ethic" which will not permit one to derive self-respect from leisure. Even though the institution of retirement implies that one deserves a reward after many years of labor, our society has never really come to look upon nonproductive leisure pursuits as a legitimate substitute for work.

Retired persons, therefore, need much more than "busywork" activities. They need opportunities to make meaningful contributions to the lives of others in their families, churches, and communities. And herein lies one of the great promises of the retirement years. Rather than being regarded as the cessation of productive labor, retirement may become the doorway to one of the most fruitful periods in life.

Retired men and women can bring a rare combination of gifts to the mission and ministry of the church. They have wisdom hammered out on the anvil of experience, technical knowledge and skills derived from a variety of occupations, and large measures of discretionary time. They represent an enormous pool of human potential, waiting to be utilized in the service of God.

> They are planted in the house of the Lord, they flourish in the courts of our God. They still bring forth fruit in old age (Ps. 92:13-14, RSV).

Notes

1. *Reader's Digest 1985 Almanac and Yearbook* (Pleasantville, N.Y.: The Reader's Digest Association, Inc., 1985), p. 962.

2. *Final Report, 1981 White House Conference on Aging, Volume 1* (Washington, D.C.: U. S. Government Printing Office, 1982), p. 9.

3. Ibid.

4. Ibid.

5. Paul B. Baltes, and K. Warner Schaie, "The Myth of the Twilight Years," *Psychology Today,* March 1974, pp. 35-40.

6. Norman Lobsenz, "Seven Myths About Aging," *Parade Magazine,* 30 Sept. 1984, p. 11.

7. *Final Report, 1981 White House Conference,* p. 9.

8. Arthur N. Schwartz, Cherie L. Snyder, and James A. Peterson, *Aging & Life: An Introduction to Gerontology, Second Edition* (New York: Holt, Rinehart, and Winston, 1984), pp. 182-184.

5

Single Adults: A New Challenge for the Church
Jerry M. Stubblefield

Introduction

One third of the adult population in America is single—always single, widowed, divorced, or separated. When I first read this statistic in the 1970s, I felt this was a new trend—that the adult population was shifting toward singleness. The census data, however, indicates only a slight movement in this direction. Table A, which analyzes the marital status of adults, shows a 3.5 percent increase in singleness since 1940. Numerically, there has been an increase of 31,466,927, growing from 30.1 million in 1940 to 61.6 million in 1980.

The greatest growth has occurred in the number and percentage of adults who have been widowed, divorced, or are now separated from a spouse. The 1980 census reported, for the first time, persons who are separated. The percentage of always single has dropped 4.2 percent since 1940. An alarming statistic is that divorce has more than doubled since 1970.

Single adults have been classified under three major headings—the never married, the widowed, and the divorced. Some have also included the separated as single adults. The separated person is difficult to identify because the person may not be living with a spouse for a variety of reasons. Separation may be caused by work, military duty, awaiting a divorce, or in hopes of reconciling the marital problems and resuming the marriage. I will use the designation of singles suggested by Britton Wood who described singles as: Single by Choice (Always Single), Single After Marriage—Without Choice (Widowed), Single After Marriage—by Choice (Divorced), and Single but Not Single (Separated).[1]

The Christian church has known how to minister to the always single and the widowed but has had great difficulty in accepting and ministering to divorced persons. This chapter will examine demographics of single adults in each category. The characteristics, tasks, and needs of each type

98

of single will be reviewed and analyzed. The implications and opportunities for the church in ministering *to* and *with* single adults will be described. Though demographic information is limited concerning the separated, a brief section will deal with this category as it pertains to single adults.

Before examining the various types of single adults, a fundamental question must be considered: "When does a person become an adult?" This issue is discussed in chapter 2, "The Young Adult Years." In recent years, persons have been viewed as adults when they reached age eighteen, completed high school, or married. In most states an individual has adult privileges such as driving an automobile, establishing credit, and voting rights by age eighteen. Some states have lowered the right to purchase alcoholic beverages to age eighteen.

Chapter 2 poses the question: "Is age an accurate index for considering a person an adult?" Legally yes, psychologically and sociologically the answer is both yes and no depending upon the person and individual life patterns.

Single by Choice—Always Single

Introduction

The always single represents the largest numerical classification of single adults. They should be viewed as being complete and whole persons who have *chosen* to be single, rather than described as "never married." While many always singles would react to Wood's phrase "Single by Choice," they have chosen to be single for whatever reason. In conferences and seminary classes, I have found the under-thirty always single feels, "Someday I will get married." Now for a closer look at the always single.

Demographics

A review of Table A reveals that at present there are 33.5 million always single in America. Percentagewise, there has been a decline from 24.3 percent in 1940 to 20.1 percent in 1980. Table B breaks down the information by decades and gives the number of males and females in each age category. Since 1940 single adult males have outnumbered females. This fact is not reflected in enrollment or participation patterns in churches. Most single adult church ministries show three to four females for every male. Information reveals that there are large numbers of single adults ranging in age from eighteen to over seventy-five. Males outnumbered females in every age bracket except fifty-five and over.

Characteristics, Tasks, Needs

Always-single adult characteristics must include those which are relevant for each period of adulthood. A careful study of each adult period will provide insight for either what the person should be experiencing or has experienced. It may also reveal why the individual is having difficulties and problems with tasks confronted during the present adult period in life.

Two men who have profoundly influenced our understanding of the human life cycle are Robert J. Havighurst and Eric H. Erikson. Both have stated that marriage plays a significant part in the well-being of adults. Havighurst's first four developmental tasks in early adulthood relate to marriage: (1) selecting a mate, (2) learning to live with a marriage partner, (3) starting a family, and (4) rearing children. Two of his tasks in middle adulthood are: (1) assisting teenage children to become responsible and happy adults, and (2) relating oneself to one's spouse as a person. Only one task relates to marriage in later maturity: adjusting to the death of a spouse.[2] Erikson, though he did not use the term *marriage,* implied marriage particularly in his discussion of intimacy vs. isolation (young adulthood) and generativity vs. stagnation (middle adulthood).[3]

Both Havighurst and Erikson place the always single at variance with what is expected for adults. Both men originally wrote their works during the 1950s. Table A reflects that in 1950 17.2 percent of the adult population were always single. The always single has been placed on the defensive by the attitude expressed in the question: "Why aren't you married?" or with the insinuation: "What's wrong with you?"

We are now experiencing an attitudinal change in the acceptance that it is "OK" to be single. Biblical studies indicate that there are examples of always single persons who profoundly influenced their world and served God.[4]

Brown stated that a sense of wholeness is the gift of God. He cited the stories of Jesus healing the man with the withered hand (Matt. 12:10-13) and the man by the pool of Bethesda (John 5:5-9a).[5] While one might not agree with his exegesis of these passages, his conclusion is correct. A person has a sense of wholeness or completeness as a result of what

God has done in Christ. The always single need to be seen as whole persons who are created and redeemed by God.

Always-single persons have the same needs as any other adult. An exercise I have used has been to ask classes to brainstorm the needs of single adults. After the list has been written on the chalkboard, I have asked them to identify those that apply only to single adults. The conclusion has been that the needs of single and married adults are alike. The difference is that the single must seek out other adults to help meet these needs while marriage provides opportunity to fill many of them.

The needs of the always single include:

- A sense of identity (good self-image)
- Meaningful relationships with members of the same sex and members of the opposite sex
- Satisfactory living arrangements (living alone, living with other single adults, living with other family members)
- Financial independence
- Fulfilling social associations
- Enjoying close relationships with individuals of the same sex and of the opposite sex
- Participation in activities that improve social conditions or meet the needs of others

Implications and Opportunities for Ministry

Each church should recognize the tremendous opportunities for ministry both *to* and *with* the always single. A church can minister by providing Bible studies and special-needs seminars, by providing a place to meet on Sundays and at other times, by purchasing curriculum materials written and designed for them. A church should minister to singles but at the same time permit them to minister to others in the church and community. They might teach Sunday School classes, participate in the church music program, work with children and youth in regular and special activities, and be elected to church committees and offices.

The church must treat the always singles as adults. One of the first questions frequently asked single adults as they plan for retreats or various activities is: "Who are the chaperons?" At first glance it seems a logical question. Many singles laugh at such statements but underneath resent it. These are adults who are financially independent, live alone or with other single adults, have responsible jobs, assume responsibility for every facet of their lives, yet the church wants to treat them as children.

Experience has proven that single adults can be responsible and handle the most difficult circumstances in a mature manner. The church should treat the always-single adults as adults because they are adults.

A third implication for the church is to give consideration to the always-single adult for various positions of leadership and responsibility in the church. Many feel discriminated against by the church because they are single. If persons are given special consideration because they are single—that would be reverse discrimination. Nicholas Christoff proposed that one third of a church's leadership positions should be filled by single adults since one third of the American population is single.[6] A church should consider for positions of responsibility and leadership the persons best qualified in terms of spiritual maturity and leadership ability. Marital status should not be the only consideration.

Another opportunity for ministry to the always single is to have a balanced provision for them in the organizational structure of the church. Churches have provided Bible study classes for the young always single, often called the college and career class. Table B reveals a significant number of singles throughout the adult life span. While the greatest number are thirty-four and under, a church should provide for the always single past thirty-five. Some have assumed that after age thirty the always single's needs can be met through existing men's or women's classes. Whenever possible, a church should have classes especially designed to meet the needs of the always single at all ages.

A shortcoming of the church has been the inability to enlist and involve men in the life and work of the church. Always-single men outnumber women in each age category until age fifty-five and over. A definite strategy must be developed that will appeal to and meet the needs of men. Most single adult Sunday School classes and ministries have an overbalance of women to men, yet the demographic evidence shows the reverse to be true. A concerted effort should be launched to reach them.

Single After Marriage—Without Choice (Widowed)

Introduction

Churches have often thought of ministering to the widowed in terms of women. While this action seems appropriate, the statistical evidence as seen in Table C shows a significant number of men who have been widowed at all ages. Churches have endeavored to minister to the widowed through pastoral care, church ministries, and existing Sunday School classes.

Demographics

Table A points out that the widowed have increased from 7.8 million in 1940 to 13.3 million in 1980 or a numerical gain of 5.5 million—an increase of 69.75 percent. This large percentage increase can be attributed to population growth. Percentagewise, the change has only been an increase of .33 percent. At every age group, there are more women than men. Significant differences are observable from age thirty-five onward.

Table C shows the total number of persons widowed in terms of age and sex. There is a significant difference between men and women, far out of balance with their numbers in the total population. While men outnumbered women slightly in 1940, there were more than twice as many widows. Since 1950 there have been more women than men, yet the number of widows is disproportionate to the number of widowers. The 1980 figures shows five times as many women as men in this category while there are only 4.4 percent more women in the adult population. For the first time in 1980, the census data listed persons who have remarried but had been widowed. Widowed men who had remarried numbered 3.6 million while there were 13 million women.

Sociologists have contended for some time that men need marriage more than women and are more likely to remarry. Table E does not confirm this fact either for the widowed or the divorced who remarry.

Characteristics, Tasks, and Needs

Characteristics, tasks, and needs of widowed persons are those that predominate through the adult life cycle. A task that is peculiar to the widowed is the need to deal with the death of a mate. The surviving spouse has the awesome task of having to deal with death. Regardless of the length of the marriage, individuals must deal with their grief. The grief process has been identified as including these steps:

- Denial—Refusal to admit that death has occurred. The survivor may experience this when a terminal illness is first diagnosed. Denial is particularly felt when death has come due to sudden or crises circumstances.
- Rage and anger—A great deal of resentment may be expressed and may be addressed either to God or the dead loved one or both.

- Fantasy—The survivor both accepts and denies the reality of what has happened.

- Depression—One begins to withdraw into a shell. Isolation is a frequent pattern during this stage. Persons trying to minister to the grief-stricken feel they are not being heard and/or cannot be helpful. Survivors state that there is no desire to live without their mates.

- Acceptance—One now accepts what has happened and gets on with the process of living. It is a mistake, however, to think that the persons have completely worked through their feelings about the departed loved one.[7]

The widowed must go through these basic steps but may not do so in the order listed. It should also be kept in mind that a person may experience these stages more than once and they may be done in a variety of ways. After the death of my father, my mother moved quickly to acceptance. However, in three or four years the depression stage was evident. This is to say that all persons will deal with these factors in their own way and in their own time.

Both society and the church help the widowed deal with their grief. Churches help persons experiencing grief by providing ministry and support at the time of death and during the grief process. Memorial services are held which help the family mark the occasion of death. Usually public notice is placed in newspapers. Churches and society have ways to respond in an affirmative manner to the widowed.

A characteristic of older widowed persons, especially women, is that they do not perceive themselves as single. They still see themselves as part of a couple though separated by death. This may be observed by the length of time these persons continue to wear wedding rings. As evidenced in Table C, the largest percent of widowed men and women is after age forty-five, with women far outnumbering men.

Implications and Opportunities for Ministry

With more than 12.8 million widowed over age forty-five, the church has a great challenge to minister to these people. Churches must consider providing Bible study groups and other special activities that will meet the needs of the widowed. Though there will be a preponderance of women, the needs of men should not be ignored. If possible there should be more than one group to care for the variety of needs in persons ranging in age from forty-five to over eighty-five. Though numerically the younger widowed group is much smaller, attempts to minister to them should be considered.

Churches can and should form support ministry groups to help persons experiencing grief through the death of a spouse. Models for this activity can be found in hospice programs, and churches can train members to be effective in helping those who grieve regardless of age. Individuals who have handled their own grief in a mature and Christian fashion could be trained to assist others experiencing grief. Periodic meetings of the widowed could be a source of strength and help with fellowship and programs designed to encourage the widowed.

A church would be wise to enlist men to share both program and leadership responsibilities so that widowed men will participate. This suggestion is not to discount what women are doing in this regard. In this situation, men respond better to men partly because they are so outnumbered by women.

Churches need to be sensitive to specific problems and concerns of the widowed. A church should not only be aware but should seek to minister to this group whenever possible.

Single After Marriage—by Choice (Divorced)

Introduction

Between 1970 and 1980 the number of divorced persons more than doubled in the United States. It was during this time that churches began to minister to single adults in its midst including the divorced. There has been a feeling among many divorced that the church had stamped a *D* on their foreheads, thus placing them in a category that the church would not minister to or accept as a vital part of the church.

This attitude has changed drastically over the last decade. Divorce is still a problem for some churches. They do not know how to respond either to the divorced person or when divorce is in process. There are some hopeful signs on the horizon. Recently, in a Sunday School Leadership Conference for Single Adults, two of my conferees were professional counselors who were specializing in counseling persons who were experiencing divorce. Both were supported and sponsored by their church.

There are many divorced persons who would disagree with the title for this section, "Single After Marriage—By Choice (Divorced)." Their quarrel would not be that they are single after marriage or that they are divorced. The problem comes in the words *by choice*. This issue is graphically illustrated by the book *Jason Loves Jane but They Got a Divorce.*[8] In many divorces, one of the marriage partners does not want a divorce. However, a number of states now have laws permitting "no-fault divorce."

The incidence of divorce has increased sharply. It is rare to find a family that has not been affected by divorce either by the parents, brothers and sisters, or aunts and uncles. Tables A and D provide statistics concerning divorce in America.

Demographics

The incidence of divorce followed basic population growth cycles from 1940 to 1970. During the next decade divorce increased more than 2.2 times. Since 1960 there are more women than men who are classified as divorced. This creates an interesting situation since for every divorce there is a man and a woman. Table E lists more women who remarry after divorce than men.

Sociologists project that there will be an increasing number of divorced persons in the American population. In starting a Single Adult ministry for a metropolitan Baptist association, I was criticized by several area pastors when we focused on the Formerly Married—the Divorced. (Ministries were also conducted for the Always Single). Their reaction was that I was encouraging divorce. In actuality, it was a recognition that divorce had occurred in many lives and was an attempt to minister to the needs of divorced persons. The need for Christian ministry for divorced persons is evident, but *each* church must decide whether this ministry is for them.

Table E points out that in 1980 there were almost 26.5 million persons who had been divorced but were now remarried. If this number were added to the 10.8 million listed as divorced, it would exceed the total number of always single in 1980.

Characteristics, Tasks, and Needs

Persons who have experienced divorce have needs that characterize the various periods of the adult life cycle. In addition to confronting the characteristics, tasks, and needs of adulthood, the divorced person must face challenges similar to the widowed and the always single plus some that are peculiar to the divorced.

Issues confronting the divorcee are the acceptance of marital failure and the lack of societal and church structures that signal the end of the marriage. When a marriage is ended by death, no one questions the quality of the marriage. The widowed receive encouragement and support both from society and the church. While the widowed and the divorced go through a similar grief process, widowhood is marked by a funeral, announcements, and acceptance by society. Divorce is marked by the admission that the marriage has failed and the lack of finality or societal rituals. Society is informed about the divorce by word of mouth.

Both the church and society have found it difficult to minister to those going through the pains of divorce or those having experienced divorced. We have excused ourselves by saying, "I don't know what to say or do." Possibly the best ministry is the ministry of presence for both the widowed and the divorced.

The divorcee experiences much that the widowed have to but with a stigma attached by society and the church. Unfortunately, the divorced begin without the support and encouragement which is extended to the widowed. Divorced women must contend with the image that they are easy sexual preys since they were sexually active during marriage. Thus, many find it harder to establish meaningful relationships of a wholesome nature.

Evidence suggests that both men and women who are divorced frequently try to establish significant relationships before they have emotionally worked through the divorce. A person who divorces at a younger age is more likely to remarry. Of the more than 105 million persons married in 1980, almost 26.5 million reported they had been divorced. A number of books have been written recently concerning the matter of remarriage.[9]

Biblical references to divorce are found in Deuteronomy 24:1-3 and Matthew 5:31-32. Jesus spoke about marriage more than divorce. These verses set forth the grounds for divorce—adultery. Jesus interpreted Moses' reason for granting divorce as the hardness of heart (Matt. 19:8). Jesus addressed His views to men since women had few rights at this time. In the modern setting both men and women have personal rights. For whatever reason, divorce must be seen as falling short of the biblical ideal for marriage. Divorce leaves scars on everyone involved.

Implications and Opportunities for Ministry

Opportunities for ministry to persons experiencing divorce are diverse and multitudinous in nature. Divorce affects both men and women in significant numbers beginning at age twenty-five. More women than men are identified as divorced at all ages. The church must endeavor to meet this challenge by providing Bible study groups for divorced persons. If the needs of the divorced are to be met successfully, seminars and special activities must be held that will provide information, encouragement, and a fellowship of caring people.

The church needs to accept the divorced as persons who have been forgiven by God and recipients of redemption. Many divorced persons perceive, accurately or inaccurately, that they are being judged and stereotyped by the church. The church should seek to treat the divorced with respect and love as it would seek to deal with everyone.

Many divorced persons can be effective in ministry through various programs and activities of the church. They should be considered on the basis of their spirituality, Christian maturity, and spiritual gifts, not merely on the basis of their marital status. Christian divorcees want the opportunity to provide ministry to persons in need—not just to be ministered to. Divorced persons desire to be an integral, vital part of the church with all the rights, privileges, benefits, and responsibilities that go with church membership.

A church can enhance its ministry to divorced persons by providing child-care service when activities and meetings for them are held at other than regular church times. They need contact with persons going through similar experiences. A church may communicate what they feel about the importance of ministering to divorced persons both by what they do to assist the ministry, and by what they fail to do which impedes the activities.

Churches can provide support and encouragement for the divorced through a divorce support ministry, modeled after that suggested for ministering to the widowed. In addition, men need to be enlisted to work with the divorced.

A church should seek to strengthen and enable people to have strong and healthy marriages. A church must take seriously its responsibility to better equip individuals for better marriages. The church must contribute to the preventive approach to the problem of divorce.

Single but Not Single (Separated)

In 1980 the census data listed persons who were married but whose spouse was absent; see Table E. The information was divided into two categories—the separated and other. Persons shown as separated were 3.9 million while 2.4 million were identified as other. There are many legitimate reasons why a spouse would be absent: military duty, work, institutionalized in a hospital, mental facility, or prison.

Separation usually means that a couple is attempting to learn something about their relationship by living apart from each other. Persons who are separated are not all moving toward divorce. Those who are separated from a spouse are functioning as a single adult but are not really single. Efforts should be made to help the separated reconcile whatever differences caused the separation.

When the separation extends over a lengthy period of time, often the separated person wants contact and fellowship with other single persons. For those separated persons desiring fellowship with single people before the divorce is finalized, certain guidelines seem to be in order:

- When one is not free to marry, one is not free to date.
- When one is not free to marry, one should inform others of one's separated status.
- When one is not free to marry, one is probably vulnerable to attention from persons of the opposite sex.
- When one is not free to marry, all heterosexual encounters and conversations need to be in group settings and never in one-to-one settings.[10]

Conclusions

The church has a tremendous challenge and opportunity to minister to large numbers of single adults. Single adult needs suggest special program structures and emphases. While such programs provide opportunities for support. They also provide opportunities for singles to use their gifts to minister to others.

The church is caught in a dilemma. More than 63 percent of adults are married; the church must minister to couples and their families. The church must hold up the highest Christian ideals concerning the family and the home. The other side is that more than one third of the adult population fits into the four categories of single. The church must offer hope and acceptance to the single. The church should offer forgiveness and support to those whose marriages have failed. The church should be a redemptive fellowship for all persons regardless of marital status.

What single adults want from the church is to be recognized as persons of worth who need ministry but who also desire to minister.

Notes

1. Britton Wood, *Single Adults Want to Be the Church, Too* (Nashville: Broadman Press, 1977).

2. Robert J. Havighurst, *Human Development and Education* (New York: Longmans, Green, and Co., 1953), pp. 259-262, 271-272, 279.

3. Erik H. Erikson, *Childhood and Society* (New York: Norton, 1963), pp. 263-268.

4. Brian L. Harbour, *Famous Singles of the Bible* (Nashville: Broadman Press, 1980).

5. Raymond Kay Brown, *Reach Out to Singles* (Philadelphia: The Westminster Press, 1978), pp. 127-129.

6. Nicholas B. Christoff, *Saturday Night, Sunday Morning* (San Francisco: Harper and Row, 1978), p. 116.

7. Elisabeth Kubler-Ross, ed., *Death: The Final Stage of Growth* (Englewood Cliffs, N.J.: Prentice-Hall, Inc., 1975).

8. Jason Towner, *Jason Loves Jane (But They Got a Divorce)* (Nashville: Impact Books, 1978).

9. Jay E. Adams, *Marriage, Divorce, and Remarriage in the Bible* (Phillipsburg, N.J.: Presbyterian and Reformed Publishing Company, 1980). E. Earl Joiner, *A Christian Considers Divorce and Remarriage* (Nashville: Broadman Press, 1983). John R. Martin, *Divorce and Remarriage* (Scottsdale, Pa.: Herald Press, 1976). Larry Richards, *Remarriage: A Healing Gift from God* (Waco: Word Books, 1981). Dwight Hervey Small, *The Right to Remarry* (Old Tappan: Fleming H. Revell Company, 1975).

10. Wood, pp. 82-83.

TABLE A

United States Adult Population 1940-1980

	Single	Percent of Adults	Married	Percent of Adults	Widowed	Percent of Adults	Divorced	Percent of Adults	Separated	Percent of Adults
1940[1]	21,996,834	24.3%	60,282,822	66.6%	7,843,814	7.46%	1,447,043	1.6%		
1950	17,653,485	17.2%	74,442,855	72%	8,998,125	7.66%	2,444,245	2.38%		
1960	16,732,586	14.6%	85,535,707	74.76%	9,952,517	7.86%	3,154,302	2.76%		
1970	22,379,107	16.96%	94,667,707	71.76%	11,746,212	7.5%	4,930,875	3.7%		
1980[2]	33,525,453	20.1%	105,277,979	63.1%	13,345,239	7.99%	10,869,463	6.5%	3,921,702	2.3%

1. Source: U. S. Department of Commerce, Bureau of the Census, Historical Statistics of the United States Colonial Times to 1970, Part I, Series A 160-171, Marital Status of the Population by Age and Sex: 1890 to 1970. U. S. Government Printing Office, Washington, D.C., 1975, p. 20.

2. Source: U. S. Department of Commerce, Bureau of the Census, 1980 Census of Population, Volume I, Characteristics of the Population, Chapter D, Detailed Population Characteristics, Table 264, Marital Status, Presence of Spouse, and Marital History for Persons 15 Years and Over.

TABLE B

Single Adults (18 and up) 1940-1980

Ages	1940[1] Males	Females	1950 Males	Females	1960 Males	Females	1970 Males	Females	1980[2] Males	Females
18-19	2,402,878	1,962,777	1,995,250	1,519,215	2,146,876	1,642,135	3,328,546	2,804,666	4,101,040	3,557,993
20-24	4,109,304	2,781,001	3,281,540	1,898,910	2,807,784	1,567,622	4,307,592	3,030,876	7,255,520	5,450,056
25-29	1,964,118	1,288,092	1,404,860	833,040	1,111,768	582,114	1,288,594	827,906	3,106,296	2,111,744
30-34	1,050,199	761,698	734,195	546,245	694,924	422,915	601,868	435,987	1,303,972	951,028
35-44	1,283,994	950,876	996,570	900,480	948,784	748,766	884,372	672,255	989,522	794,047
45-54	885,004	654,312	725,355	680,150	749,390	738,266	711,099	662,506	657,622	547,702
55-64	577,170	462,407	551,185	525,405	605,187	648,264	574,425	669,051	552,236	568,840
65 and up	433,641	429,363	479,155	581,930	564,373	753,418	631,768	947,686	364,922	549,681
75 and up									199,028	464,204
Totals	12,706,308	9,290,526	10,168,110	7,485,375	9,629,086	7,103,500	12,328,264	10,050,843	18,503,158	14,995,295
Combined Totals	21,996,835		17,653,485		16,732,586		22,379,107		33,525,453	

1. Source: U. S. Department of Commerce, Bureau of the Census, Historical Statistics of the United States Colonial Times to 1970, Part I, Series A 160-171, Marital Status of the Population by Age and Sex: 1890 to 1970. U. S. Government Printing Office, Washington, D.C., 1975, p. 20.

2. Source: U. S. Department of Commerce, Bureau of the Census, 1980 Census of Population, Volume I, Characteristics of the Population, Chapter D, Detailed Population Characteristics, Table 264, Marital Status, Presence of Spouse, and Marital History for Persons 15 Years and Over.

TABLE C

Widowed Adults (14 and up) 1940-1980

Ages	1940[1] Males	1940[1] Females	1950 Males	1950 Females	1960 Males	1960 Females	1970 Males	1970 Females	1980[2] Males	1980[2] Females
14	60	110	1,670	565	163	391	2,451	5,421		
15-17	311	1,729	3,460	2,055	897	1,874	5,057	12,382	992	2,757
18-19	720	4,694	1,535	3,205	887	2,877	3,472	10,657	1,089	3,691
20-24	8,934	32,751	9,060	25,280	4,780	17,252	12,878	56,508	5,970	24,746
25-29	20,973	71,878	15,485	57,490	9,548	37,047	19,196	71,530	11,759	51,751
30-34	36,714	128,256	20,945	91,945	17,246	74,109	19,574	86,494	16,531	79,480
35-44	155,405	537,584	94,865	409,250	76,436	374,216	75,546	353,760	53,374	279,304
45-54	328,130	991,448	240,755	967,595	182,260	921,258	186,144	942,796	152,424	815,634
55-64	488,620	1,365,044	495,140	1,636,660	380,508	1,819,043	364,665	1,988,096	367,249	2,104,980
65 and up	1,104,285	2,566,708	1,380,935	3,540,230	1,399,185	4,632,540	1,441,949	6,087,637	602,790	3,482,027
75 and up									892,643	4,396,048
Totals	2,143,612	5,700,202	2,263,850	6,734,275	2,071,910	7,880,607	2,130,932	9,615,280	2,104,821	11,240,418
Combined Totals	7,843,814		8,998,125		9,952,517		11,746,212		13,345,239	

1. Source: U. S. Department of Commerce, Bureau of the Census, Historical Statistics of the United States Colonial Times to 1970, Part I, Series A 160-171, Marital Status of the Population by Age and Sex: 1890 to 1970. U. S. Government Printing Office, Washington, D.C., 1975, p. 20.

2. Source: U. S. Department of Commerce, Bureau of the Census, 1980 Census of Population, Volume I, Characteristics of the Population, Chapter D, Detailed Population Characteristics, Table 264, Marital Status, Presence of Spouse, and Marital History for Persons 15 Years and Over.

TABLE D

Divorced Adults (14 and up) 1940-1980

Ages	1940[1] Males	Females	1950 Males	Females	1960 Males	Females	1970 Males	Females	1980[2] Males	Females
14	25	57	1,320	215	379	406	1,821	1,945	2,766	7,768
15-17	180	1,803	2,280	3,500	1,578	5,627	4,793	8,640	2,766	7,768
18-19	842	7,181	2,630	12,815	3,912	15,670	7,926	22,156	9,198	33,752
20-24	17,590	55,768	50,855	97,090	53,112	101,107	110,967	212,804	237,712	446,973
25-29	48,525	100,681	103,255	158,990	94,894	145,937	195,830	294,340	644,906	890,566
30-34	70,579	126,250	116,180	176,175	127,354	191,170	182,948	290,789	758,322	1,005,534
35-44	173,421	249,175	264,085	387,865	303,880	471,753	405,882	646,547	1,046,349	1,490,310
45-54	157,931	167,678	250,790	302,185	311,253	446,360	427,425	663,011	778,534	1,120,776
55-64	97,963	80,806	173,105	160,945	232,050	296,022	332,718	492,146	553,414	831,141
65 and up	57,367	33,221	106,860	73,105	170,792	181,046	256,287	371,900	274,795	448,000
75 and up									99,309	189,338
Totals	624,423	822,620	1,071,360	1,372,885	1,299,204	1,855,098	1,926,597	3,004,278	4,405,305	6,464,158
Combined Totals	1,447,043		2,444,245		3,154,302		4,930,875		10,869,463	

1. Source: U. S. Department of Commerce, Bureau of the Census, Historical Statistics of the United States Colonial Times to 1970, Part I, Series A 160-171, Marital Status of the Population by Age and Sex: 1890 to 1970. U. S. Government Printing Office, Washington, D.C., 1975, p. 20.

2. Source: U. S. Department of Commerce, Bureau of the Census, 1980 Census of Population, Volume I, Characteristics of the Population, Chapter D, Detailed Population Characteristics, Table 264, Marital Status, Presence of Spouse, and Marital History for Persons 15 Years and Over.

TABLE E[1]

Separated, Married Widows/Divorced 1980

Ages	Separated		Widowed Now Married		Divorced Now Married	
	Males	Females	Males	Females	Males	Females
15-17	4,357	12,332	1,377	3,380	3,938	10,247
18-19	11,889	39,897	1,306	4,231	11,861	46,272
20-24	143,934	285,965	8,407	34,101	356,946	732,203
25-29	247,007	377,355	22,300	83,783	1,216,741	1,709,508
30-34	241,829	355,089	41,487	145,930	1,804,313	2,151,327
35-44	334,155	514,292	139,808	467,128	3,004,854	3,299,604
45-54	256,432	372,322	345,230	1,160,645	2,388,814	2,583,571
55-64	186,538	248,953	747,482	2,659,249	1,867,010	2,090,116
65-74	98,530	114,602	1,055,877	3,923,945	1,005,210	1,254,412
75 and up	38,395	37,829	1,235,018	4,572,431	373,919	587,187
Totals	1,563,066	2,358,636	3,598,292	13,054,925	12,033,606	14,464,447
Combined Totals	3,921,702		16,653,217		26,498,053	

1. Source: U. S. Department of Commerce. Bureau of the Census. 1980 Census of Population, Volume I, Characteristics of the Population, Chapter D, Detailed Population Characteristics. Table 264, Marital Status, Presence of Spouse, and Marital History for Persons 15 Years and Over.

6

Senior Adults: Expanding Opportunities for Ministry/Service

Lucien E. Coleman

We were visiting an aging relative in a nursing home. As our teenage son followed us down the hallway, a shrill voice startled him: "Sonny, do you have a pocketknife?" He turned to see the small figure of an elderly woman hunched over in a wheelchair. A four-foot strip of muslin tethered her chair to a nearby handrail. "Cut this thing loose," she said, "they've got me harnessed up here like a mule!" One of the staff nurses came over and spoke to her sweetly. "Now, now, honey. You know you can't go rolling around everywhere. You'll hurt yourself."

At the time, we were amused. But later, as I reflected on the incident, I realized that we had witnessed a parable of the experience of aging in our society. Many older persons feel harnessed up, constrained, incapacitated by forces which they cannot control. And, as in the case of that aging woman in the nursing home, the harnesses are frequently fashioned by those who think they are acting in the best interest of the elderly, to protect them from themselves.

The more visible restrictions are physical. Older persons can be immobilized by physical handicaps, by inability to purchase transportation, or by fear of danger on the streets. But there are more subtle constraints operating in the realm of the psyche, fettering the spirit, devitalizing the will.

Consider the assumption, so deeply rooted in our culture, that incompetence is synonymous with old age. Stephen J. Miller has argued, for example, that a stigma of "implied inability to perform" is associated with retirement, and this stigma is carried over into all of the individual's remaining roles.

While those who work with older persons in the church would not consciously endorse such a disparaging attitude, they sometimes lend credence to it by sidestepping older persons themselves when planning and implementing programs for senior adults. The following excerpt from a letter written by an older church member tellingly illustrates the point. The writer, who had been attempting in vain to serve responsibly as a member of a planning task force for senior adults, wrote:

I must admit I enjoyed the luncheon for us but was shocked when I saw the slides of some programs that would soon be initiated. I, nor any of the other planning members, had any input. Since coming on the planning task force we have not had an opportunity to contribute or to do a thorough job of planning. We have been asked to rubber-stamp programs. I cannot conscientiously allow myself to be held responsible. Please accept my resignation.

Carroll B. Freeman, who quoted the letter, told of attending conferences in the field of gerontology where not a single older person was a leader or a participant. Reflecting on this experience he wrote:

I could hear, "We need to help senior adults because they are not wise enough and sufficiently articulate to get the job done." What a contradiction! Neither will we be effective if we give a token nod in their direction because we recognize the above problem. The crucial question is, "Do I believe that senior adults are able to accomplish many laudable tasks with only a minimum of assistance and moral support?"[1]

Ministry *With* Older Adults

Some church leaders call it "ministry to older adults." Others say, "ministry *with* older adults." The difference in wording is significant. The two prepositions represent distinctly different philosophies of older adult work. "Ministry to" implies a unidirectional program, treating older adults as dependent recipients of the services of others. "Ministry with" implies a two-directional flow of services and resources, treating older persons as givers, not just as recipients. The latter view implies that the responsibility of the church toward older adults is precisely the same as its responsibility toward any other age group, "to equip the saints for the work of ministry, for building up the body of Christ" (Eph. 4:12, RSV).

Elbert C. Cole, Methodist minister and executive director of the Shepherd's Center in Kansas City, Missouri, echoed this sentiment when he wrote:

A false assumption is made that older adults are not able to lead themselves and therefore need younger leadership to provide for them. . . . Older adults are quite capable of providing their own leadership. After all, who knows more about what is needed and how to go about achieving the desired goals of older adults than older adults themselves?[2]

The Shepherd's Center is a pioneering ministry with older adults built on the concept that, with some help from others, older adults can minister to one another. According to Cole, this program was initiated to help older adults answer two fundamental questions: First, how can I get help when I need it in order to remain independent as long as possible? Second, what can I do in later years to find meaning and purpose for my life? In the Shepherd's Center program, older men and women find their own answers to the second question even as they *provide* answers to the first question for others.[3]

Elaborating on this idea, Cole wrote:

> The Shepherd's Center focuses on people, not on programs or activities. The concept is based on a "people base" (a population base of older people living in a specific geographical area), and involves a covenant relation between center leaders and people assuring that every effort will be made to assist the people in achieving those goals needed or desired in their later years. In turn, the people provide the program leadership and participate in whatever way possible in maintaining a supportive network capable of helping themselves survive while finding some meaning and purpose in life.[4]

A Reservoir of Untapped Power

The aging of the American population (see chapter 4) is rapidly moving us toward a social problem of monumental proportions.

The Social Security system is one of the more visible evidences of the problem. In 1940, when the first monthly Social Security benefits were paid, there were fewer than 9 million people who had lived to sixty-five. By 1980, there were more than 25 million. In 1940, only 1.6 percent of the older population drew Social Security benefits; by 1976, 92 percent of the older population were receiving Social Security checks. Today, more than 31.7 million receive retirement benefits through the Social Security program. By the year 2030, that figure will have more than doubled.[5]

The ability of the Social Security system to support the elderly depends increasingly upon the contributions of the young and middle-aged adults in the work force. (Since 1950, the maximum Social Security tax paid by employees has rocketed from $45 to $2,855 per year.) But, even as the number of older people continues to escalate dramatically, the proportion of people in the work force (ages 20 to 64) is expected to decrease proportionately. At present, there are about three workers for every Social Security beneficiary. But by 2010, when the post-World War II baby boom will have begun to retire, there will be only two persons in the work force for every Social Security beneficiary. We are rapidly approaching the time when the younger population simply will not have the resources to support the retirement system as it is presently conceived.

Now, let's translate that problem into the church context. As the older adult population grows over the next several decades, the church will feel the impact of that development in numerous ways. Older persons will require more educational space, more leadership, a greater share of budget resources. There will be more aging persons in need of services, more older adults in evangelistic prospect files. Churches will need more staff ministers and volunteer workers with training in gerontology. Eventually, the sheer numbers of older adults will far outweigh the church's ability to minister to them.

But there is a solution. Perhaps it is the only viable solution to the problem. While churches will soon lose their ability to minister *to* older adults, it is entirely feasible for them to find adequate resources to minister *with* older adults. To put it differently, rather than simply adding to the problem, older adults in the church must be given increased opportunities to function as solutions to the problem.

As Cole has put it, "There are hundreds of causes just waiting for the abilities and energies of retired people. Many problems will not be helped or solved unless volunteers in their retirement years take them on and make them their own crusades."[6]

It is already happening in some places. In Kansas City, a man in his seventies tutors disadvantaged children; another carries on a significant ministry with the families of terminally ill patients. A former paint salesman coordinates a large work force of handymen, all retirees, who are available to make repairs in the homes of the elderly. An eighty-year-old delivers hot meals to the homebound.

In Fort Worth, a dedicated band of older adults keep their church's benevolence ministry going, dispensing clothing, food, financial assistance, advice, love, and the gospel of Jesus Christ to hundreds of needy people every year.

Every word in the heading, "A Reservoir of Untapped Power," was chosen with care. Power is associated with such things as guns, and bombs, and rocket engines. But, in a broader sense, power is "the ability to get things done." One dictionary definition of the term is the "ability of a living being to perform in a given way or capacity for a particular kind of performance."[7] And that is precisely the point. In the past, traditional attitudes have tied too many older adults to the handrail, limiting their contributions to church and society.

Sitting around the game tables in our "Keenage Klubs" is a great pool of "capacity for performance," largely unused—a store of creative energy waiting to be unleashed. And, in the unleashing, we will help older men and women achieve the destiny of the psalmist's righteous man, who is "like a tree/planted by streams of water,/that yields its fruit in its season,/and its leaf does not wither" (Ps. 1:3, RSV).

Guidelines for Ministry with Older Adults

As the tidal wave of aging Americans hits the church with full impact in the years ahead, Christian leaders will be called upon to develop more creative and sophisticated ministries to meet the needs of older adults. Such programs will vary in shape and texture, changing from one situation context to another. But they should have the following common denominators:

1. Older adults have basic survival needs, but they also have a deep need to be independent and to be useful to others. Church programs for the aging should keep all these needs in focus.

2. Older adults should be given an opportunity to plan and implement programs for people their own age as well as programs for other age groups in the church.

3. Churches should learn to assess the competencies and interests of older adults carefully, to give them opportunities to exploit their strengths in Christian ministries, rather than providing only limited opportunities to function in unchallenging conventional roles.

4. Church programs for older adults should be comprehensive, encompassing every aspect of the life of the congregation (music, recreational activity, evangelism, Bible study, discipleship training, benevolence ministries, worship) and not be confined to a single "senior citizens" club.

5. Older adults should be regarded as "people on pilgrimage," capable of growth and infinite change as followers of Jesus Christ. There is no such thing as retirement from Christian discipleship.

Notes

1. Carroll B. Freeman, *The Senior Adult Years* (Nashville: Broadman Press, 1979), p. 197-198.

2. Elbert C. Cole, "Lay Ministries with Older Adults," *Ministry with the Aging,* ed. William M. Clements (San Francisco: Harper & Row, Publishers, 1981), p. 255.

3. Ibid., p. 256.

4. Ibid., p. 255.

5. Arthur N. Schwartz, Cherie L. Snyder, and James A. Peterson, *Aging and Life* (New York: Holt, Rinehart, and Winston, 1984), 170-172.

6. Cole, *Ministry with the Aging,* p. 254.

7. *Webster's New Collegiate Dictionary* (Springfield, Mass.: G. & C. Merriam Company), p. 895.

7

Perspectives on Adult Faith Development
Bruce P. Powers

Religion, belief, and faith—these words often are used interchangeably in Christian education. And, yet, they do have significant differences. Religion relates primarily to the collected traditions of people who follow the same Deity. The religion one has is explained by the customs one follows and seeks to pass on. This common heritage binds adherents together in common purpose—fulfilling the expectations of their particular religious tradition.

Religion exists among all peoples who seek to understand and explain the nature of creation; the meaning of life and death; the relationship among past, present, and future; and the supernatural powers in the universe. Religion and Christianity are not necessarily the same thing.

Belief, also, is an ambiguous word. It can be *our* belief, *my* belief, *their* belief, or even *that* belief. Actually, belief is primarily a way of expressing that which a person holds to be true. It usually is a statement, creed, doctrine, or description of personal value that *illustrates* the commitments held by a person. Beliefs are open to judgment. They may be highly individual and are assumed to be chosen by the person professing them. Conversely, beliefs may be part of religious tradition and be adopted by individuals simply because of the customs. Regardless, belief is the way we express our feelings about our religion. Again, belief may or may not be Christian.

Faith probably is the most-used word of these three. It gives an impression of depth, power, and the essence of personal being. It is the way in which we express our innermost feelings about communion with Deity and about the ultimate issues in life. Whereas religion primarily is observable and formalized, and belief is primarily an expression of personal feeling, faith is more of an umbrella, paradoxical term. It is religion, but it is not; it is belief, but it is not; it is knowing, but it is not. Faith is a general term that helps us bond deity and humankind, that allows us to project ourselves into and within the essence of the Almighty.

122

Faith, also, is not distinctively Christian. It is a process that expresses the heart and will of any person who actively places his or her trust in a greater power.

This may make us a bit uncomfortable, for we use these three words so freely, not only in church but in business and civic affairs. In this chapter, you will be exposed not only to the cultural use and application of these terms but to the distinctively Christian dimension of the word *faith*. I have chosen *faith* rather than *religion* and *belief* because faith is the essence of belief and practice. It is the beginning point of personal commitment, and as such is central to understanding and developing an effective ministry with and through adults.

By definition, faith is an expression of trust in the unknown. Where there is certainty—when everything can be explained and understood in human terms—there is no real need for faith. Faith is my way of knowing that God exists, that Jesus is God as well as my personal Redeemer, and that the Holy Spirit is the direct presence of God in my life.

Faith has degrees of understanding and conviction. I used to think that a person either had faith or did not. But as I have come to see, *everyone* has a way of (1) relating to God, (2) some beliefs about this, and, therefore, (3) religion of some type that gives form to their lives. And this basic framework that helps people to understand their existence guides their day-to-day actions. From my viewpoint, the question is not whether or not a person has faith. What really counts is the *content* and *quality* of the faith that ultimately is a part of every person.

How Does Faith Grow?

This question focuses on the growing image long associated with Christians as illustrated in Ephesians 4:11-16: we are to grow into the likeness of Jesus Christ. How *does* a person develop as a disciple of Jesus Christ?

When does a person begin in the faith, and what happens as a person experiences a growing faith? A beginning point, for example, might be a family-oriented faith that is passed on from parent to child simply through the day-to-day routine in a Christian home.

This nurture-oriented faith might then mature to a time of learning and accepting doctrines and beliefs which have been passed down from others (parents, church, community, and so forth). An advanced expression of this would occur as a person acted on or demonstrated skill in using doctrines, beliefs, and practices in the same way as his or her models/teachers.

Additional spiritual growth depends on a Christian's ability and/or freedom to personalize his or her beliefs. This growth step requires not only mastering the content of one's faith but examining these beliefs in light of alternatives and personal experience. That is, the believer tests *what* he or she has come to believe against the realities of personal study, reflection, and experience. Out of this encounter between what others have valued and one's personal conscience develops convictions regarding the *why* and *how* of that person's faith.

So faith may be viewed as *what* a person believes, but at a more mature stage it must also include *why* and *how* a person believes, acts, and lives.

Three Related Perspectives

Faith development has elements of all of the phases described above, and there are, as you know, various ways of viewing the roles of learners, teachers, and the community of faith. I want to share with you three perspectives that will help you interpret the faith development among adults in an evangelical church. Each of these ways of looking at the process focuses on the way in which a person comes to profess faith in Jesus Christ as Savior: (1) developmental-conversion, (2) crisis-conversion, and (3) process-conversion.

Developmental-Conversion

This is closest to the growing image. It assumes that there are rather distinct phases in the spiritual growth of persons. The usual development begins in a Christian home and proceeds through the following phases:

- Nurture (about ages 0-6)
- Indoctrination (about ages 7-older adolescence)
- Testing (older adolescence-adulthood)
- Making Choices (adulthood)
- Active Devotion (adulthood)

Nurture. This consists of a person's basic exposure to and awareness of the meaning of life. It is gained from those who are the primary caregivers of a person. For the very young, this begins with the family, then gradually expands through the years to include significant persons who exert influence in church and community.

These impressions are oriented largely toward feelings. For example, in my own life, I can't remember too much about what I was taught during this time, but I do remember how much my parents and teachers cared for and loved me. As such, the imprints from this period form the foundation for and create the potential—or lack of potential—for future growth.

Indoctrination. Indoctrination is that phase of learning which enables a person to become an accepted and functioning member of a cohesive group. For our purposes, this is the period during which a person learns how to be an accepted member of his or her church. I recall seeking avidly to learn and perform as others did. The indoctrination I received came from the Bible, curriculum materials, the modeling I observed among the more mature Christians in our congregation, and what my parents, teachers, and other significant persons told me was true. I memorized much material, learned how to act as a Christian, discovered what I could and could not say at church, and otherwise formed the foundation for knowing and believing in an acceptable way in my church.

Usually, a person is confronted during this phase with the need to make a public profession of accepting Christ as personal Savior. The Scripture studied, the rituals, the traditions, the focus of church teaching —all point to the need for learning and accepting the fact that Jesus was born, died, and resurrected to provide a means for personal salvation to those who confess Him as Lord. One does not have to interpret or understand, only accept and believe the Scripture message and the preached Word of God.

Persons who have experienced indoctrination in the best sense will know what is valued in the beliefs and practices of their church, will have responded to the encouragement to profess the beliefs and participate in the practices, and will have formed a firm foundation for beginning a *personal* journey into knowing God.

Whereas the indoctrination and nuture phases have been directed primarily by parents, church leaders, and other authority figures, future spiritual growth has to rely on individual capacity for making personal choices and developing individualized ways of practicing one's faith. The reason for this is that what we teach through indoctrination is second-hand learning. Others tell us or show us, and we learn it as knowledge.

For example, during this phase the learner generally appropriates the content, experiences, and forms of his or her church experience as literal and normative—that is, they are the right ways to believe, act, think, and feel. These answers are adequate so long as one does not consider other equally good interpretations of Christian belief and practice. But when one begins to think for oneself, and ventures beyond that which has been passed from authority figures, one encounters the threshhold of a new phase of spiritual growth.

Reality Testing. During this phase a person ventures into the larger world of places, ideas, and experiences. The journey begins with the set of values and beliefs received from others. It does not take long to discover that many things that had worked well and been explained easily when authorities were giving the answers don't always apply. So, almost without thinking, a person begins the process of testing. What proves real in *my* experience? Can I affirm that which was passed to me, or must I adapt it? Or must I look for other answers?

As a person deals with personalizing faith, he or she is faced with using the knowledge, attitudes, and skills learned earlier. Whenever the person successfully relates these previous items to current experience, there is reinforcement that helps to make the learning a personal, self-chosen principle for life. Whenever there is difficulty in using previous learning, an individual then is faced with either trying to make the previous answers fit by rationalizing the situation, or by trying to relearn in light of new information.

As one is exposed to the broader dimensions of work, society, education, different cultures, and historical perspectives, there is a gradual disillusionment as the individual becomes aware that parts of his or her past are inconsistent with present experience. In this phase, you find out what makes sense and what doesn't. If it makes sense, you keep it; if it doesn't, you begin to look for other answers.

You begin this phase with high idealism—thinking that you have all the spiritual answers for all times and all places. By the end of this period, you will have acquired a realistic appraisal of yourself and be convinced that what you know, feel, and do must be consistent with life as you understand and experience it.

Making Choices. This phase comes into focus as you begin to realize that whatever choices you make to direct life must be yours, and that every choice has consequences. Whereas the previous phase exposed the inconsistencies between present experiences and the answers which were passed to you by your home, church, and culture, now you resolve these issues. You make choices.

I recall two very distinct urges—or pulls—during the transition to this phase. The first was to reach out and grab many of the new ideas and ways of doing things which promised easy, even radical, answers to my questions.

The other feeling came a bit later, probably in response to my easy acceptance of some answers which were quite different from those of my childhood. This urge was the opposite of the first—*to grasp the answers I had always known and to hold very tightly.* I was struggling to meet a very basic human need, *security.* I was uncomfortable in the tension of not knowing exactly what, why, when, and how about my faith, my church life, my vocation, my family, and my future.

My growth point came when I realized how both these pulls were working on me, that they existed side by side, and that they were a natural part of the maturing process. The question I faced was: Do I succumb to *either* pull? Each was an answer, an easy answer. But I realized that both represented viewpoints held and decisions made by others. *They were not mine.* I decided I would have to endure the tension —the pulls from these two directions—and begin to make *my* choices.

This decision led to the first testing point. When I made choices, I had to take the consequences. I could no longer blame others; my church, parents, teachers, and ministers no longer had the responsibility.

For many people, this phase is another type of conversion. Whereas one's initial profession of faith is an act of accepting that to which others have testified, this phase focuses on reaffirmation as one consciously chooses from a variety of alternatives, many often quite attractive. The earlier decision was more *when* to affirm publicly one's identity as a Christian. This experience is more drawn out, and focuses on choosing *what, how,* and *why* a person believes and lives.

The process of developing, testing, and clarifying personal choices is a significant time of maturing for the Christian. It is during this phase that personal commitment is refined and a person establishes the critical essence that comprises faith. For some, the decisions are momentous and the consequences radical—a type of "Here I stand; I can do no other!" For others, the decisions may result in following the path that so many others have chosen—reaffirming those beliefs and practices that have been passed on from others.

Either direction can be a growth step, as long as the individual examines, tests, and freely chooses what, how, and why he or she will commit to God.

The choices in this phase are similar to the experience of the rich young man in Matthew 19:16-22. Here was a person searching for direction, who could not sufficiently reorient his values. He asked Jesus how he might have eternal life. As you may recall, he declared that he had kept the religious commandments from his youth up; but he could not sell his possessions, give to the poor, and follow Jesus unreservedly.

Another example is in John 12:42 where we are told that individuals believed on Jesus but did not confess it lest they be rejected by others.

Active Devotion. As a person begins to resolve the crucial issues about faith commitments and life purpose, there is a gradual shift toward concern for living one's convictions. Not that all of the struggles and searching is left behind, but rather there seems to develop a sense of satisfaction that comes from having worked through some of life's most crucial issues. A person's philosophy of life seems to move from *try things and see what feels good* to *I know what I stand for, and I am going to live that way.* For the Christian, this means finding ways to practice your commitments in every part of life. There is no option; you are what you have chosen.

As I have experienced this phase, I have become aware that I no longer feel as defensive about my beliefs as I did in earlier phases. This probably comes from having made my faith my own through examining options, looking at consequences, and testing it out in the day-to-day realities of life.

I have the conviction that my faith is my own: that it is strongly rooted in the gospel of Jesus Christ; that it is right for me; and by growing through to this point, I know how to examine and renew it as situations change. So I have no need to defend my faith from the close examination of others, nor do I hesitate to share it as something that has been a life-changing experience for me.

Some Considerations

Research suggests that this type of Christian growth may be relatively superficial as in the case of persons who for the most part stagnate at the indoctrination level (whether by conscious choice or simply because that is the level of the status quo or of cultural religion). Or this process may be a continuing conversion experience as persons rework and enlarge their understandings and commitments in ever-widening dimensions.

This understanding of faith development is based on certain assumptions, which also form the foundation for the other two approaches.

Before going on, let's review the basic biblical and theological principles that form the foundation for faith development among evangelical Christians.

1.   The Christian way is community (for example, body of Christ, people of God, loving neighbor as self).

2.   *Coming to faith* and *growing in faith* are inseparable components of Christian discipleship.

3.   Faith is a *gift*. There will always be an element of mystery concerning how and why God works.

4.   All levels, or phases, represent faith. There is no greater or lesser. The key question is: How is one being *faithful* in the maturing process?

5.   Phases represent *opportunities* for growth. There is no assurance that one will progress.

6.   Integration of leadership theory and practice comes as we identify the outcomes desired (For example, I always ask: What am I trying to do to people?) and design appropriate ways to assist persons in spiritual growth at any phase.

     Note: The ways in which you seek to assist persons are not always *age related,* especially among adults. For example, many adults who become converts without exposure to traditional beliefs/practices that are expected in a particular Christian community may have extreme difficulty in interpreting and/or understanding why certain beliefs and practices are important. Effective nurture and instruction would be necessary for assimilation into the body.

7.   Faith development is more a *patterning* than a sequential process, with advances and retreats—sometimes existing in different stages in various dimensions of the same person's life. What makes sense of all this may be the ongoing learning process of Action—Reflection—Evaluation that undergirds and informs the faith development process.[1]

Crisis-Conversion

A second approach to faith development is rooted in unusual or painful circumstances. Whereas developmental-conversion depends on an individual responding to and developing a trusting relationship with his or her community of faith, this approach describes what happens when a person's faith development is influenced more by suspicion and distrust of others.

The crisis-conversion route of discipleship development is most apparent among persons who have a background of confused impressions related to their family, community, peer group, or even church. These persons tend to speak of their background in legalistic terms and often have made a major break with persons who formerly influenced their lives.

When they encounter new situations that do not match up with their way of understanding life, they have difficulty handling the ambiguity. Instead of feeling secure about solving problems and trusting self and others to search openly for good solutions, they might become disillusioned. In the absence of a sense of personal security and a trusted community, such persons are open for easy answers and strong leadership that promises caring and understanding of the person's plight. In extreme situations, persons reject their background and go to what they perceive as better answers. This may be *to* religion or *away* from religion, depending on interpretation.

Conversion under these circumstances is, in effect, equated with salvation. The route often followed finds the person transferring total dependence to the newfound answer and total rejection of one's former spiritual experience. This, in effect, is a new cycle of *indoctrination.*

If a person has a rather *weak* personality structure, the reinforcement of the new group or leader will be a continuing need—and must function as *authority* in the individual's life. Otherwise, disillusionment will set in, and the person will look for another easy answer/paternalistic leader.

If a person tends to have a *strong* personality structure, he or she eventually will see discrepancies between the answers provided by leadership and self-determined choices. Searching will set in, and the individual will have to make choices concerning the beliefs and practices supported by the leader/group. If group controls are too restrictive—and searching is not allowed—again there will be a rejection and the person's basic distrust of community will be reinforced.

If the *answer* to which one turns tends to be transcendent in expression (such as private prayer/confession periods, silent meditation, and individual Bible study), dependence on God becomes the highest good. Thus, meaningful relationships with others become increasingly less important in the person's life.

In this process, the focus of *authority* is the key issue. Where is one's major influence? For the God-dependent person, the key to spiritual growth is to learn to trust and relate to the faith community as a full participant. For the community-dependent person, the key is to learn to trust and relate to the transcendent dimensions of spirituality.[2]

Process-Conversion

This third approach grows out of the others but interprets the process of faith development as a continuum of receptivity to the claims of Christ. Indeed, one may be involved in a turning toward Christ long before accepting Christ as Savior.

For example, a person may be anti-Christian but in light of a particular circumstance *turns about* in his or her attitude and/or conduct. It may be that such a person turns from persecution to a new attitude of tolerance. It may have been brought about by some crisis, but whatever the cause, the individual, instead of walking away from Christ and His church, now begins movement toward the One who has called. The person has not yet arrived at the point of becoming one of Christ's own body, but nevertheless has changed direction.

In reality, this moment of change may be called a *conversion* because it is a turnaround, but it can also easily be confused with *regeneration.* However, while this *may* be the moment of regeneration, as in Paul's case, it is not necessarily so. One may change direction and still be far from salvation. To say that one is born again may, in this case, be premature, and failure to comprehend this may account for many drop-outs in churches. This is especially so in mission settings where there is little cultural and historical understanding of what it means to give one's life to Christ.[3]

Spiritual growth from this perspective must take persons at the point of need, as in the *developmental-conversion* process, and assist them in reorienting their lives. Faith development might well be related to guiding babes, regardless of age, as they come to claim and act on their own beliefs as disciples of Christ.

Working With Developmentally Oriented People

Traditionally, work among adults has been most effective with those who have come from Christian-home, Bible-belt, evangelical-church situations. These are the ones who, for the most part, are oriented toward a developmental growth process. To the degree that they are able to function within the system without too much conflict, they will respond to the nurture and education of a local congregation.

The approaches to Bible study and the types of groups that might be provided are listed in Figure 1.

The important thing is to provide spiritual growth opportunities for persons at all levels, not just one or two. By orienting them to the possibilities and helping them discuss their individual needs, you can begin to structure an overall program that will meet people where they are and provide for them as they mature. As pointed out in earlier chapters, many needs can be met through existing, ongoing programs. Naturally, the focus will be on bringing people to faith and introducing them to the foundational beliefs and practices of the local congregation.

As people move beyond basic educational experiences, their Christian development can be encouraged by providing specialized short-term

Figure 1

Approaches to Bible Study

Level of Need	Type of Bible Study	Focus of Group
Nurture	Inspiration	Fellowship
	Personal testimony	Caring
	Devotional approach	Support
	Tell the great biblical stories/experiences	
Indoctrination/ Instruction	Information	Sharing
	Convey knowledge about the content	Task oriented
	Interpret doctrines and practices	
Testing/ Making Choices	Interpretation (What is the Bible saying to me?)	Searching Encouraging
	Assist persons in making application to life	
Active Devotion	All of the above as appropriate	Mission action Christian service
	Leader serves as equipper, helper, and encourager	Ministry support Vocational ministry Lay ministry
	People at this level can benefit from a variety of approaches as long as they point toward active living for Christ	

study opportunities; individualized sharing, searching, and ministry groups; and mission-service projects that allow persons to channel their gifts into Christian service.

Another possibility is to build on the strengths of more mature Christians who are willing to assume increased leadership responsibilities. Enlist those who have gifts in relating to persons at the various levels. Provide special training and give them opportunities to lead groups and provide ministry.[4]

Working With Crisis-Oriented People

Persons with a crisis background who have learned how to accept and deal effectively with their inner feelings usually move within a congregation unnoticed. They have made peace with themselves, and are on their Christian pilgrimage just like everyone else.

Persons who have not worked through their feelings and claimed a personal faith, however, do not move freely. They often are on the fringes of church ministry or family life, ready at any moment to reject all that the congregation or family stands for. Without someone reaching out who knows how to meet their needs, they likely will turn to the first easy answer that promises relief.

While there is not any one way to identify those who come from a crisis orientation, you can be alert to certain characteristics.

- Highly dependent
- Distrusts larger groups
- Feeds on a relationship with one or two people who have similar characteristics
- Background of transition/crisis
- Suspicious of group decision making
- Excessive legalism
- Manic-depressive
- Talks of *direct* experiences with God while discounting community worship
- Disillusioned with parents, peers, church, and so forth.
- Seeks quick, easy answers to complex problems

Usually, you will see these persons as they look for authority and support figures to meet their security needs. Some may be seeking to *replace* those authorities who met their needs in another setting (church, home, college, peer group, and so forth). Others may not know what they are looking for, but instinct tells them to find someone or something *tangible* to lean on. Early in this process most adults do not respond well to spiritual encouragement; they might hear you tell them to lean on Jesus, but they will want to lean on you.

If you respond as a paternalistic judge, you will fill that need and the person will lean on you until you disappoint him. If you or someone in your church does not respond, the individual will look for a center of emotional support and authority elsewhere.

The key to meeting needs of these persons is to surround them with direct leadership and a few understanding, nurturing peers for a period of orientation and assimilation. During this time, which may extend from a few weeks to several months, the aim is to develop trusting relationships while gradually moving from total dependency to an *inter-dependency* among the crisis-oriented person(s), others in the group, and those in positions of leadership. Then, channel the person(s) into mainstream educational activities at the nurture level with some accepting people and one of your best class or group leaders.

In extreme cases, you will be dealing with individuals who have participated in or are ripe for a Bible cult. The appropriate response, apart from professional assistance, is to be clear and direct with the person. Acknowledge the disillusionment the person has that would drive him to an extreme answer. Listen and dialogue; don't condemn. Ask what alternatives have been considered, then help the person evaluate them.

Set up a way for the person to be exposed to a holistic, informed reflection on possible ways to meet his concerns. The best way would be for this person to meet with someone who has gone through this experience and has returned. Another is to provide reading material related to the symptoms being experienced. Then seek a commitment for involvement in the assimilation activity already described.

Of course, the best approach is preventive. Be open to searching and choice making as a natural part of each person's spiritual growth. Discuss the needs and responses of persons at various points in their lives. Study the structure of Bible cults, the role of leaders, and what happens to participants. Contrast that with a wholesome, well-designed ministry to and with persons of all types and ages.[5]

Working With Process-Oriented People

Pick out these persons as you hear their life stories, as they give personal testimonies, when an adult makes a profession of faith, from the records of new adult members that tell of a recent conversion elsewhere, when persons come to your church from another faith, and other expressions that indicate a *significant change from one set of moral and religious values to another.* Do not assume—as the person might assume—that the individual is at the same point of understanding and practice of faith as those in the mainstream activities of your church.

This person needs a chance to begin as a babe in Christ—to move through the experiences beginning with *nurture.* The sequence may be rapid or slow, but a person with this orientation cannot skip steps. He may *imitate* others, but it is simply stimulus-response learning until the person actually circles through the meaning of faith and practice from the beginning.

Try setting up special groups with trained leaders who can nurture and instruct. Build some discipline into the program to meet the authority needs that come early in the process. Give opportunity for persons to expand their understandings as they become ready by moving to new groups, increased independence, and assumption of leadership responsibilities.

Note: The needs of people in this group are very similar to those of persons who are *developmentally oriented* but have never moved beyond a nominal adoption of cultural religion. Thus, provisions for those in this category and for those in the *nurture* and *indoctrination* phases might be the same.[6]

Your Role

It is difficult to meet the needs of all adults, and you won't. You can, however, focus on a mainstream educational program and have enrichment and assimilation provisions for those who do not fall into the general category. It will be important to view all provisions as *regular* educational ministry, avoiding any impression of a "we vs. they" attitude among the participants.

Where do your energies go? My guess is that with effective recruitment and leadership training you can focus about half of your time on administration of mainstream activities such as Sunday School, Church Training, mission groups, worship leadership, and outreach activities. The rest

Figure 2

Fowler's Stages of Faith

Stage One: Intuitive-Projective Faith

This stage involves much imitation and fantasy based on the examples and expressions of parents and other significant persons.

Stage Two: Mythic-Literal Faith

At this point, a person begins to take part in and adopt the stories, beliefs, and observances which are a part of one's faith community; this happens through informal exposure as well as through intentional, structured experiences. Learning focuses on literal interpretations with distinct rules for judging right and wrong. Security and cohesion are primary values, with authority and tradition being stronger influences than the desire for peer approval. Conformity is a virtue.

Stage Three: Synthetic-Conventional Faith

Faith at this level begins to extend beyond a close-knit group that has determined the individual's faith concepts. As one moves in ever-widening circles, faith is adjusted so that it ties life together; this is synthesis. Since this faith is a reflection of the various parts of a person's environment and society, it is best described as *conventional*. Beliefs and practices are determined largely by authority figures.

Stage Four: Individuative-Reflective Faith

The distinguishing characteristic of this stage is that a person assumes responsibility for his or her own commitments, taking whatever steps are necessary to *individualize* the previously held conventional faith. When one has genuinely moved to this stage, there is an open and honest struggle to deal with the ambiguous tensions in one's life, such as:

Being an individual	vs. Belonging to a group
Truth as I view it	vs. Truth as it is given to me
Self-fulfillment	vs. Service to others

One who has not successfully achieved this stage collapses to one of the extreme positions rather than holding them in tension. Faith is caught in a cross pull between expressions which are conventional and other-directed, and those which are individualized, self-chosen, and self-directed. Along with self-choice in this stage is a corresponding acceptance of responsibility for the decisions one makes.

Stage Five: Conjunctive Faith

At this stage, the ambiguities are accepted as paradoxes that must exist. One recognizes the possibility of truth in the positions of others, and finds that one can affirm and live out personal commitments while honoring that which may be true in the lives of others. Stage five is the point at which faith comes to grips with being ethically responsible: one must remain committed to practicing one's faith regardless of the consequences.

Stage Six: Universalizing Faith

This stage builds on all that has gone before, providing a sense of oneness with the Creator and Sustainer. There is an ability to transcend the human elements of physical, social, and personal concerns to focus on the broader issues of truth, justice, and goodness. One dwells in the world as a transforming presence but is not *of,* or controlled, by the world. Persons at this stage seem instinctively to be able to relate to others affirmingly and supportively, demonstrating a style of life and commitment that challenges and intrigues.

of your time would be divided between actual contact time with the enrichment/assimilation activities and the administrative responsibilities you have in your work.

Faith Development Theory

As you have no doubt noticed, one of the major implications from this material on faith development is that if a person makes a commitment at one point in life, it will have to be renewed or deepened at a later time. Commitments that are not renewed and actively expressed in one's life will gradually fade and die.

As suggested in the chapter on adult development, there are phases through which we all move. These relate to physical, emotional, and cultural influences in our lives. Research in adult faith development has focused on the interrelationships between the spiritual dimension of a person's life and these other phases of development. As you might expect, there is disagreement about the nature of Christian growth vs. the natural development that occurs in an individual's life. Consider the theories for what they are: a human interpretation of the marvelous process of coming to and growing in faith. They must not be considered final answers, only guideposts to give structure to our human efforts to understand and provide assistance to those on the journey.

The information I have shared with you is a type of theory. Although it is highly descriptive—it tells what people experience—the material I have presented became a theory as I attempted to fit the pieces together to help us understand how best to relate to adults in our churches. Other writers have sought to develop a much more systematic theory based on extensive research over many years. Two writers often mentioned in faith development discussions are James W. Fowler and John H. Westerhoff III.

James Fowler, professor of theology and human development at Emory University, Atlanta, Georgia, is the dominant theorist at the present time. He has focused his research on intensive interviews with persons to examine their journey of faith. After compiling the results from several hundred sessions, he began to notice patterns that coincided with previous research done in related fields. Comparing these responses with the stage theories of Jean Piaget (how people learn), Lawrence Kohlberg (how people develop moral values), and Erik Erikson (how people deal with developmental tasks in life), Fowler developed what he came to call *stages* in faith development.

In this theory Fowler proposed a series of six stages (see Figure 2) "which he sees as hierarchical (increasingly complex and qualitative), sequential (they appear one after the other in the life span), and invariant (they follow the same order for all persons)." This work, according to the director of a major interdenominational research project on adult faith development, is not only one of the first, but "undoubtedly the most complete organization of concepts of faith within the framework of human development."[7]

Fowler has been criticized rather strongly by those from a formative spirituality perspective (faith grows from within in response to the call of God), as well as from a biblical-theological perspective (a process of spiritual growth based on an interpretation of New Testament passages). In the first case, life-cycle influences are considered incongruent with both the unfolding process within the individual and the corresponding transcendent relationship one has with God.[8]

In the second case, Fowler is charged with focusing broadly on a general development of values rather than on a distinctively Christian expression of New Testament faith.[9]

To draw your own conclusions about Fowler's theory, see his book *Stages of Faith.* To see how he is answering his critics, read the sequel, *Becoming Adult, Becoming Christian.* Fowler, an ordained Methodist minister, is anxious to describe in this later book specifically how adult developmental theory and Christianity are related.[10]

John H. Westerhoff III is a professor at Duke University Divinity School. Instead of a comprehensive theory, he has dealt primarily with issues, relating theory as appropriate. Whereas Fowler has done extensive field research and sought to present a well-defined theory, Westerhoff has focused more on interpreting biblical and theological issues and how they relate to the teaching dimension of a congregation's life. Consequently, his theory is not as well defined, nor is it the primary focus of his writing. Instead, what he has written makes sense to so many people that he has become a major influence in this field.

Westerhoff describes faith development in the form of a visual impression: faith grows like the rings of a tree with each ring adding to and changing the tree somewhat, yet building on that which has grown before. He builds on this tree analogy, suggesting four rings which are involved in the growth process.[11] (See Figure 3.)

Experienced Faith—that which we first experience represents our interpretation of faith during this time. This is what we gain from our earliest years either in life or, if one has a major change in beliefs, as we move into the new religious orientation. We adopt *feelings* about the faith and pick up the values of those who nurture us. This core of experience is refined in subsequent phases.

Affiliative Faith—this occurs as one gradually takes on the beliefs, values, and practices of one's primary faith community and becomes an accepted member.

Searching Faith—this form of faith begins as one becomes aware that one is beginning to develop, express, and accept responsibility for a personal interpretation of the faith which has been received from others. Those who move into this phase inevitably question the content and expressions that were important during the affiliative period. This phase is characterized by struggle, yet it is the way that people must pass in order to make personal commitments, deepen convictions, and prepare

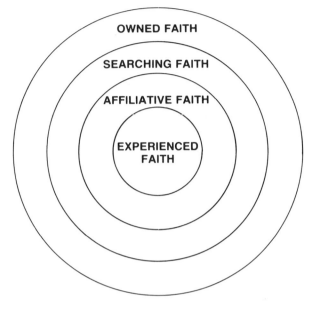

Figure 3

themselves for actively expressing and accepting responsibility for their faith.

Owned Faith—this occurs when one has successfully reoriented one's life and now claims personal ownership of and responsibility for beliefs and practices. The searching associated with the previous phase does not disappear entirely but is resolved in a trusting acceptance that the commitments made are a faithful response to the call of God. Characteristics of this phase include close attention to practicing one's faith as well as believing it; increased attention to in-depth Bible study, devotional experiences, and personal ministry efforts; and a natural sharing of one's faith with others. This, says Westerhoff, is God's intention for everyone.

What Now?

The information in this chapter is just an overview. It will prove most helpful if used (1) as stimulation for further research related to your particular situation, and (2) in the overall planning of ways to structure adult ministry in your institution.

I have deliberately steered away from too much secondhand reporting on theorists in faith development. Their work is interesting and provides much stimulation, but you can read their work for yourself.[12] Here, I wanted you to look at an experiential approach, one that can easily be related to the adults in your church. Now take it, and make it your own. Adapt what you wish, and begin to find your own unique ways to enrich your educational ministry with adults!

Notes

1. See Bruce P. Powers, *Growing Faith* (Nashville: Broadman Press, 1982), chap. 2, p. 27.

2. Many church leaders are familiar with the illness/death and broken-family crises that cause people to question their faith. There are many pastoral care resources to help with these problems. Not as well known are the crises that lead people from a Christian background to turn to unusual religious groups, rejecting family, friends, and church. Excellent resource to help church leaders understand and deal with this problem are Harold L. Bussell, *Unholy Devotion: Why Cults Lure Christians,* (Grand Rapids: Zondervan Publishing House, 1983); Glenn A. Igleheart, *Church Members and Nontraditional Religious Groups* (Nashville: Broadman Press, 1985); Robert D. Dale and Delos Miles, *Evangelizing the Hard-to-Reach* (Nashville: Broadman Press, 1986).

3. For a discussion of this, see Edward C. Pentecost, *Issues in Missiology: An Introduction to the Conversion Process* (Grand Rapids: Baker Book House, 1982), p. 118f.

4. A good resource for helping persons understand their own faith development and the needs of others is my book, *Growing Faith* (Nashville: Broadman Press, 1982). I wrote this to provide a study guide for and experience in personal faith development.

5. For a study of this topic, refer to Harold L. Bussell, *Unholy Devotion.* A helpful study guide for persons who could assist you in leading assimilation groups is my book, *Christian Leadership* (Nashville: Broadman Press, 1979).

6. Excellent resources in this area are published by the Church Training Department and by National Student Ministries of the Sunday School Board, SBC. Request information from the appropriate department, 127 Ninth Avenue, North; Nashville, Tenn. 37234. Another recent publication that could be used is *Dynamic Discipleship,* by Paul W. Powell (Nashville: Broadman Press, 1984).

7. Kenneth Stokes, ed., *Faith Development in the Adult Life Cycle* (New York: William H. Sadlier, 1982), p. 35.

8. For an example of a theory of formative spirituality, see Adrian van Kaam, *Formative Spirituality,* vol. 1: *Fundamental Formation* (New York: Crosroad Publishing Co., 1983).

9. Some scholars are proposing alternative interpretations of faith development. For example, see Neill Q. Hamilton, *Maturing in the Christian Life.* (Philadelphia: The Geneva Press, 1984).

10. For a summary of Fowler's work and an interpretation of the Christian implications, see Bruce P. Powers, *Growing Faith* (Nashville: Broadman Press, 1982), pp. 40-59.

11. Westerhoff has continued to write in the field. The ideas presented here were first published in *Will Our Children Have Faith?* (New York: Seabury Press, 1978), pp. 89f.

12. Several key resources are listed here and in the bibliography for those who desire to do in-depth research into the theories of prominent writers. For a variety of perspectives, read Fowler, Westerhoff, Stokes, and Hamilton.

Bibliography

Erikson, Erik (ed.). *Adulthood*. New York: W.W. Norton, 1978.

Fowler, James W. *Stages of Faith*. San Francisco: Harper & Row, 1981.

_____. *Becoming Adult, Becoming Christian*. San Francisco: Harper & Row, 1984.

Gallup, George, Jr., and Poling, David. *The Search for America's Faith*. Nashville: Abingdon Press, 1980.

Groome, Thomas. *Christian Religious Education*. New York: Harper & Row, 1980.

McCoy, Vivian Rogers, et al. *The Adult Life Cycle*. Lawrence, Kans.: University of Kansas Press, 1978.

Munsey, Brenda (ed.) *Moral Development, Moral Education, and Kohlberg*. Birmingham, Ala.: Religious Education Press, 1980.

Muto, Susan Annette, and Van Kaam, Adrian. *Am I Living a Spiritual Life?* Denville, N.J.: Dimension Books, 1978.

Powers, Bruce P. *Adventures in Christian Service*. Nashville: Convention Press, 1982.

Westerhoff, John H. III. *Bringing Up Children in the Christian Faith*. Minneapolis: Winston Press, 1980.

PART II:

Meeting the Needs of Adults

Meeting the needs of adults through Christian programs and activities requires an understanding of the adult life cycle, Part Two views various programs and activities churches have used to meet the needs of adults.

Chapter 8, "Program Planning Models for Adult Christian Education," serves as a foundational base for designing adult Christian education programs and activities that will assist adults to grow spiritually and personally.

"The Bible Teaching Program" (chapter 9) is described from the standpoint of rationale, philosophy, objectives, and goals for adults. Organizational and practical issues and concerns are addressed.

The adult need for discipleship training in addition to that provided when one becomes a Christian, is the subject of chapter 10. It is discussed from a biblical, theological, and educational background. Tasks and goals are reviewed with practical suggestions for implementing an adult discipleship training program.

The need of adults for mission education and involvement is considered in chapter 11. The fulfillment of being a disciple can be partially achieved as the adult participates in and learns about missions.

America is facing a family crisis with skyrocketing divorce rates, family problems, and so forth. A church's ministry to families is analyzed in chapter 12.

Many churches do not perceive that their adult music ministry and activities is a part of the church's educational ministry to adults. Music provides an opportunity for the personal growth of adults plus many opportunities for service and ministry. Chapter 13 is "Adults and Music."

Adults continue to study and to learn. The church can assist adult growth and personal spiritual development by scheduling and encouraging adults to keep on learning. Suggestions for helping adults continue to learn is the topic of chapter 14.

8

Program Planning Models
for Adult Christian Education
R. Michael Harton

Once as an eager, well-intentioned young minister of education, I decided to provide some much-needed training for the youth leaders in my new church. I had observed the Youth Sunday School on several occasions and concluded that what was being done was largely ineffective. So I sat down at my desk and outlined a five-session training course for the youth leaders. I included a wide variety of topics from understanding the youth themselves to an array of teaching methods. Each Youth Sunday School worker was enlisted to attend. At the appointed time and place, the training began and for the duration of the five sessions this green educator, chocked full of seminary knowledge, waxed eloquent. The leaders attended faithfully. Quite frankly, they surprised me at how much they already knew about what I was "teaching" them. The training concluded, and a satisfied minister of education waited expectantly to observe the vast improvement in Youth Sunday School. After one month nothing had changed!

It was nearly six months later that I realized in conversation with some of the youth teachers that the problem they were having was simple: They did not know how to use the curriculum materials! Three years earlier, vast changes had been made in the materials by the denomination. Without warning or training, these leaders suddenly had a director's book, a teacher's guide, and a large envelope full of materials (resource kit) that they were expected to use. They had no idea how these materials were coordinated or to be used. They had struggled with the new approaches suggested for three years. It was quickly agreed by the workers and their minister of education that what was needed was a "curriculum workshop." Also needed was a weekly planning meeting to facilitate proper use of the materials.

In reflecting on that experience I recall several observations. First, the early training was planned chiefly to meet *my* need to do *something* to justify my existence. The leaders attended out of loyalty to the new staff

144

member and a desire to be supportive. Second, I had *guessed* at their needs (and missed), unilaterally decided how to meet those needs, and planned the event without any input from the group. Thus I wasted precious resources (including *their time*) and placed my credibility in question.

I share that experience with the confidence that many readers can identify with it. Either you have perpetrated the same crime, or you have been a victim! McKenzie calls this approach to planning "preemptive" because the needs of the educator preempt the needs of the learner.[1] It is my contention that one of the primary reasons for low participation in adult Christian education is that little or no attempt is made to *get in touch* with learners' needs. Instead, we rely on guesswork or the needs of the educator. It was indicated in chapter 1 that research on nonparticipation indicated that many adults report that programs do not meet their needs, and thus they stay away. One of the reasons the programs do not meet their needs is that no one bothered to discover those needs!

Assessing Educational Needs

The rationale for assessing the educational needs of our constitutents can be stated in both practical and ideal terms. Practically speaking, we want to avoid wasting valuable resources—for example, the time, money, and materials which programs consume. We want adults to be responsive to the educational offerings we provide. Simply stated, we want them to attend! All other details properly attended to, they are more likely to participate if they perceive that the educational activity will meet an educational need or interest they have identified.

Ideally, we assess needs because we want to be responsive to the concerns and issues facing adults. The Christian educator who wants to provide an equipping, enabling ministry attempts to help adults identify approaches and resources to facilitate growth. First, however, the educator must be in touch with the growth needs of the individual. The educator may make some assumptions about the needs of her constituents, but until these assumptions have been verified through feedback from the individuals themselves, the educator has not gone far enough.

Some Observations About Needs and Needs Assessment

Perhaps before proceeding, the concept of *need* should be defined. Simply stated, a need is a lack or deficiency experienced by the individual. For our context, needs which may be alleviated in part or in whole through education are our focus. Thus we address *educational needs*. This is no trite distinction, for persons may have needs which cannot appropriately be satisfied through education. A person may have a ministry, counseling, or other need which may be more adequately addressed through direct intervention. In general, we may say an educational need exists when a person has identified a goal, the attainment of which can be facilitated through education.

Another way of stating this same concept is by describing a need as the gap between what the learner perceives *should be* and what actually *is*. The "should be" becomes the goal. The task of the learner and the educator is to determine whether this is a need which can be satisfied through education.

$$
\text{Need} \begin{cases} \text{"What Should Be"} \\ \text{gap} \\ \text{"What Actually Is"} \end{cases}
$$

A further caution is in order. Instructional development specialists point out that what may appear as an educational or training need may actually be an organizational problem. For example, leaders may be unable to function according to expectations but not because they lack the competence. Rather, they may be hampered by problems with structures, communication, personnel, or resources (or lack of resources).

One further distinction is helpful. When the educator makes assumptions about the educational needs of adults, he is *ascribing needs* to individuals. Ascribed needs may provide a starting point. But ultimately, adequately planned educational programs must be built on the *perceived* needs of learners. That is, adults must themselves come to the realization that a need exists. Ultimately, guilt and loyalty to the educator aside, adults will respond on the basis of their perception that the educational activity provided will alleviate a need which they perceive they have.

Sources of Information About Needs

Needs assessment is a starting point for programming. But how can the educator determine persons' educational needs? Several sources might be consulted. First, the literature on adult development and life tasks are rich with insight into life needs of adults. Though individual differences must always be accounted for, persons do progress through fairly predictable ages and stages. Thus familiarity with the works of Erikson, Havighurst, Buhler, Valiant, Levinson, Gilligan, and other developmental and life-span researchers will enable the educator to ascribe needs with a considerable degree of accuracy. Position descriptions, constituents' expectations, and so forth provide further information. Once again it must be emphasized that this is a *beginning point* for developing educational programs.

Adults themselves are, of course, the best source of information about individual needs. It is not safe to assume, however, that one need merely ask adults to describe their learning needs, for they cannot always do that. Individuals may not be aware that they have learning needs related to a given subject. On the other hand, they may recognize or sense a need, but not recognize that it is basically a learning need. These kinds of difficulties complicate getting firsthand information on learning needs and are no doubt some of the reasons many educators do not bother with attempting to collect firsthand data.

Knowles provides examples of several paper and pencil instruments for collecting information on learners' needs. He suggests checklists, interviews, as well as questionnaires and surveys.[2] Since these last two are the more commonly used approaches, they warrant further discussion.

The adult educator wishing to avoid the preemptive approach to needs assessment may decide to consult potential participants using a survey and/or questionnaire, often with given parameters defined by organizational or program tasks. This is admirable. Unfortunately, the educator often sets about to construct the instrument unilaterally. The problem with this is that the educators are limited to their own ideas on developing checklists, or they limit questions to areas covered by known resources. For example, a checklist may be developed from curriculum sources with which the educator is familiar. This is like saying to the respondent, "You cannot be interested in any but the following topics." A more sensitive and responsible approach will be described in the section on program development.

A word needs to be said about administration of surveys and questions. Construction and administration of these instruments is almost a science in itself and helpful resources are readily available. Generally speaking, the instrument should be as brief as possible (as in one or two pages). A brief explanation of the rationale for the survey and instructions on its completion should be included. For best results, the survey should be anonymous (unless you are asking for persons willing to assist in a task). Some personal data about the respondent is often helpful in the interpretation of the data received. Thus information on age, sex, marital status, and so forth, may be gathered.

Often the highest return rate is obtained by handing the instrument to persons and asking them to complete and return it on the spot. Thus an instrument may be distributed, instructions given, and time allowed for completion. The educator can collect the instruments after sufficient time and have the results in hand. Even then he or she may be surprised to discover less than 100% return, or that some turned in blank surveys! However, he can be assured that if persons are handed the survey and are asked to bring it back later, the return rate will probably be very low depending upon the time lapse.

Decision Making in Your Parish by Leon McKenzie contains helpful information on instrument construction, cover letters, and so forth, including how to draw a random sample. (It is surprising how small a sample is required, even from a large population, to gain reliable, representative results.)[3]

Developing Educational Programs

A difficulty which occurs in discussing program development is related to how *program* is defined. Are we talking about institutionalized programs such as the Sunday School? Or are we refering to freestanding, somewhat independent educational activities which may be short- or long-term in duration and without any formalized programmic identification? The models for which an overview is provided below may actually be appropriate for both types of educational activities. Let us first examine several approaches to programming, then make some possible applications.

Knowles promotes what he describes as an "organic" model for program development consisting of the steps in the andragogical process:

1. Climate setting
2. Establishing a structure for mutual planning
3. Diagnosing needs/interests
4. Formulating objectives
5. Designing a pattern of activities
6. Carrying out the activities

7.   Evaluating the results and rediagnosing needs and interests

This model becomes the "macro" structure for broad (as in community) based programs as well as a "discrete" model for individual learning activities. This model will be part of the basis for a model illustrated in the latter part of this chapter.

The PIE approach to *planning, implementation,* and *evaluation* finds application in some human resource development settings (as in military and industrial training programs). This model is illustrated in Figure 1.

Outcomes, methods, and resources are the key ingredients of this model. As may be seen from the diagram, planning proceeds from outcomes through methods and resources. Implementation proceeds in reverse order. When resources have been secured, methods implemented and outcomes achieved, evaluation begins, once again, from outcome through resources. This is obviously a more conceptual model and does not provide the nitty-gritty details for program planning. It is, nonetheless, helpful in gaining a global view of the whole process of program development.

One of the pioneers in distinctly adult Christian education planning

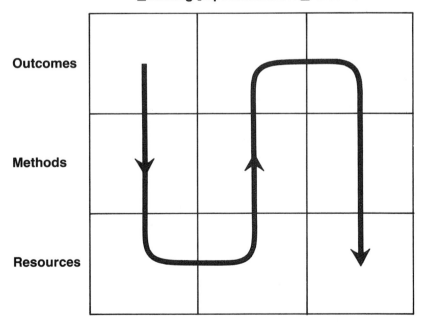

Planning Implementation Evaluation

Outcomes

Methods

Resources

Figure 1

was the "Indiana Plan," so named because it was developed by two professors at Indiana University. Paul Bergevin and John McKinley developed an elaborate, carefully worked-out plan for developing a comprehensive program of church-based adult education. The fully developed plan was published in 1958 under the title *Design for Adult Education in the Church.*

The Indiana Plan had three phases: Starting the Plan, Expanding the Plan, and Consolidating the Plan.[4] The starting phase involved enlisting a representative group of adults from various church organizations and committees to comprise the planning group. This group received extensive training in group process and team building. Beyond becoming an effective team, the goals of this initial planning group were to discover educational needs and to ultimately become the first learning group.

The expanding phase involved moving the planning group beyond its own concerns to the discovery of wider educational problems and needs of the church. The group then zeroed in on a need and planned a "trial" program to meet that need. The primary goal was to give experience in using the skills developed in phase one.

The consolidating phase attempted to provide continued training for increased numbers of adults in the planning processes and to develop an ongoing, self-perpetuating program.

If one word could be used to describe the Indiana Plan, that word might be *collaborative.* It involved leaders and participants alike in the planning and development of the adult Christian education program. In fact, the two identified goals were the development of collaborative effectiveness and group autonomy.

The plan went through several revisions. Bergevin retired as professor of adult education at Indiana University, but McKinley continued to work on the plan with the aid of his students. By the mid-1960s "institutes" had become popular, their purpose being to provide intensive training for leaders in the use of the plan. Ultimately, under McKinley's guidance and authorship, the plan became known as Participation Training and broadened its appeal beyond church educators to business and industry. Two basic phases were included: learning participation skills and applying these skills in a collaborative planning group for the purpose of planning development.

A seven-step planning process characterized the PT model:

1.   Identification of interest/need area

2. Selection of program content by possible topic
3. Identification of desired outcomes (goals and development of content outline)
4. Identification of resources
5. Selection of techniques
6. Operation of program
7. Evaluation and reassessment

In the PT Institutes conducted by certified trainers, the procedure is used from the beginning as a laboratory experience for developing skills in collaborative effectiveness and group autonomy.

The Participation Training model of program development would appear to be useful for an adult study group responsible for choosing its own topics and materials for study. The model has been demonstrated as effective for a large group where the group was divided and each subgroup planned a program for the other. Thus, in effect, the programs were self-perpetuating, and needs assessment and planning was an ongoing process.

James R. Schaefer proposed a model of program development for Christian adult education that is similar to the PT model. Dubbed the "GIFT" model (Growth In Faith Together), the process is designed to consume the better part of thirteen weeks and involves three phases: research, reflection, and response.[5] While Schaefer's is not a lockstep process, the components of his model seem to be:

1. Identify the planning team.
2. Assess needs of adults and competence of available resources.
3. Select themes and topics.
4. Devise program plan (learning modes).

This model is similar to the PT approach in that it involves participating adults in the assessment of needs, interests, and in the selection of themes and topics to be explored. In this regard, both models seem to assume an established or predetermined grouping of adults. The Schafer model omits the step in which objectives for the activities are selected because these are predetermined by the governing body.[6] A further distinction is that this model assumes participants are not astute enough to select their own learning approaches, so this is done by the educator.

The *research* phase of this model is conducted via a "Survey of Religious Beliefs and Concerns" mailed to participants' homes. After data from the survey are collected, participants meet in small groups for *reflection* upon their faith together. This reflection is intended to elaborate on concerns expressed in the survey and to surface other issues. Over a five-week period, the concerns are ordered into a priority list.

The *response* phase is initiated by the planning team as they actually plan programs and design activities.

While this model may appear to be a bit more restrictive in the direction the group's learning may take, it may be realistic for a group which meets within the context of an identified program organization. For example, where the educational program of a church consists of various organizations with predetermined tasks or missional statements, content areas may be somewhat predetermined. In other words, parameters may be predetermined for the content or topical areas the group can consider.

A third model of program development will be discussed before returning to illustrate a "hybrid" model for adult learning groups.

An intriguing "Interactive Model" of program development is proposed by Edwin L. Simpson of Northern Illinois University.[7] The model is intended to compensate for the deficiencies of linear, lockstep models which simply list the steps one is to follow in program planning. Simpson asserts that in practice the process of developing an educational program is rarely strictly sequential, nor are the steps equal in functional importance. For example, two planners may achieve very different ends using a linear model, depending on whether they are focusing on *function* or *process*. The interactive model is thus designed to attend to both function *and* process. By forcing interaction of planning steps with philosophy and objectives the *what* and the *why* of a program are compared. (See Figure 2.).

The interactive nature of the model is indicated in the first step of the process. Needs assessment is accomplished through interaction with target audiences, whether individuals, groups, institutions, or whole communities. The needs discovered are checked against the normative criteria (philosophy-purpose and goals-objectives) for consistency.

Assessing learning styles is the next step. In this step the learning orientation of the constituents is determined. Unfortunately, this step is not well developed by Simpson. The matter of learning styles is a complicated issue and is the subject of much current research, but as yet there is no practical approach to such assessment for the practitioner. Witkin[8] and Kolb[9] have found that persons involved in certain fields tend to have

Adult Education Program Planning:
An Interactive Model

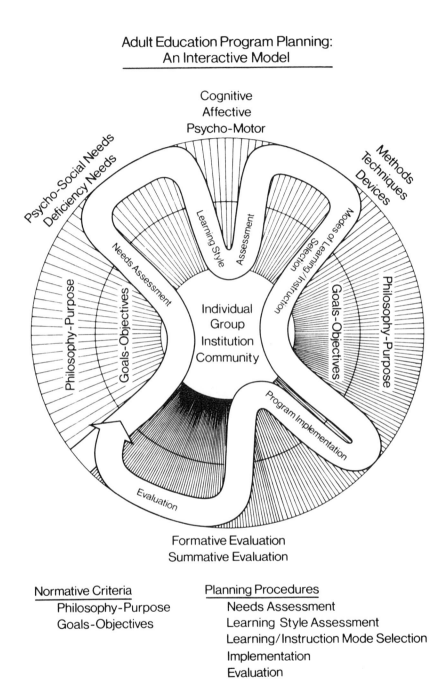

Cognitive
Affective
Psycho-Motor

Psycho-Social Needs
Deficiency Needs

Methods
Techniques
Devices

Needs Assessment

Learning Style

Assessment

Modes of Learning/Instruction
Selection

Philosophy-Purpose

Goals-Objectives

Individual
Group
Institution
Community

Goals-Objectives

Philosophy-Purpose

Program Implementation

Evaluation

Formative Evaluation
Summative Evaluation

Normative Criteria
   Philosophy-Purpose
   Goals-Objectives

Planning Procedures
   Needs Assessment
   Learning Style Assessment
   Learning/Instruction Mode Selection
   Implementation
   Evaluation

Figure 2

fairly common orientations to learning. The more individual the design, the more individual assessment is possible.

"Learner analysis" may be a more appropriate approach for this step in which the educator attempts to define constituents in terms of demographics (age, income, education) and prior knowledge of the subject area. All of these factors affect the rest of the planning process.

Based upon the assessment of needs and information gained concerning the learning orientation of adults, instruction/learning modes may be selected. This is actually an interactive step in linear models since approaches to learning, techniques, and methods are ideally selected only after purposes are defined and needs assessment and learner analysis are completed.

Program implementation and evaluation complete the model. Two kinds of evaluation are important: summative and formative. Summative evaluation determines if the results of the program achieved the desired end, consistent with the identified purpose. Formative evaluation is conducted throughout planning and implementation and focuses on process. Simpson claims formative evaluation contributes to the interactive nature of the model.

Perhaps the most heuristic contribution of this model is that it provides a conceptual framework for viewing the interactive nature of the steps in any program-planning process. At each point along the way the educator consults, formally or informally, consciously or subconsciously, the purposes, goals, and needs as identified.

A Program Planning Model Illustrated

The more planning models one examines, the more certain elements or steps recur. Collaborative planning, attention to goals/objectives, and assessment of needs and interests seem common to most models. The model illustrated here contains these features and is essentially a hybrid of several of the models aforementioned. It is "generic" in the sense that it may be used by an established, ongoing adult learning group or by a group which comes together for a specific purpose at a given point in time and then disbands. It may fit into a specific "macro" program organization context or be used by a self-sustaining learning group for which no prescribed parameters are given.

The model begins with Knowles's learning climate consideration and concludes with evaluation, a step common to most models. The steps are:

1. Create a conducive learning climate.
2. Develop a collaborative planning group.
3. Establish purpose/philosophy.
4. Assess needs/interests.
5. Make consensus decision on topic/content.
6. Formulate desired outcomes.
7. Select/secure resources.
8. Determine appropriate learning modes and techniques.
9. Develop activity outline/Operate the program.
10. Evaluate.

The model is longer in terms of the number of steps included because it does not make assumptions about steps that seem "given" (for example, planning group identification). Elements necessary to comprehensive program development are given due consideration (for example, program operation).

For purposes of illustration, let us assume two separate tracks for planning: one in which no set, ongoing group exists, the other in which programs are conducted for and by a self-perpetuating learning group. First, envision a scenario in which the adult Christian educator wishes to minister through education to the broad range of adult needs as they may be discovered. The educator, by word and by deed, will seek to establish an atmosphere for adult learning which is characterized by mutual trust, respect, recognition of learner's life experience, encouragement of independence, freedom, and participation in decision making. This last ingredient indicates the interactive nature of the model since one means of actualizing this element is through step two, development of a collaborative planning group. This group should, to every extent possible, consist of a cross section of constituent groups. In our example, this means representatives of all age and special interest groups (for example, single, senior, handicapped adults, and so forth).

When the planning group is formed, the function of the adult educator becomes that of trainer for the group in principles of effective adult education and in the process of program development. The planning group thus becomes responsible for subsequent steps in the process, including consideration of philosophy and purpose. Included in the training should be consideration of the process of group development, team building, consensus building, and how to do needs assessment. These can actually be built around a laboratory experience utilizing the planning model itself. The underlying assumption is that groups develop faster when they work collaboratively on a task. The assigned task may thus be to plan a "prototype" learning activity, followed by evaluation and debriefing of the planning experience.

Sound principles of adult education will be reflected in the group's development of purpose and philosophy which will guide the program. The statement of philosophy will include consideration of the nature of adult learning, the purpose of adult Christian education, a description of the ideal adult learning climate, and an affirmation of the ability of adults to be self-directing, given appropriate guidance and resources. As an illustration of the importance of developing a statement of philosophy, consider a potentially controversial question, "Must all our program offerings be religious as defined by the content? Or may we offer courses which do not have an explicitly religious content but may be defined as religious education by virtue of our intent ('effective parenting' for example)?" Such an issue can be clearly dealt with in the governing philosophy developed by the planning group.

Having been trained in the process and various approaches to needs/interest assessment, the planning group proceeds with the next step. The group may conduct surveys, interviews, and discussion with adults and may develop competency models in given areas from experts and the literature. Data is collected, collated, and analyzed giving a picture of the concerns, issues, felt deficiencies, and/or interests of adult constituents.

Priorities among subject areas can be determined from an evaluation of data collected from the assessment, enabling the planning group to begin the process of developing consensus on topical approaches to the priority needs/interests expressed. Consideration of demographic characteristics of respondents may actually necessitate the development of several topical areas for special interest or needs groups. For example, a high priority among young adults as expressed in a survey may be effective discipline with preschoolers. Consensus concerning a workable topic covering this area may result in a program entitled "Effective/Ineffective Approaches to Discipline with Preschoolers."

Pursuing this example, when the topic area has been defined, attention can be focused on what the program is to accomplish, that is, on the desired outcomes. Desired outcomes refer to the skills, competencies, and understanding participants will have gained at the conclusion of the learning program. Thus, one desired outcome of the program on approaches to discipline might be stated as follows: "At the conclusion of this program parents will be able to identify constructive approaches to discipline in several specific situations." A second possible outcome might be: "At the conclusion of the program parents will have a better understanding of how the concrete thinking level of preschoolers affects the choice of appropriate disciplinary actions."

McKenzie points out that anticipated program outcomes should always be stated in terms of terminal competencies of the learners and not with "woolly expressions of what the instructors are going to do during the program."[10] It is a common mistake of educators to confuse desired outcomes with intended teacher behavior. Outcomes focus on what the learner will take away from the activity, *not* with actions the leader will take *during* the activity.

Stating desired outcomes is essential to the rest of the process because it guides the selection of resources, selection of learning modes, and the conduct of the learning activities.

What are the available resources for use in a program on discipline with preschoolers? Research in the community, local public library, church library, and a survey of the congregation may reveal audiovisual resources (films, videotapes, and so forth), doctors, college professors, or trained preschool teachers within the congregation. Availability, affordability, and appropriateness are all considerations in the selection of resources.

Learning modes are the formats or settings in which the activities will take place. Thus a one-day workshop or conference, a demonstration, or a course are among the choices of formats for the program on discipline.[11] Techniques are used in the chosen format or mode to establish a relationship between the learner and the content. Lecture, discussion, role play, and/or case study are among techniques that may be chosen to help achieve the desired outcomes.

An activity outline is a "road map" to guide the conduct of the program. It may also be seen as a time budget to insure that sufficient time is allocated to the essential ingredients of the program. A sample outline of the program on discipline (in a workshop format) is shown in the example at the end of this chapter.

Operating the program may be the easiest step when previous steps have been well developed. It does warrant some discussion, however. Operating the program successfully means giving attention to the following:

Scheduling

Fee arrangements (if necessary)

Publicity/registration

Physical environment (comfort, accessibility, appropriate equipment, and so forth)

Psychological environment (openness, "psychological safety," acceptance, and so forth)

Providing appropriate learning resources

Managing the time schedule

Refreshments (if desired)

Evaluation

Note that evaluation is included, even though it is listed as the last step of the whole model. Formative evaluation should be taking place, assessing and critiquing the conduct and effectiveness of each program element, as well as checking on learner progress toward desired outcomes.

One specific element of program operation may be singled out for attention. Publicizing the program is actually the first consideration of this phase. Strange as it may seem, many well-planned, well-intentioned, well-resourced programs are poorly attended because planners failed to "get the word out" about the program. Educators are well aware of the busy schedules of adults. Potential participants must have enough advance notice of the activity to build it into their calendars. "Lead time" refers not only to allowing sufficient time for planning but also to giving sufficient time to publicize the event. Anticipated benefits, a concept noted by Allen Tough,[12] must be highlighted in the publicity. The "y'all come" or "you need this" approach combined with a dose of guilt is rarely effective in this day and time. Adults want to know what benefits will accrue to them. Thus, publicity should include, along with time and place, and so forth, a summary of desired outcomes. For example, publicity may state that "As a result of participating in this workshop parents of preschoolers will be able to . . . " and to every extent possible go on to state specific skills and understanding included in the desired outcomes. Sales people call this "selling the sizzle."

It has already been noted that evaluation, the essential final step, actually has two parts. Formative evaluation continues throughout the planning and implementation process. Summative evaluation attempts to determine first if the desired outcomes were achieved. If a preassessment was included in introductory activities of the program, a postassessment may be given and the two compared as an assessment of learning. A most interesting and helpful approach might be role play or case analysis where learners have opportunity to test skills or knowledge gained.

Besides assessing learning, summative evaluation also considers the program development process as a whole. At this point the educator gets a better picture of whether the appropriate resources were selected, if techniques used were effective, and so forth.

A Similar but Different Application

It was suggested at the beginning of this illustration that there were at least two tracks for planning: one for a "free-standing" program and one for an ongoing, self-perpetuating learning group. The collaborative planning group formed in the above example may continue in existence to plan additional programs, guided by the purpose/philosophy originally stated. The same process may be applied to an ongoing group of adults (such as a discipleship group or Bible study group). In such a case steps one, two, and three may be taken once, with the succeeding steps of the process repeated for each program.

The group may actually be divided into two or more planning committees to plan programs for each other. Thus, while one group is operating a program, another group may be participating in that program and also planning the next program. This makes the group and programs self-perpetuating. Besides the benefit of ongoing program development, groups hone their skills in group dynamics, collaborative effectiveness, and planning. This was one of the key features of the Indiana Plan described earlier in this chapter. It puts the planning and programming under the control of the learners. The educator becomes both trainer and resource, or in current adult education lingo, a "facilitator of learning."

Conclusion

Several models for planning educational programs with adults have been overviewed in this chapter. One model has been illustrated. In practice, models simply provide a framework for touching the necessary "bases." Whatever approach the educator uses, several "givens" must be included—learning climate, needs assessment, and participation of adults in planning where possible. In a day when record numbers of adults are seeking quality educational experiences in an increasingly competitive market, the "seat-of-the-pants" approach so long characteristic of much adult religious education will no longer suffice.

Program Prototype

Target audience: Parents of Preschool children

Expressed Need/Interest: "Right ways" to discipline preschoolers

Topic/program title: "Effective/Ineffective Approaches to Discipline with Preschoolers"

Desired Outcomes:

1. Parents will have a better understanding of preschoolers developmentally.

2. Parents will gain insight into how the concrete thinking of preschoolers affects the choice of appropriate disciplinary actions.

3. Parents will be able to identify constructive approaches to discipline in several specific situations.

Resources: videotape

film

guest lecturer

"Parent Attitude Inventory"

Participants

Learning mode: workshop

Techniques: Lecture

Question/answer

Group discussion

Role play

Case study

Publicity: Church newsletter

Local paper

Announcements in young adult classes

Direct mail

Time and Place: Sunday, May 20, 5 to 7 PM

Conference Room

Activity Outline: Get acquainted activities ....10 minutes

Overview of workshop.............................. 5 minutes

Guest Lecture ....20 minutes

Question and Answer ....15 minutes

Break ....10 minutes

Film ....20 minutes

Case study analysis/discussion ....10 minutes

Role play/videotape/discussion ....20 minutes

Summary/evaluation ....10 minutes

Evaluation Process: Oral comments

Paper/pencil critique (including suggestions for future workshops)

Notes

1. Leon McKenzie, *The Religious Education of Adults* (Birmingham, Ala.: Religious Education Press, 1982), p. 139.

2. Malcolm Knowles, *The Modern Practice of Adult Education,* 2nd ed. (Chicago: Association Press, 1980), pp. 93-115.

3. Ibid., pp. 237-238.

4. Paul Bergevin and John McKinley, *Design for Adult Education in the Church* (Greenwich: Seabury Press, 1958).

5. James R. Schaefer, *Program Planning for Adult Christian Education* (New York: Newman Press, 1972) pp. 198 *ff.*

6. Ibid. See chapter 2.

7. Chester Klevins, *Materials and Methods in Adult and Continuing Education* (Los Angeles: Klevens Publications, Inc., 1982), p. 94. Used by permission.

8. H. Whitkin, "Cognitive Styles in Academic Performance and in Teacher-Student Relations," ed. Messick, *Individuality in Learning* (San Francisco: Jossey-Bass, 1976).

9. David Kolb, *The Learning Styles Inventory: Technical Manual* (Boston: McBer, 1976).

10. Leon McKenzie, *Adult Religious Education: the 20th Century Challenge* (West Mystic, Conn.: 23rd Publications, 1975), p. 53.

11. Knowles provides a typology of formats for individual and group learning in chapter 11, *The Modern Practice of Adult Education.* In this chapter he also provides a typology of learning techniques organized by category: presentation, audience participation, and discussion technique.

12. Allen Tough, *Intentional Changes* (Chicago: Follett Publishing Co., 1982).

9

Bible Teaching Program
C. Ferris Jordan

The major activities a church provides to teach the Bible are included in what may be termed the Bible teaching program of the church. The activities may be conducted at any time and any place persons can be assembled to study the Word. However, the major responsibility for the Bible teaching program in most churches is borne by the Sunday School. The vitality of the Sunday School is one of the most accurate barometers for measuring the health of the church, and the strength of adult work is a primary determination of the Sunday School's well-being.

The focus of this chapter is upon the Bible teaching program with special reference to adult Sunday School work. The significance of Bible teaching generally and of adult Bible study specifically, the tasks of the Sunday School, guidelines for organizing, leadership suggestions, and tips for planning will be among the topics presented.

Understanding the Importance of the
Bible Teaching Program

Harry Piland, director of the Sunday School Department of the Southern Baptist Sunday School Board, said, "the Sunday School is at the heart of the mission of the church. It is central—not a side issue; it is major—not minor."[1] With these words, the leader of the Bible teaching program in a major denomination described the importance of the program in the life of the church. The significance of the program will be discussed here under two headings, namely, the biblical emphasis on teaching and the place of teaching in the mission of the church.

The Biblical Emphasis on Teaching

God has revealed in the Bible the importance of teaching as a function of God's people. The note was sounded clearly among the Hebrews in Deuteronomy.

> And these words, which I command thee this day, shall be in thine heart: And thou shalt teach them diligently unto thy children, and shalt talk of them when thou sittest in thine house, and when thou walkest by the way, and when thou liest down, and when thou risest up (Deut. 6:6-7).

With these words God commanded that His law be taught, and He gave parents responsibility for teaching in the home formally and informally. God also admonished the leaders of His people to give attention to teaching in the gatherings of His people.

> When all Israel is come to appear before the Lord thy God in the place which he shall choose, thou shalt read this law before all Israel in their hearing. Gather the people together, men, and women, and children, and thy stranger that is within thy gates, that they may hear, and that they may learn, and fear the Lord your God, and observe to do all the words of this law: And that their children, which have not known anything, may hear, and learn to fear the Lord your God, as long as ye live in the land whither ye go over Jordan to possess it (Deut. 31:11-13).

Teaching God's commandments was absolutely essential for Israel's well-being. If they were to prosper as a nation, they had to fear the Lord and obey all His teachings. These commands in Deuteronomy have strong implications for the contemporary Bible teaching program with regard to both reaching people and teaching them.

The strong biblical emphasis upon teaching is seen in various places in the Old Testament. Only a few can be cited here. In the days of Jehoshaphat in Judah, the king commanded his princes "to teach in the cities of Judah" (2 Chron. 17:7). He sent priests and Levites with the princes, "And they taught in Judah, and had the book of the law of the Lord with them, and went about throughout all the cities of Judah, and taught the people" (17:9). King Hezekiah had a good word for all the Levites who "taught the good knowledge of the Lord" (2 Chron. 30:22). The psalmist spoke of the Lord as the one who had taught him from his youth (Ps. 71:17). In various passages in Psalms 119, the psalmist asked the Lord to teach him His statutes (vv. 12,26,64,68,124,135).

In keeping with the strong emphasis upon teaching in the Old Testament, the Messiah came teaching as well as preaching. A casual glance at a concordance will reveal how numerous are the references to Jesus' functioning as teacher. "He taught daily in the temple" (Luke 19:47), "He entered into the synagogue and taught" (Mark 1:21), and "He taught them as one that had authority" (Mark 1:22) will suffice to illustrate Jesus' attention to teaching and His unsurpassed competence as Teacher.

The unfolding history of the New Testament church saw the early leaders carrying on in the tradition of Jesus giving much attention to teaching. Paul's sessions in the synagogues in which he "reasoned with them out of the Scriptures" (Acts 17:2) suggest a dialogical teaching format more than mere proclamation. The possibility of a similar format is certainly suggested when Paul went to Athens. There "disputed he in the synagogue with the Jews, and with the devout persons, and in the market daily with them that met with him" (Acts 17:17). Teaching was highlighted in the New Testament church. Timothy was admonished, "And the things that thou hast heard of me among many witnesses, the same commit thou to faithful men, who shall be able to teach others also" (2 Tim. 2:2).

God has been teaching His people through the centuries. He has called others to teach. He has provided His Scriptures that men may learn of Him, know Him personally by faith, and live full lives as they obey His guidelines and live in His power.

The Place of Teaching in the Mission of the Church

God's concern for teaching was given clear expression not only in Israel but also in the New Israel, His church. He has sent them on mission in the world, and teaching has a prominent place in that mission. The church's divine mandate to teach was set forth by Jesus in the Great Commission.

> Go ye therefore, and teach all nations, baptizing them in the name of the Father, and of the Son, and of the Holy Ghost: Teaching them to observe all things whatsoever I have commanded you: and, lo, I am with you alway, even unto the end of the world (Matt. 28:19-20).

The prominent role of teaching in the Lord's commission is indisputable. Through the centuries the church has been held accountable for her faithfulness to her mission. She is still under divine orders to teach the Scriptures, and any congregation that takes that assignment lightly will bring upon themselves the Lord's reproach.

The importance of teaching in the church's life and ministry may be viewed not only from the perspective of her mandate but also from the view of the benefits that accrue when Bible teaching is done faithfully and effectively. A passage in 2 Timothy states clearly God's intention with regard to the Scripture's function in the body of Christ. "All Scripture is given by inspiration of God, and is profitable for doctrine, for reproof, for correction, for instruction in righteousness; That the man of God may be perfect, throughly furnished unto all good works" (2 Tim. 3:16-17).

Where attention is given to Bible teaching, a church is more likely to be doctrinally sound, and the people will be growing in the ways of the Lord. God gave the Scriptures so that men might know Him, rely upon Him for salvation, and press toward maturity in Him, fully equipped for every good work. That purpose cannot be accomplished if a church gives mere lip service to the Bible. But God's intention will be realized when the Scriptures are proclaimed from the pulpit, taught in the church's classrooms, and searched daily in the homes of God's people. The lost being saved, the saved being developed, families being strengthened, and the church being unified and committed to mission are the kinds of results a congregation can expect when the divinely mandated emphasis upon teaching the Scriptures is honored.

Assigning Priority to the Adult
Bible Teaching Program

The Bible teaching program of any church is important. What place does reaching and teaching adults have in that program is the question to be addressed now.

In the contemporary period, the Sunday School has been the primary expression of the Bible teaching program, but Sunday School has not always been for adults. During the first 110 years of its history, Sunday School focused on children and youth. In the early years adult participation in Sunday School was hindered, not only by the childhood focus of the movement from its inception, but also by the attitude of many churches toward the Sunday School. Church leaders and congregations often looked with suspicion upon anyone who attempted to teach the Bible without having received ordination to religious work and formal theological training. Sunday School classes often were denied the privilege of using the church building for their Bible teaching sessions. The Schools were looked upon as "auxiliaries" to the church rather than as an integral part of the church's life and work. With these kinds of attitudes toward Sunday School and with the focus on children, it is little wonder that adults failed to take an interest.

But slowly change was effected. During the 1880s an adult class was started at the Calvary Baptist Church in Washington, DC. By 1889 the work had prospered to the extent that an adult department was created. In 1890 and 1893 respectively, the Baraca and Philathea Bible class organizations began to promote the establishment of adult Bible classes.[2] The promotion began in Syracuse, New York, the home of founders Marshal Hudson and his daughter. Soon the movement spread. As years passed, the classes grew large. They tended to become independent in spirit, often selecting curriculum and projects independently of the church. The classes operated across denominational lines. In some places a strong competitive spirit existed among the classes, and the emphasis upon inspiration, fellowship, and projects took precedence over quality Bible study.

Gradually, Sunday Schools began to exercise more control over their adult classes, and churches began to see the potential in reaching adults for Bible study. Adult departments were established to provide better coordination among the classes and cooperation with the church. Today, Adult Sunday School work is more likely to be perceived as a vital part of the entire Sunday School, and the latter is generally seen as the church at work accomplishing specific assigned tasks.

Reaching and teaching adults not only should have a place in the Sunday School but also should be given priority in the church's Bible teaching program. That priority should be assigned for several reasons. First, there appears to be an implied strategy in the Scriptures that says that persons of all ages are reached best when priority is given to reaching adults. Second, adults represent the largest percentage of a church's prospects and thus deserve a priority commensurate with that potential. Projections are that the adult population will continue to grow in the United States so that by 2050 there will be 260 persons sixty-five years of age and over for every 100 teenagers.[3]

A third consideration is the significant leadership roles filled by adults in all areas of life. Adults choose public officials, control the media, teach in the school classrooms, lead in government at all levels, serve as heads of households, determine the financial climate, set the tone in churches, and perform many other functions. Persons so strategically situated with ability to wield such power need to be enrolled in a regular study of God's Word, so their lives can be molded by His teachings. Finally, a casual survey of church history reveals a direct relationship between the church's vitality and the priority assigned to Christian education of adults. When adult education has been strong, the church has been most vital. The lessons of history dictate that the contemporary church must give priority to adults if she is to have strength.

Defining the Tasks of the Bible Teaching Program

To carry out the Great Commission, a church must develop strategy and assign specific responsibility. It is at this point that the Sunday School comes into clear focus. The work of the Sunday School may be described in terms of tasks to be done—tasks that grow directly from the mission of the church. Southern Baptists, for example, have defined six tasks of the Sunday School.

Reach People for Bible Study

The first task focuses on leading persons to enroll and participate in Bible study. Through planned visitation and outreach programs, the Sunday School reaches out. Every church member should be enrolled in Bible study. Special attention must be given to enrolling lost persons. Every adult class should be involved in finding, cultivating, loving, and enrolling persons. The small number of lost adults enrolled in Sunday School today is tragic. The large number of adult church members not enrolled in Bible study is appalling. The Sunday School must reach.

Teach the Bible

The church charges the Bible teaching program to teach the meaning and message of the Bible. Teaching the Bible to every member and prospect is crucial for every church. The goal of the teaching must be the application of Bible truths to every area of life and the assimilation of those teachings into the life-style. When that goal is being achieved, adults will be saved and maturing in Christ.

Witness About Christ and Lead Persons to Salvation

Enrolling persons in Bible study and teaching them the Bible are essential. But, in the case of lost persons, the Sunday School has a responsibility to provide a verbal witness about Christ and to lead persons into a saving relationship with Him. Personal evangelism is a task of the Sunday School. Once individuals have received Christ, the Sunday School leaders and members must help them understand the value of scriptural baptism and membership in a church.

Minister to Sunday School Members and Nonmembers

God is concerned about the total person. He expects His churches to meet the needs of persons in Jesus' name. The efforts to fulfill those expectations are referred to as ministry. Adult Sunday School classes and departments should be ministering units, and the recipients of their love and care ought to be members and nonmembers.

Lead Members to Worship

Worship is primary in the lives of believers. Through worship persons encounter and adore God. They hear His message, discover his will, and find power for service. A significant task of the Sunday School is to lead members to worship corporately with the church family, in their homes as family units, and individually in private devotions.

Interpret and Undergird Church and Denominational Work

The Sunday School has more members than any other organization of the church. It has more leaders and prospects. The organization and structure are such that it can do a significant part of the church's work. Thus it is reasonable that the sixth task assigned to the Sunday School should be interpreting to its members the work of the church and the denomination and undergirding that work with the support and participation of leaders and members.

Organizing for Adult Sunday School Work

Thus far in this chapter, attention has been focused upon understanding the importance of the Bible teaching program, assigning priority to the adult aspect of that program, and defining the work of the program. Now the focus shifts to organizing for Adult Sunday School work.

Definition of Organization

Perhaps it would be helpful to establish a definition of organization. One Sunday School leader wrote, "Simply put, organization involves having a task too big to perform by one person, dividing that task into reasonable parts, and asking persons to do parts of the whole."[4] Another writer has suggested that organization refers "to the ways leaders and members can work together to accomplish mutual objectives in Adult Sunday School work."[5] For persons who have failed to appreciate organization because they believe it is not spiritual, it may be helpful to define organization as the way by which God's people, under the leadership of the Holy Spirit, labor together to meet the challenge of Adult Sunday School work. Organization that serves the people and provides the means for achieving the purposes of the Sunday School is both practical and spiritual. "We can help more adults in more ways through organization than we can through disorganization or no organization."[6]

Relation of Organization to Sunday School Tasks

So much for definition of organization. How does adult Sunday School organization relate to the tasks assigned to Sunday School? The tasks are the mutual objectives which adult Sunday School leaders and members are seeking to accomplish. The units of organization needed and the leaders required are determined by the tasks to be done and the objectives to be achieved. The units of work employed must be conducive to reaching, teaching, ministering, and evangelizing. The leadership roles must include persons who will assume responsibility for the various task areas.

Recommendations about Units of Organization

The two units of organization needed to get the Sunday School work done are the department and the class. The primary unit is the class. The department exists to strengthen the classes and to help them get their work done. Consider each unit separately.

1. *The adult class.* A class is needed for each twenty-five possibilities or less. The term *possibilities* means both members and prospects. An estimate of the number of classes needed can be determined by dividing the total possibilities by twenty-five. The actual number of classes provided will be determined by the space and other resources a church has available.

Why is twenty-five suggested as the maximum class enrollment for adults? That number has been selected because a teacher and other volunteer leaders can do their best work in all the Sunday School tasks with a group approximately this size. Absentees and prospects can be more easily contacted in a group of this size. Furthermore, about 40 to 60 percent of the class enrollment is present on a given Sunday. Ten to fifteen persons comprise an ideal group for Bible study that employs interaction and member involvement in learning activities. Although twenty-five is the suggested maximum class enrollment, seldom should a new class be started full grown, and every effort should be made not to allow a class to reach the maximum enrollment before consideration is given to creating new units. When the class is not full-grown, there is greater psychological encouragement for growth.

Larger classes may be effective if the teacher maintains a wholesome attitude about the work of the class and guides class leaders in giving attention to all the Sunday School tasks. However, certain weaknesses seem to be present as a class enrollment grows beyond twenty-five. John Sisemore has identified some of those weaknesses:

(1) Large classes curtail the informality and freedom essential to the teaching-learning process.

(2) Large classes tend to minimize the personal touch of the teacher and to dissipate the opportunities to be a friend and counselor.

(3) Large classes usually weaken the urge to visit, to win souls, and to render personal service.

(4) Large classes tend to destroy compassion for the lost and unreached multitude around them.

(5) Large classes frequently decline in their interest in the affairs of the church, and at times even compete with church activities.

(6) Large classes usually are not conducive to developing new workers and sending them out in service.[7]

Not only the number of adult classes needed but also the basis on which the adults will be grouped is important. No perfect grouping plan exists. Age grading seems to be the best plan in terms of efficient administration and meeting the needs of adults. While age grading has its critics, it does allow churches to provide for every adult, to assign every prospect to a class, and to form Bible study groups in which members are more likely to have common needs.

Whether separate classes should be provided for each sex or coeducational grouping be allowed within each assigned age range is a question that evokes differences of opinion. Separate classes for men and women do offer some advantage in teaching and reaching. Some adults relate best to a teacher of their own sex. Ministry needs may be met best in classes of one sex if members are more comfortable sharing their problems with class leaders and members of the same sex. On the other hand, coeducational classes seem to have special appeal for single adults and young married adults. If the teacher of the coed class can guide in a manner that will deter the members from a tendency to become primarily social in orientation and to shy away from life-centered learning that focuses on needs and grapples with life's issues, perhaps coed classes will allow a church to reach some adults whom it could not serve otherwise.

Perhaps a church that can organize classes and departments on an age basis and provide classes for both coed and separate constituencies is in best position to reach *all* adults. Making dual provision can create problems, however, unless carefully defined guidelines are followed. Consider some guidelines in dealing with the complexities of providing both co-educational classes and separate classes for men and women:

(1) Organize coeducational classes within a department structure.
(2) Maintain coeducational classes on an age-graded system based on the age of one of the spouses, a median age, or the age of the younger spouse.
(3) Encourage the maximum size of twenty-five enrolled and provide for periodic reorganization or annual promotion to maintain the grading system.
(4) Provide bona fide choices of classes for men and women who prefer separate provisions.
(5) Assign prospects to both kinds of classes based on preference of the prospects rather than allowing the classes to be in competition with one another. If the preference is not known, make the assignment to the separate classes for men and women.
(6) Encourage cooperation of classes within a department to assist persons in making a choice based on need, rather than "building up" a particular class.
(7) Provide groups for men with a man group leader and groups for women with a woman group leader so that individual ministry needs may be met more adequately.
(8) Encourage the use of the term *coeducational* rather than "couples" to provide for persons whose spouse serves in a leadership position in another area of the Sunday School and for persons whose spouse cannot or will not attend.[8]

2. The Adult Department. The class is one unit of organization in Adult Sunday School work; the other is the department. Usually an adult department is created when there are at least two classes and includes a maximum of six classes. The suggested enrollment ceiling for departments is 125. A department and its leaders exist to help the classes function efficiently. At lease four objectives for adult departments may be cited: (1) to unify and correlate the work of the classes with the program of the Sunday School and the church; (2) to create and maintain as many classes as are needed to reach the total possibilities within the age range assigned by the church; (3) to increase the efficiency of the classes by overseeing the work of visitation, other outreach activities, ministry, and other projects related to Sunday School tasks; and (4) to improve teaching through the department section of the weekly workers' meeting and other training opportunities

Identifying the Leaders Needed in
Adult Sunday School Work

The units of organization require leaders with clearly defined duties. Each leader should be prayerfully enlisted, carefully trained, and continuously supported. The importance of well-chosen leaders who function effectively can hardly be overestimated. Leaders with vision and the ability to share it with members who will voluntarily work with them to make it a reality make all the difference in Adult Sunday School work. They supply inspiration, provide resources, and offer encouragement. Leaders who pray, express compassion, and work diligently provide a model for co-workers and members.

Characteristics of Effective Leaders

In addition to their being born-again believers with genuine commitment to Adult Sunday School work, what characteristics mark effective leaders of adults? As persons, leaders will be progressing toward maturity in Christ. They will care for those under their leadership to the extent that they feel a sense of responsibility that compels them to give watchful attention and to suffer inconvenience. Leaders who truly lead are marked by keen sensitivity to the needs of others, readiness to understand and to act in the best interest of others and the work, and a nonjudgmental stance that accepts persons where they are and works with them for God's glory.

In terms of leadership skills and techniques, quality leaders plan their work regularly. They include members in their planning, soliciting and respecting their suggestions. Mastering the art of delegation and learning to commend others appropriately always have high priority in their thoughts and practices. Evaluation receives constant attention from growing leaders.

Suggested Leaders and Their Duties

Who are the suggested leaders in Adult Sunday School classes and departments? The leaders and class organization are defined in Figure 1.

Adult Sunday School work embraces teaching, reaching, ministering, witnessing, leading persons to worship, and informing adults about the work of their church and denomination. A task so varied in scope cannot be done by the teacher alone. The wise teacher will become a partner with a corps of class leaders and work through a TEAMREACH concept to get the work done.[9]

In the approach to the work of the adult class, the teacher and class outreach leaders are church elected. They share responsibility for selecting, enlisting, and training the other class leaders. The church holds the teachers ultimately responsible for the total work of the class and expects them to guide the members in quality Bible study. The *outreach leader* guides in reaching prospects, in witnessing to the lost, and in strengthening the organization. Ministry to class members and prospects, weektime class activities, and building class fellowship are assignments given to the *class activities leader*. *Group leaders* work with an assigned group of four

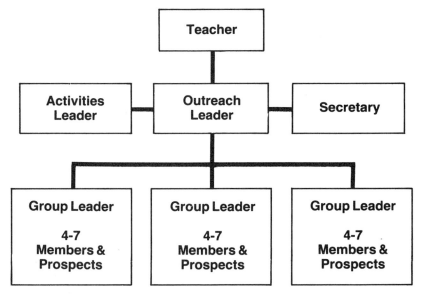

Figure 1

to seven members and prospects in ministering to members and encouraging members in witnessing and in worshiping. The *class secretary* performs the important function of keeping accurate records.

Adult departments function under the oversight of a director. A department outreach leader, an activities leader, and a secretary work with the director. As the primary department leader, the *director* is responsible to the Sunday School director for planning, conducting, and evaluating the work of the department. Organizing the department for reaching, teaching, witnessing, ministering; enlisting and training leaders; leading department planning meetings, and administering the department are the director's duties. The *department outreach leader* is responsible to the director for planning and administering the department's efforts in outreach and evangelism, and serves as the link between the general outreach director of the Sunday School and class outreach leaders. The *department activities leader* will work with the outreach leader to assist class activities leaders in their ministry responsibility and to provide weektime opportunities for social activities and Bible study. The *department secretary* supervises all matters related to department records and assists class secretaries.

Guiding the Sunday Morning Session

The Sunday morning session in adult departments should be lively. It should be marked by warm fellowship, appropriate focus on reaching and ministering, and life-related Bible study. The time allotted by the church should be at least one hour, preferably an hour and fifteen minutes. The assigned time may be spent in a large group experience, a combination large group/small group setting, or exclusively in the small group. The suggested basic schedule is one fourth of the time in the large group (department period) and three fourths in the small group (class period). Deviations from the basic schedule to alternate or flexible schedules should always be made for a definite purpose and as a result of the combined planning efforts of department leaders and teachers.

In the large group, the department director and/or other department leaders are in charge. They will give attention to welcoming visitors and new members, to informing the members about department, church, and denominational activities, and to administering department concerns related to outreach, ministry, and witnessing. A brief feature that utilizes the talents and services of members may be used to focus on an ongoing church concern or the small-group Bible study for the morning. The large group (department period) can be used to prepare the members socially, mentally, emotionally, and spiritually for Bible study.

The class period should be used primarily for Bible study. However, five to ten well-planned minutes may be designated for welcoming newcomers, receiving records and offerings, hearing reports from group leaders, and assigning prospects. The Bible study period should afford maximum contact with the Bible. Through well-planned learning activities, teachers will seek to guide members in achieving readiness to learn, exploring the biblical content purposefully, and in making application of Bible truth to their own lives. To provide a study experience that produces maximum learning, the teacher will rely upon such basic approaches as lecture, discussion, question and answer, case study, brainstorming, and small-group activity. From time to time, more innovative approaches such as role play, debate, panel/forum, monologue, and creative art activities will be used.

In all the activity, the teacher will seek to stimulate members to meaningful involvement in discovering, understanding, and applying Bible truth. The teacher's primary roles are those of guide and resource person. The members' responsibilities include advance preparation, active participation, and application of truth with appropriate follow-through.

Planning for Adult Sunday School Work

Adult Sunday School work that counts most is that orchestrated by careful and prayerful planning. It does not just happen! The chief partner and resource in the planning is the Holy Spirit. When department and class leaders participate in planning sessions in which they seek His counsel through earnest prayer and when they rely upon His leadership in implementing their plans, no activity will be wasted and no spiritual resources will be lacking. Planning takes place at both the department and class levels.

Ideally, department planning occurs weekly. If that frequency is not possible, carefully administered monthly planning will enhance the work. Usually department planning is done as a part of the weekly workers' meeting provided for all Sunday School leaders. In many churches the weekly meeting is held prior to or following a midweek church prayer meeting. One hour is needed for effective department planning. The department director is in charge. Approximately one third of the hour may be devoted to administering department concerns related to enrolling new members, outreach, witnessing, ministery, and fellowship activities. The department outreach leader and activities leader share this time with the director under the latter's leadership.

The remaining two thirds of the hours is devoted to improving teaching and preparing for the following Sunday session. Focus is upon how the Sunday morning session will be divided between the large- and small-group periods, how the feature in the department period will be conducted, and ideas related to Bible study in the class period. Teachers will profit from exploring the Bible content for Sunday's lesson, and from sharing ideas about formulating central truth and teaching aim statements, creating learning readiness, and guiding in purposeful Bible study and application to life. Prayer periods in planning meeting will build team spirit, provide encouragement, and supply power.

Class planning occurs at two levels: class leader planning and planning with leaders and members together. Class leader planning may occur monthly. The leadership team comes together with the outreach leader presiding. The group follows an agenda previously determined by the teacher and outreach leader who have considered items submitted to them by other class leaders. Agenda items may include: (1) the secretary's report on enrollment increase, average attendance, and total weekly contacts with members and prospects; (2) the outreach leader's report on progress in visitation, in prospect cultivation, and in training members for more effective witnessing and outreach; (3) group leaders' reports on the work of their groups in reaching and ministering; (4) plans for the coming month in relation to each of the Sunday School tasks; and (5) plans for leading the class to cooperate with the work of the church and the Sunday School.

At least quarterly, a class planning meeting should be held in which the outreach leader presides. Class members will hear reports from their class leaders about their work in outreach, witnessing, and ministry. Plans will be shared for class participation in the coming quarter in visitation, ministry projects, and Sunday School and churchwide events. Goals for class growth will be discussed and adopted. The teacher will have a time to commend the class for past accomplishments and to challenge them for the future. The class meeting may include Bible study and should always provide a social time for fellowship.

Providing Weektime Bible Study
Opportunities

Although the main thrust of the Bible teaching program for adults occurs on Sunday morning through Sunday School, other aspects of the program are offered on weekdays. Several examples will be sighted here.

Adult Vacation Bible School is receiving good response. A good blend of informal, intensive Bible study units designed to enhance growth in some specific aspect of adults' Christian lives, and fellowship opportunities may comprise the curriculum. The Bible School may be geared to specific target groups such as senior adults, parents who bring their children to Vacation Bible School, college students, and adults who work at night. The setting may be in the church building, in apartment complexes, in college dorms, mobile home parks, or retirement centers, to mention only a few. A director, a study leader, a publicity/enlistment committee, and a fellowship committee will satisfy leadership requirements.

Bible conferences may also be a part of the program. The conference may be planned for a single church or a group of churches. The conference may offer a number of alternate Bible conferences on Bible books or Bible themes.

Home Bible studies offer another opportunity. Southern Baptists offer a Bible correspondence study. Adults may use a study guide, submit papers, receive graded papers, and earn achievement awards.

Outreach Bible Study may be another opportunity to involve persons, especially unsaved adults, in studying the Scriptures. The work will be assured of good coordination if an Outreach Bible Study director functioning as a general officer of the Sunday School provides oversight. This leader will locate specialized needs for Bible study, lead in selecting leaders and in determining curriculum according to church policy, propose meeting times and location. Among the clusters of adults whom a church may address in this way are: Sunday workers; ethnic, language, or other cultural subgroups; adults in specialized settings such as resorts, hotels, nursing homes; clusters of families engaged in intergenerational Bible study; and adults, who by their own choice of life-style, are oriented away from the church.

Conclusion

The most compelling reason for involving adults in Bible study is that doing so is at the heart of Christ's Great Commission to the churches. No effort expended to train leaders, provide organization, and conduct planning sessions that will assure a strong Adult Sunday School program and other Bible study opportunities is too great. Few challenges confronting churches in the final decades of the twentieth century are greater than the opportunity to provide life-centered Bible study for *all* adults.

Notes

1. Harry M. Piland, *Basic Sunday School Work* (Nashville: Convention Press, 1980), pp. 15-16.

2. Marshall A. Hudson, "The Philathea Bible Class," *The Sunday School Times,* 1914, p. 11.

3. Population Reference Bureau, January 1984, cited in *Digest,* Research Division of the Home Mission Board, SBC, 6, No. 6, June 1984, p. 3

4. Piland, p. 35.

5. Charles Livingstone, compiler, *Adult Sunday School Work* (Nashville: Convention Press, 1969), p. 15.

6. Ibid., p. 14.

7. John T. Sisemore, *The Sunday School Ministry to Adults* (Nashville: Convention Press, 1959), p. 35.

8. Larry Shotwell, *Basic Adult Sunday School Work* (Nashville: Convention Press, 1981), p. 70.

9. Ibid. The class and department organizations are discussed in detail in chapter 5, and the duties of leaders are presented in chapter 6.

10

Discipleship Training

Jerry M. Stubblefield

Introduction

Discipleship training is crucial for the growth, development, and maturity of *all* Christians if they are to grow to Christlikeness and do the work of Christ in the world. A disciple is a learner. A Christian disciple is a person who seeks to learn from Christ and to try to be like Him.

Although many churches believe that children and youth should be involved in discipleship training, some churches do not provide regular, ongoing discipleship training for adults. However, it is popular to provide discipleship training for new believers whatever their age. Discipleship training for a new believer emphasizes the establishment of Christian disciplines. Attention is focused upon maintaining a daily quiet time with God, Scripture memory, systematic Bible reading and study, intercessory prayer, engaging in ministry and service, and being involved in personal evangelism. Such discipleship training has been developed to function on a one-to-one basis with the anticipation that the one being discipled will become a discipler of a person whom she has helped to become a Christian. It operates on the multiplication principle. A similar plan should be a part of the ongoing church program—available to all adults.

Biblical Background

The word *disciple* comes from the word *discere* which means *to learn*. Our word *disciple* comes from the Latin *discipulus*. A disciple is a learner, scholar, pupil, and sometimes an apprentice. Disciple always refers to the pupil of someone, not to the master or teacher when it appears in the Greek language. The inference is that persons not only accept the views of the teacher, but seek to practice the teacher's instruction. A disciple is one who accepts the teachings of another not only in belief but in practice.[1]

The Hebrew language also has a similar word *lamad*. It is found in 1 Chronicles 25:8 describing pupils in the Temple music school and carries the idea that "learning" involves practice as well as theory. The word *disciple* is used only once in the English Old Testament in Isaiah 8:16. The context and resulting ideas are important. Isaiah recognized that the people had rejected his message. He determined to entrust his message to a band of followers who were not only to preserve it, but to seek to make it effective for days to come. The similarity between Isaiah's disciples and those of Jesus is clear.

In the New Testament the word *disciple* is used only in the Gospels and Acts where it is found more than 250 times. Except for reference to the disciples of John the Baptist, it refers to Jesus' disciples. In the Gospels Jesus' disciples are not called "the disciples" but "His disciples." In most cases disciples is used in the plural except where John refers to the disciple whom Jesus loved (John 19:26). It is not always clear whether the disciples were a small group living in close fellowship with Jesus or was a reference to the larger body who accepted Jesus as their teacher and leader.

Surprisingly, the word *disciple* is not found in other New Testament writings. However, it is found in later Christian writings in the same sense in which it is in Acts—to describe those who believed in Christ.[2]

Philosophy

Theological Foundations

There are three key theological ideas upon which a philosophy of discipleship training can be built. The concepts are: each individual is of supreme worth in the sight of God; the nature and essence of the Christian life demands growth; the church is a spiritual democracy, and its successful ministry demands an informed membership and training leadership.

The Bible teaches repeatedly that each individual is of supreme worth in the sight of God. Every person is of infinite worth and possesses the dignity of personality. This idea is affirmed at creation when God made humans in His image. Of all the created order, human beings are the only creatures who have the ability to commune with God and enter into a vital relationship with Him. God gave persons dominion over the world.

The highest example of God's value of people is expressed in John 3:16: "For God so loved the world, that He gave His only begotten Son, that whoever believes in Him should not perish, but have eternal life" (NASB). Because each individual is of supreme worth in the sight of God, a person must become all that is capable of becoming under God. Therefore, discipleship training is essential for every Christian.

Another theological foundation is that the nature and essence of the Christian life demands growth. There is more to the Christian life than making a profession of faith or giving one's life to Christ. Discipleship training offers the opportunity for growth to take place in the Christian's life. A freshman college student said, "My faith as a child does not seem adequate for me now." She was not questioning her earlier faith or commitment but was acknowledging her need to continue to grow and mature as a Christian.

Many Christians have acted as if growth in the Christian life were an optional matter. I accepted Christ as Savior at the age of ten. How thankful I am that God has continued to deal with me throughout my Christian life. Many Christians act as if growth in the Christian life were an optional matter. Addressing college students, Kenneth Chafin invited some of them to take a step to update their faith. It was said of Jesus, "And Jesus kept increasing in wisdom and stature, and in favor with God and man" (Luke 2:52, NASB). Would that it were said of every Christian!

The third theological foundation is that the church is a spiritual democracy, and its successful ministry demands an informed membership and trained leadership. My religious involvement has been in a denomination that practices congregational polity. I have been influenced by the meaning of Ephesians 4:11-12 which describes various types of ministry and their purpose. For a church to be effective and successful in doing the work of God, the people of God need to be equipped, enabled to do the work of ministry so that the church (the body of Christ) can be built up. This is the essense of discipleship training. To be involved in the work of ministry, a Christian must know what the ministry is and then be trained to do the task effectively.

Educational Foundations

Two educational principles form the foundation for discipleship training—learning by doing and individual development through individual participation. Often we feel we know how to do something because we have studied or read about it. I have been a part of discipleship training since a child. I had said "grace" at mealtime but had never prayed in public. Through discipleship training I was led to pray in public, speak before a group, and even attempt personal evangelism, in the context of persons like myself. How encouraging it was to exercise these aspects of the Christian life among fellow disciples—learners.

Study is very important in understanding the Christian life and what it means to be a Christian. Evidence that one has learned the concept comes by demonstrating it. Jesus spent a lot of time teaching His disciples, but then came the time when He sent them out—first the twelve and then the seventy. After both experiences Jesus spent additional time teaching them.

A Christian grows, matures, develops through participation. We have learned to experience things vicariously—through the experience of others. A person enjoys such times but probably grows very little or does not improve or become more skillful. Thousands of Christians have studied personal soul-winning, perhaps have received credit for the study, but have never known the challenge and joy of sharing one's faith with another. It is estimated that 80 percent of church leadership positions are held by 20 percent of the membership. Is it possible that 80 percent of the membership have never been trained or challenged to participate meaningfully in the life and work of Christ through His church?

Discipleship training helps a Christian to grow through learning by doing and individual development through individual participation.

Tasks of Adult Discipleship Training

What can and should adult discipleship training do for a church? What are its functions? What will adult discipleship training do to help individual Christians live more effective lives and thus strengthen and enhance a church's ministry? Adult discipleship training has four primary tasks.

Equip Adults for Discipleship and Personal Ministry

Being a disciple means that the adult Christian has made a lifelong commitment to the person, teaching, and spirit of Jesus Christ. Letting Christ be Lord of one's life means that the Christian is involved in progressive learning, growing in Christlikeness, applying biblical truth to various areas of life, responsibly sharing the Christian faith, and accepting responsible church membership. While these aspects of discipleship may be learned and shared in group experiences, the focus is upon helping each adult grow and develop into Christlikeness. As each adult Christian grows, there must be corporate understandings, skills, and relationships that build up the church. Church members must know how to work in harmonious relationships with other Christians to strengthen and build up the church.

This task can be realized through teaching the biblical meanings of discipleship. Opportunities for training need to be designed to help Adult Christians gain basic knowledge and understandings in discipleship, personal growth, spiritual gifts, and skills necessary to live an effective Christian life.

**Teach Christian Theology, Doctrine, Ethics, History,
and Church Polity and Organization**

The purpose for teaching Christian theology and doctrine, Christian ethics, Christian history, and church polity and organization is to assist the adult Christian in exploring the realities of the Christian faith. The study of theology is to help the adult develop a valid system of beliefs about God and God's relationship to persons. Christian ethics should help the adult grow in Christian character, and communicate and apply ethical principles in every relationship of daily living. A study of Christian history should aid the adult in discovering and appropriating meaning and values from the past. Examining church polity and organization will help adults work together effectively in achieving Christ's objectives for the local church and for the denomination.

Studying Christian theology will help adult Christians deepen their understanding of biblical teachings and develop their beliefs into a personal theology. An adult should be able to know and communicate to others what he believes. These beliefs should be applied to daily living.

Every adult should have a knowledge of the ethical teachings of the Bible. Each Christian is responsible to God for moral choices. Christian ethics is concerned with God's ideals for living. These ideals are set forth in the Bible and provide the "oughtness" of the Christian life. The purpose of Christian ethics is to speak to every issue with which the Christian is confronted—to every issue that influences conduct—and to help all Christians act according to Christian principles.

Christian history commences with the revelation of God in Christ. The biblical witness is the primary source of the origin of the church and its earliest development. The first documents of Christian history are found in the New Testament. The Old Testament is important as it gives the context out of which the church arose. Christian history addresses the problems of church and state, economic motives in Christian behavior, and the influence of society upon the life of the church. A part of Christian history is the church struggling with its own internal problems of discipline.

A study of church polity and organization can help adults to know how and why a church does its work. With this knowledge adults are more likely to be motivated to be good stewards of their time, talents, and money in fulfilling the church's mission. One is also better able to participate in the affairs of the church and the denomination.

Equip Church Leaders for Service

Equipping church leaders for service involves general training for any type of leadership role usually held by church members, training potential leaders, and basic job training. Training results in adults developing increased competence to serve effectively and efficiently. Church leaders must have an understanding of the type of leadership role in which a person is likely to be most effective.

A key part of adult discipleship training is a concern that every adult discover a meaningful place of service in the life and work of the church. Focusing upon potential leader training allows a person to explore various areas of gifts and interests. The emphasis is upon general leadership skills that one can use working in the church. There is no commitment that the person will be asked to take a leadership position in the church once the training has been completed. Both the person and the church must feel that this is the place where God would have that person serve.

Training should be provided for a person to function in a specific leadership position. This training seeks to help a person achieve a basic level of competence to satisfactorily do the task. This training may be done prior to a person's beginning to function in the task or while the person is involved in doing the work. A combination of both pre-service and in-service training should be provided.

Trained leaders help guide Christians to achieve the church's goals. Most churches have difficulty providing enough trained, qualified leaders each year. Training leaders grows out of the biblical concept of volunteer leadership in the church. This idea is consistent with Christ's democratic call to discipleship. A church would do well to help its adult members seek to discover their spiritual gifts and then provide the training necessary to effectively use their gifts to build up the body of Christ—the church.

Support and Undergird Church and Denominational Work

Church members should know what is happening both in the local church and in the denomination. Without this knowledge, it is difficult to work together toward worthy goals and objectives. Coordination and cooperation are possible when lines of communication are kept open. Through working together adult Christians can participate meaningfully in the life and work of the church and the denomination.

Every church program and activity should endeavor to strengthen what the church has established as its objectives, goals, and priorities. This can only be done when people are adequately informed about what is happening and what needs to be done.

No church is large enough to do all that Christ wants done in and of itself. Most churches are aligned with fellow Christians to achieve those goals and tasks that cannot be done alone. Both the church and the denomination need each other so that the work of Christ can be more effectively and efficiently completed.[3]

Goals of Adult Discipleship Training

The goals of adult discipleship training primarily should be to help Christians in their daily walk with God. Too often church programs have tried to emphasize what a particular program can do to benefit or help the church accomplish its goals rather than what it can do for the person who participates. Discipleship training should endeavor to strengthen or help the believer be a more effective Christian. There are five goals of discipleship training—three which relate to the individual and two which benefit the church but only as individuals are able to be involved in what the church is striving to do.

Growth in Christian Discipleship

A fundamental goal of adult discipleship training is to help the believer grow toward Christlikeness. Everything about the person—attitude, conversation, behavior—is moving toward being what Christ would have been had He lived on earth in the twentieth century. The very essence and nature of the Christian life emphasizes growth in the direction of being like Jesus.

Comprehend and Apply Biblical Doctrine

The need for a Christian to understand and to be able to apply biblical doctrine is very evident today with the cults and other forces clamoring for one's loyalty and allegiance. All Christians need to know what they believe and be able to explain it in their own words. Many people have a faith which they do not own—it is what they have gotten from others including one's family or friends. Everyone has a theology because no one can live life without believing in someone or something. A person should have definite beliefs gleaned from an understanding of the Bible.

Once a person has understood what he believes, then the beliefs should be evident in the way he lives. Biblical doctrines should form the core out of which one shapes one's life. Participating in a Bible study program is crucial for the Christian. Being a part of a discipleship training program helps the Christian put it all together into a belief system which helps him in daily living. The old adage "It doesn't matter what you believe" is not correct. It does make a difference what you believe because your actions will be reflections of your belief system.

Live Biblical Principles

A Christian's life should be based clearly on the teachings of the Bible. Much of life is based on tradition or what other people tell us. Christians should be such students of the Bible that their lives are based on biblical principles and teachings. This means that a Christian's life will be different from the standards of the world. When one lives such a life a frequent statement will be: "You're different. There is something unique about you." This will provide a natural opportunity to share one's faith—to tell why life is being lived on a different level.

Know and Participate in Church's Ministry

Adult discipleship training helps the person be knowledgeable about the life and work of the church. When one knows what the church is striving to do, one is more apt to want to be a part of it. The church provides opportunities for personal and spiritual growth. Through the church's ministries the adult will be able to minister to others.

Build Up the Church

A church seeks to do the work of Christ as it witnesses, worships, ministers, and educates. Through discipleship training, adults not only grow and mature as Christians but also have opportunities to help others experience what happened in their lives. Through using one's gifts in the life and work of the church, the adult knows that God is using him to advance His work in the lives of people to whom he ministers.

Conclusion

An adult discipleship training program is not an optional matter for the church that wants to see its members grow and mature in Christ. It cannot be a sporadic program but must be a continuing activity. It is not enough to believe that discipleship is what is done when a person makes a profession of faith in Jesus Christ as Lord and Savior. That may be the beginning point, but discipleship training seeks to help the believer be and live like Christ.

An effective discipleship program will not just happen. It will require planning, promoting, enlistment, and resources if it is to be successful. Discipleship activities have to be relevant to the lives of the Christians— whether new or old. An adult discipleship training program must be imaginative and creative to assist Christians to show forth Christ in every facet of living—work, home, play, community, and church.

Notes

1. James Orr, gen. ed., *The International Standard Bible Encyclopedia,* vol. 2 (Grand Rapids: William B. Eerdmans Publishing Co., 1943), pp. 851-852.

2. Alan Richardson, ed., *A Theological Wordbook of the Bible* (New York: Macmillan Publishing Co., Inc., 1950), pp. 69-70.

3. Roy T. Edgemon, comp., *Equipping Disciples Through Church Training* (Nashville: Convention Press, 1981), pp. 15-18.

11

Mission Education and Involvement

Bruce P. Powers

The church exists for mission. At the heart of its being is the witness to Christ, His redemptive message, and His healing presence. There is no option for the institution, nor for those individuals who make up the local as well as the universal body.

The teaching ministry of the church has long sought to keep an appropriate focus on this primary concern. For to the degree Christians are committed to and actively involved in being on mission for Christ, they will be fulfilling their commitment to be disciples.

In this chapter, I will review some of the important issues that must be considered when working with adults: an understanding of discipleship, the process of educating adults for mission involvement, and an overview of mission organizations that assist churches in this field of ministry.

What Is Discipleship?

Jesus said in John 8:31, "If you continue in my word, you are truly my disciples" (RSV). It is this simple expression that suggests a quality and way of living that describe discipleship. I like to describe discipleship as *being, doing,* and *telling* the gospel.

A good explanation of discipleship is given by John Hendrix and Lloyd Householder in *The Equipping of Disciples.* Discipleship was a matter of great concern to Jesus during His earthly ministry. This concern was manifested in the teachings of Paul and others throughout the New Testament and through the early history of the church. For the purpose of this work, Christian discipleship is defined as the Christian's lifelong commitment to the person, teaching, and Spirit of Jesus Christ. Life under Jesus' lordship involves progressive learning, growth in Christlikeness, implementation of biblical truth, and responsibility for sharing the Christian faith.[1]

Mission education for adults must begin with a commitment to pro-

188

vide an ongoing focus on these two key issues: What is discipleship? and What does discipleship involve?

The next step is to develop a process that can be the framework for planning, organizing, and otherwise administering an adult program that supports mission involvement. Here is a possible structure that could be adapted for use in any church.

Leading Adults into Mission

As illustrated in Figure 1, there are five steps involved in leading adults into mission. Ideally, everyone could move through these steps together, arriving at the point of involvement in and support for Christian service. However, while this may be possible for a small group, the usual approach is to view the five steps of the overall plan as a road map. There must always be a variety of ways provided among the steps to get to the desired destination. While some may begin the journey at one time, others will come later. And some will move rapidly while others stop and go many times.

Administratively, a variety of educational opportunities should be provided to meet the needs of adults wherever they might be. At the same time, the overall emphasis is on ongoing discipleship development that leads to involvement in the support of the mission of Christ.[2]

Learning How Discipleship Grows

The opportunity for growth in discipleship begins the moment a person accepts Jesus as personal Savior. There is no expectation that a person will immediately be a mature disciple either in what he knows or what he does. But there is a clear understanding that a disciple, when fully taught, will be like the Teacher (Luke 6:40). This is the idea of a

Figure 1

Steps for Leading Adults into Mission

1. Learning How Discipleship Grows.
2. Understanding God's Call.
3. Accepting Discipleship.
4. Choosing a Ministry.
5. Supporting Cooperative Ministries.

Christian's growing toward the likeness of Christ as expressed in Ephesians 4:13.

The development takes place in phases like this:

Phase 1: Awareness. During this phase a Christian recognizes a personal growth need related to God's call. Awareness of a problem or recognition of a need are examples of this phase.

Phase 2: Understanding. Once aware of a need, a person seeks to understand God's call and the possibilities for responding. Responses will vary from person to person, but the focus will always be: How is God working in my life, and what can I do about it?

Phase 3: Conviction. This phase of Christian growth involves making a decision that certain actions must be taken. Whereas the previous phases are related primarily to *knowing* about things, this step requires evaluation of alternatives and development of a commitment that a particular course of action will be followed.

Phase 4: Application. Once a person reaches this point, growth results from using one's knowledge and talents in Christian living and service. Such actions produce two results: The Christian is (1) practicing the teachings of Jesus (being, doing, and telling the gospel), and (2) discovering new areas in which growth is necessary, which sends the disciple back to phase 1—awareness. So discipleship must be viewed as a growth process—a continual development toward being like Christ, the Teacher. Visually, discipleship development looks like the diagram in Figure 2.

Understanding God's Call

The way in which we respond to God is similar to the way in which we respond to any other call. We ask many of the same questions and, in responding, feel that our lives are much in tune with God and His will. The call of God is most often understood in two ways: a call directed to individuals and a call directed to the church.

God's Call to Individuals. The personal call relates directly to the message of Christ (1) that belief in Him is the only way to God, and (2) that believers will keep Christ's commandments. (See John 14:6-7,12-17.) The crucial concern for each individual in understanding God's call is to determine how best to apply Christ's teachings in his own life. The questions that must be answered are: *Who* is calling me? *Why?* To do *what?*

God's Call to the Church. Individuals who have responded to God's call can focus on an added dimension to His message: that those who

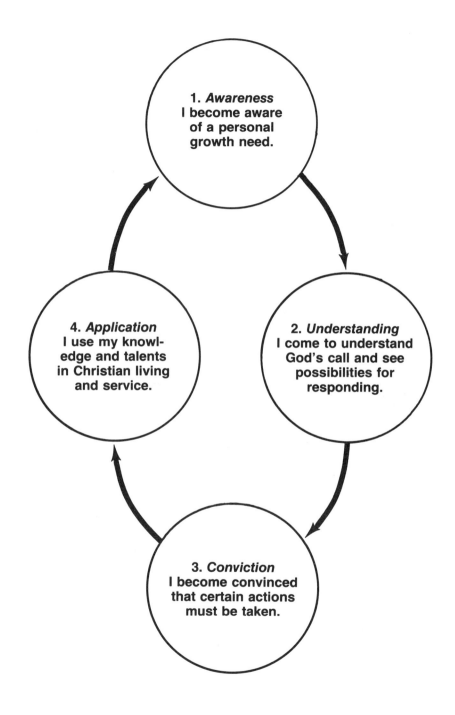

1. *Awareness*
I become aware
of a personal
growth need.

2. *Understanding*
I come to understand
God's call and see
possibilities for
responding.

3. *Conviction*
I become convinced
that certain actions
must be taken.

4. *Application*
I use my knowl-
edge and talents
in Christian living
and service.

Figure 2

follow Christ are to unite themselves in a body—the church—to carry out God's will. What is the call to the church? It is the same as God's call to each individual: to be His people and to continue the earthly ministry of Jesus. The church must be the means, or the channel, through which the eternal purpose of God is declared. The mission education and involvement of a congregation is a direct expression of this call.

Accepting Discipleship

A local church that has been formed in response to the leadership of God possesses in some form all of the gifts—that is, human and spiritual resources—that are essential for that body of believers to carry out their portion of God's mission in their particular area.

Here is a key to mission involvement: believing that God has not only called His people into service, but also provided whatever gifts might be necessary for them to minister in their time and place. So this phase of the educational process requires that individuals join with the larger congregation in placing priority on discovering, developing, and using their gifts in Christian service. For the individual, being involved in this process is being within God's will.[3]

As for the church, there is a twofold leadership responsibility: (1) to involve individuals in discovering, developing, and using their gifts, and (2) to encourage and support organizations and groups for the purpose of eliciting, combining, and directing the use of gifts in Christian service. For resources to assist with this process, see the bibliography.

This phase also requires that persons be exposed to the necessity for cooperative relationships among churches such as associations and conventions. Through these efforts we are able to combine gifts to perform many ministries not possible by one congregation, like foreign missions and benevolent institutions. Christians must come to view their calling as a personal, a congregational, *and* as a cooperative venture on behalf of their Lord.

Choosing a Ministry

The purpose of this phase is to assist believers in matching their gifts with congregational and community needs. Bill Clemmons described this in *Adventures in Christian Service* as helping Christians develop eyes to see need. This, he suggested, is "a seeing with the eyes, a seeing with the mind, but more importantly a seeing with the heart."[4]

The initial steps include:

- Determine needs in church and community.
- Evaluate needs in terms of priority.
- Select possible approaches for meeting needs.[5]

As persons get involved in this process, there often is a sense of being overwhelmed. Where can a few people with limited resources make much of a difference for very long? The reaction then might be either one of despair, or of conviction that we *must* do it all. Either decision illustrates our finiteness; some never start, and others burn themselves out emotionally and physically.

The important outcome of this phase is to "encounter the needs of the world out of your particular set of gifts."[6] Everyone is *not* called to do everything all the time. But each *is* called to find needs to which he or she can seek to meet in the name of Christ. Just as there is a variety of needs, there is a variety of gifts. And as we make choices for Christian service, we will find that some ministries will call for individuals; others will be more suitable for a small group or the entire congregation.

After determining the priority of needs, adults must:

- Evaluate their ministry gifts in light of the needs.
- Determine who will focus where.
- Consider what combination of gifts will be needed for projects requiring more than one person.
- Claim area(s) of ministry and share commitment with congregation; call others to join as appropriate.
- Prepare for and implement the chosen ministries.

Church educational organizations usually facilitate this process. In the early stages, Sunday School and Church Training organizations provide foundational experiences that prepare all participants for specific involvement in mission. Mission education organizations help to keep needs in front of the congregation and solicit support on behalf of existing mission involvement.

In supporting specific mission activities, churches usually provide administrative assistance either through the mission organizations or a standing church committee.

Supporting Cooperative Ministries

The last step in the process is an ongoing one. It is an educational and promotional effort by church leadership to assist the congregation in being a full partner in local, national, and worldwide mission efforts.

Whereas the local congregation will care for many nearby needs, these cooperative activities will keep the congregation active in the overall ministry of the body of Christ.

Significant, ongoing support of cooperative ministries generally has a positive impact on all other phases of the mission education and involvement steps listed above.

Mission Organizations

The congregation itself is the heart. There is no more important mission organization. This must be taught and practiced in all segments of the local body and reaffirmed with every proclamation of the gospel in joint worship services.

To enrich and enhance the overall focus on mission, most churches provide special organizations. In some churches, there are ongoing groups for women and for men. Other possibilities include a church mission committee, periodic meetings with a mission focus planned by the minister or concerned church members, or mission groups formed by interested church members.

The most effective way to promote and support missionary education and involvement is through ongoing organizations. For example, Southern Baptists offer Baptist Women and Baptist Men. These organizations are devoted to the following tasks on behalf of the congregation:

Teach Missions. Persons are led to explore with growing understanding the nature, implications, and evidences of God's missionary purpose and to respond to that purpose in personal commitment and obedience.

Engage in Missions Activities. This is the organized effort of the church to channel the gifts of persons into specific areas of ministry. Activities include personal and group mission projects, individual witnessing, mass evangelism, and efforts to remedy social and moral problems.

Support Missions. To support means to promote a cause or to keep something going. In this case, the focus is on the mission work of the congregation through its local ministries as well as through all cooperative endeavors.

Provide and Interpret Information About the Work of the Church and Denomination. This task is the same for all church program organizations. It is designed to provide a consistent channel through which common concerns can be discussed, interpreted, and acted on so as to build a united body dedicated to the mission of the church.

Information concerning mission organizations may be found in the appropriate organizational manual listed in the bibliography. For assistance in starting or improving one of these mission organizations, contact either the appropriate agency or the denominational office in your association or state.

Notes

1. John Hendrix and Lloyd Householder, eds., *The Equipping of Disciples* (Nashville: Broadman Press, 1977), p. 17*ff*.

2. The procedure described in this chapter is adapted from Bruce P. Powers, Robert D. Dale, and William Clemmons, *Adventures in Christian Service* (Nashville: Convention Press, 1982). This resource is available in a learning kit and can be used for a series of studies with adults. Order from Materials Services Department; 127 Ninth Avenue, North; Nashville, TN 37234.

3. For an extensive discussion of this, see my book *Christian Leadership* (Nashville: Broadman Press, 1979), Chapter 6.

4. Bruce P. Powers, Robert D. Dale, and William Clemmons, *Adventures* p. 46.

5. A helpful guide for this process is the Church/Community Needs Survey Guide, jointly produced by the Brotherhood Commission, Home Mission Board, and Woman's Missionary Union. See address for each organization in the bibliography.

6. Powers, Dale, and Clemmons, p. 49.

Bibliography

Belew, Wendell. *The Purpose and Plan of Baptist Brotherhood.* Memphis: Brotherhood Commission, 1979.

Cosby, Gordon. *Handbook of Mission Groups.* Waco: Word, Inc., 1975.

Martin, Mickey, *Woman's Missionary Union Manual.* Birmingham, Ala.: Woman's Missionary Union, 1981.

Miller, Ruth Wagner. *The Mission Action Plan Book.* Birmingham, Ala.: Woman's Missionary Union, 1983.

Smith, Ebbie C., et al, *Discovering Your Spiritual Gifts.* Nashville: Convention Press, 1981.

Sorrill, Bobbie. *WMU–A Church Missions Organization.* Birmingham, Ala.: Woman's Missionary Union, 1981.

Staff. *Mission Action Projects Guide.* Memphis: Brotherhood Commission, n.d.

Addresses:

Brotherhood Commission, 1548 Poplar Avenue, Memphis, TN 38104

Foreign Mission Board, 3806 Monument Avenue, Richmond, VA 23230

Home Mission Board, 1350 Spring Street, NW, Atlanta, GA 30309

Woman's Missionary Union, P.O. Box C-10, Birmingham, AL 35283

12

Family Life Education
C. Ferris Jordan

The role of family life education in the educational program of the church has sometimes been questioned, more often misunderstood, and most often neglected. However, the church committed to adult ministry must give attention to family life education. Adults and family are vitally linked. Many adult concerns which the church needs to address are related to family. Families are established and led by adults. In family relationships, adults satisfy or fail to meet most of their intimacy needs. Adults who have children face no greater challenge than developing their parenting skills. Through families and family members, adults can make their most lasting contributions to society and to the Kingdom.

Church and family are partners. They need to grow together.[1] John Howell has pointed out that church and family share a common origin in the creative purpose of the Father, face similar concerns in society as they fulfill their respective roles in God's redemptive purpose, and share common objectives in developing persons for life together.[2] One way the church can fill its role in the church-family partnership is by offering a program of family life education that will provide stimulation and instruction for family members. Before some possible components in such a program with supporting resources are presented, a brief overview of the family scene in America is appropriate.

The Contemporary Family Scene in America

The family scene in the last decades of the twentieth century is more complex than some church leaders may recognize as they contemplate the need for family life education. To all too many leaders, *family* still refers to husband, wife, and one or two children living at home. Such family units are a vital part of church and society. They do exist, and they need ministry. But they represent a minority of the families today. By the end of the 1980s, fewer than one third of all American households will be conventional families.[3] Only three million to four million of the

197

twenty million new households expected to be established between 1975 and 1990 will be married couples, researchers have predicted. The remaining households will be headed by the never married, divorced, or widowed population.[4]

The family scene is affected by the alarming divorce rate. The year following World War II, 1946, saw an alarmingly high divorce rate. The years 1946-50 saw that rate cut almost in half, and it remained at the 1950 level for about seventeen years. In 1967, divorce took an upward surge that has resulted in over one million divorces being granted per year since 1977.[5] The record year was 1981 when 1,219,000 divorces were granted. The divorce rate declined slightly for the following three years reaching 4.9 percent in August 1984. Although divorce is still much too prevalent in America, the sustained decline is significant.

Divorce and other factors are contributing to the single-parent household phenomenon in contemporary America. The dissolution rates of the late 1970s imply that about one of every three white children and two of three black children born after marriage will experience a parental marital dissolution by age sixteen. Most children of divorced parents live with their mother, and the majority will experience living in a fatherless home for at least five years. About a quarter of children who were six and under in 1970 lived for at least a year in a fatherless home by 1979.[6] In 1983, 19 percent of households with children under eighteen were headed by a woman with no husband present. If that prevalence of female-headed families persists, estimates are that 40 to 50 percent of all children will live in a fatherless home for some time before they reach eighteen.[7]

Family life in America includes the reconstituted family. Approximately 80 percent of persons who divorce remarry within five years.[8] The rising rate of remarriage blends about eighteen million stepchildren from remnants of families affected by divorce. Learning to live in these step relationships is a challenge. A church ministry to stepfamilies is desirable.

The number of the nation's mothers employed in jobs outside the home is having its impact on the family scene, too. Forty-three percent of the nation's mothers are employed outside the home.[9] One-worker, husband-wife households will have fallen from 43 percent of all households in 1960 to 14 percent by 1990 according to Harvard researchers Masnick and Bane.[10] In 1980, wives contributed about 25 percent of family income. The contribution may increase to 40 percent by 1990.[11]

The refilled nest and homing trend must be considered in an overview of American families. The 1980 census reported that about 18 million adult children in the United States lived at home with their parents. Population studies at the University of Chicago and Harvard show the "refilled nest syndrome" is on the upswing.[12] Some experts have attributed the trend to hard times in which escalating housing costs and tough competition for jobs have brought adult children home. Others attribute the rerooting instincts to the fact that the rebellion of the 1960s and 70s is over, and the family is being reconciled. Young people waiting later to get married want to live at home in the meantime. Divorcing adults in their twenties and thirties often feel the need to go back home for financial and moral support.[13] The circumstances created by divorced adults returning to the nest was labeled "the homing trend" by syndicated columnist Bob Greene.[14] When adult children return home, schedules are affected, financial resources may be hard pressed, and interpersonal relationships are subject to strain.

Single persons must be considered in planning family life education. The number of single adults has been on the rise for several years. They comprise one of the most rapidly expanding groups in the United States. The number and nature of single adults in this country have changed radically from 1950 to 1982. The number has risen from 4 million to 19.4 million in that period. Those who have never married account for 31.3 percent of the total; the widowed 40.6 percent; and the divorced 19.6 percent. The remaining 8.5 percent represents persons married whose spouse is absent.[15] The ranks of the never married are being swelled by the fact that more people are delaying marriage. Fifty-six percent of women aged twenty to twenty-four in 1983 had never been married compared to only 36 percent of women this age in 1970.[16] Career goals and prolonged educational pursuits are two factors accounting for the delay.

Life expectancy is lengthening in the United States. The population is growing older. These factors are having their influence on the family scene. The longer life span will make it possible for many more couples to celebrate their golden wedding anniversary and beyond. Adding years to marriage will require that couples give continuing attention to enriching their marriages. Longer lives may also mean a longer period of time to live alone for persons who outlive their spouses. Among the general elderly population, 80 percent of the men and half the women still have a spouse.[17] The proportion of older unmarried Americans living alone has increased from about one in ten in 1900 to two out of three in 1983.[18] The institutionalization of the elderly is usually the solution of last resort, and most of the institutionalized are the very old with serious physical impairments. Only about one in ten of the institutionalized elderly still have a surviving spouse and about half have surviving children.[19] Ministry to senior adult family needs must be included in the family life programs of a church.

A final consideration in this discussion of the family scene today is the alternative marriage forms that are present. There was a time when the only socially approved life-styles could be basically defined as singleness or marriage. Roger Libby and Robert White identified and sought to define several alternative marriage forms based on actual practices. Their list includes: contract marriage, ad hoc marriage, homosexual marriage, a co-marital relationship, mate-swapping, polygamous marriage, a communal marriage, and a multilateral marriage.[20] Faced with these realities, the church has responsibility for communicating biblical teachings about the purpose of marriage and family, and for upholding Christian principles about monogamous marriage.

Family life education in the church must be multifaceted in its emphases and in the constituency served. Married couples of all ages; couples with children; never married, divorced, and widowed persons living alone; and single parents are to be included in planning and delivering family life education.

Some Components in a Balanced Family Life Education Program

Most often churches provide no identifiable family life education program. When an attempt to address the need is made, only one or two areas of need are addressed. The suggestions offered here are designed to assure balance in the offerings.

Preparing Persons for Maturing Adulthood[21]

The Bible is growth oriented as it presents God's redemptive purpose for people. He has gone to the limit to provide life in Christ and resources in Him to make abundant life a possibility for everyone. The church is under divine mandate to help persons achieve their full potential in Christ. This assignment requires that younger people in the constituency be given assistance in moving toward adulthood and that adults be guided in their continuing pilgrimage toward mature adulthood. Efforts to provide this kind of ministry are a part of family life education, for strong family units (both single-person families and multiple-person families) await the presence of persons who are equipped for maturing adulthood.

How does a church prepare persons for maturing adulthood? It does so by utilizing educational principles and sound biblical teachings to provide children, youth, and adults with helpful insights into their self-concept, sexuality, friendships, and ultimate choices about singleness or marriage. As for self-concept, the church must seek to teach self-worth based on persons having been created in the image of God and on God's redemptive activity in Christ. A high view of personhood and selfhood is absolutely essential for the development of well-adjusted persons who can relate well to other family members and to all persons.

Education for responsible sexuality includes instruction about the biological facts of sexual growth and reproduction. But sex education goes beyond that to include the process of helping young people and adults to develop and live by a set of values about sex and its place in human development. Sex education programs appropriate for children in preadolescence years, for youth, for young single adults, for married adults, and for parents seeking to provide sex education for their own children can be offered through the educational organizations of the church, through retreats, through seminars, and through workshops. Resources are available to help churches provide sex education. Check with your denominational publishing house and religious book stores for help in this area.

The primary responsibility for sex education rests in the home. Churches can help parents feel more comfortable in their role through sex education programs that are an integral part of family life education.

Preparing persons for maturing adulthood also includes assisting them in making life-style choices between singleness and marriage. While marriage was the assumed goal for young adults in the biblical world and remaining unmarried was unusual in the cultural world of the Bible, there is a biblical tradition of singleness that includes widowed, divorced, and never-married persons. Jesus and Paul chose voluntary celibacy as a part of their commitment to the will of God

By reemphasizing Jesus' teaching that it is OK for a person to choose celibacy, the church can make it clear that wholeness as persons is not determined by marital status. Churches can teach singles that it is possible for them to be committed to God and lead productive lives while still upholding marriage as a God-given relationship through which couples can do God's will. Single adults need acceptance, fellowship, and love. The church can provide all of these. The church can also offer singles information about dating, courtship, and marriage so that those who choose to marry are better prepared for the married life-style.

Premarital Guidance

A second component in a balanced family life education program is premarital guidance. This element is designed to help engaged couples make preparation for the wedding ceremony and their life together as husband and wife. Generally, the pastor has three to six sessions with the couple. In churches having a large number of weddings each year, lay-persons may be trained to conduct the sessions.

In the prescribed sessions, effort is made to help the couple gain insights into their maturity for marriage, explore their role understanding, acquire appreciation for communication skills, and learn basics in conflict resolution. Plans for the wedding are made. The biblical teachings about the nature and purpose of marriage are explored. Potential problem areas in marriage can be identified, and personal concerns of the couple as they approach marriage can be discussed.

Some pastors use a workbook approach, utilizing resources like *Two as One* by George E. Von Kaenel and Martin G. Olsen or *Preparing for Christian Marriage* by Joan and Richard Hunt. The latter has a pastor's manual by the same title authored by Antoinette and Leon Smith. Having couples read preassigned chapters in a book prior to each session may also be helpful. *Harmony in Marriage* by Leland F. Wood, *Christian Marriage: Growing in Oneness* by John Howell, *How to Get Married and Stay that Way* by Cliff Allbritton, and *Marriage Readiness* by Bobbye and Britton Wood are possibilities. When there are several couples preparing for marriage at the same time, the premarital guidance may be done in group sessions over a period of weeks or in a retreat for engaged couples.

Marriage Enrichment

Enriching marriages that are already in existence is a vital part of family life education. In fact, one of the best ways to contribute to strong families is to strengthen spouse relationships. Marriage is the process of becoming "one flesh." That expression is a total experience including every aspect of the marital relationship; it is not confined to the physical sex relationship. One of the major tasks of marriage education is to provide couples with incentive and skills to be "one."

What areas need to be addressed in efforts to assist couples in enriching their marriages? A major concern needs to be improving the quality of communication. The interaction and exchange between spouses must occur at a level that encourages shared feelings and self-disclosure. True self-disclosure must operate within the scriptural bounds of saying only those things that will edify (Eph. 4:29) and the commands to speak "the truth in love" (Eph. 4:15, RSV) and to put off "falsehood" (Eph. 4:25, RSV). Verbalizing one's feelings in a selfish manner merely to ventilate or manipulate is a far cry from the intimate sharing that is a high expression of love.

Handling conflict is another topic to be addressed in marriage enrichment. Conflict between two adults living in the intimacy of the marriage relationship is inevitable. How to resolve conflicts constructively is the issue. Negative ways of nagging, blaming, criticizing, avoiding the issues, kissing and making up must be avoided. Positive approaches to conflict management will include open discussion resulting in compromise that shows mutual respect.

Having couples to think about roles in marriage and to find their solution to the confusion that exists about various approaches to roles is vital in marriage enrichment. Guidance in understanding the value of commitment, as opposed to romantic love, as the firm foundation for marriage is an essential element in marriage enrichment. Romance is important in marriage, but it is not the basis for marriage. Commitment can hold together two persons brought together by romantic love. Couples need help in understanding how to develop and maintain the commitment characteristic of mature love.

Marriage enrichment activities are not designed to provide therapy for troubled marriages. They are educational experiences directed toward making good marriages better. Contributions toward marriage enrichment may be made in retreats, in ongoing and short-term groups planned as a part of the church's training program, and in family life conferences.

Family Enrichment

Another component in family life education is family enrichment. Even as marriage enrichment focuses on strengthening spouse relationships, family enrichment activities are targeted toward the entire family and seek to address various issues that arise in the dynamics of family members relating to one another. Family finances, parent-child and parent-teen relationships, communication within the family, family devotions and family worship, problem-solving techniques, parent roles in teaching religious and spiritual matters in the family, and understanding the physical and emotional needs of the family are only a sampling of family concerns the church may address.[22]

Approaches to family enrichment may be varied. Well-planned family life conferences that include larger sessions given to broad topics and workshop sessions devoted to specific age-related interests can make a good contribution. Retired adults, adults in their middle years, parents with teenagers, parents of children in their preteen years, young married adults, single adults who are looking forward to marriage, teenagers, and children (preteen) are groups for whom special workshops may be offered.

In addition to family life conferences the family enrichment needs may be addressed through seasonal, temporary, and occasional intergenerational experiences;[23] through family clusters based on the model suggested by Margaret Sawin;[24] and through family camping.[25]

Parenting Enrichment

Still another aspect of family life education in the church is parenting. While developing good parenting concepts and skills is definitely a part of family enrichment, this component of family life education deserves a brief, specific focus in this chapter. Most parent enrichment programs work in the areas of self-understanding, concepts of Christian parenting, understanding children, communication and problem-solving skills, and approaches to discipline. A seminar or workshop format may be used effectively in parent enrichment.

Enrichment for Single Adults and Senior Adults

While single adults and senior adults certainly should be included in a churchwide family life conference, their very numerical strength in contemporary America and their unique needs require that special projects designed to meet the needs of each group be planned. Seminars, conferences, workshops, and retreats that offer opportunities for spiritual growth, for fellowship, and for help with very practical matters such as budgeting, hobbies, and making new friends may be provided for both single and senior adults. The efforts with single adults should include specific help with divorce adjustment, single parenting, and the question of remarriage.[26]

Conclusion

The church, as the family of God, should provide a good model for family relationships. She must work hand in hand with families as their partner in ministry, their ally in the continuing battle with evil forces, and their source of help in coping with the routines and crises that comprise family living. Providing family life education that addresses the various components presented in this chapter is one way the church can be a good partner.

Notes

1. For a good discussion of church and family as partners in ministry needing to grow together, consult John C. Howell, *Church and Family Growing Together* (Nashville: Broadman Press, 1984).

2. Ibid., pp. 14-24.

3. "The Nation's Families: 1960-1990," a study sponsored by the Joint Center for Urban Studies of the Massachusetts Institute of Technology and Harvard University and conducted by George Masnick and Mary Jo Bane, Harvard associate professors.

4. Ibid.

5. Howell, p.13.

6. The information about children of divorce is from the *Population Bulletin,* Vol. 38, No. 4, October 1983, published by the Population Reference Bureau, titled, "The Changing American Family" by Arland Thornton and Deborah Freedman. Statistics cited here are from the "Digest" published by the Research Division of the Home Mission Board, SBC, Vol. VI, No. 1, January 1984.

7. Ibid.

8. Howell, p. 14.

9. Charles M. Sell, *The Enrichment of Family Life Through the Church* (Grand Rapids: Zondervan Publishing House, 1981), p. 26.

10. George Masnick and Mary Jo Bane, "The Nation's Families: 1960-1990." See note number 3 above.

11. Ibid.

12. Norma Peterson, "Is the Rebellion Over?" *Parade,* 31 Jan. 1982, p. 10.

13. Ibid.

14. Bob Greene, "The Homing Trend—Divorced Adults Returning to the Nest," *Times Picayune,* Jan. 1979.

15. "Eleven Million Singles: Their Joys and Frustrations," *U. S. News and World Report,* 21 Feb. 1983. Statistics are from the U. S. Department of Commerce.

16. Thornton and Freedman, Ibid.

17. Ibid.

18. Ibid.

19. Ibid.

20. Roger W. Libbey and Robert N. White, *Renovating Marriage* (Danville, Calif.: Consensus Publishers, Inc., 1973), pp. 283-85.

21. This heading and the ideas it introduces are taken from Howell, pp. 53-81.

22. The Family Life Equipping Center includes several modules that are good resources for family enrichment. These are described in the *Church Materials Catalog* issued by the Sunday School Board of the Southern Baptist Convention.

23. Lela Hendrix, *Extended Family: Combining Ages in Church Experience* (Nashville: Broadman Press, 1979).

24. Margaret M. Sawin, *Family Enrichment with Family Clusters* (Valley Forge, Pa.: Judson Press, 1979).

25. Elizabeth and William Genne, *Church Family Camps and Conferences,* rev. ed. (Valley Forge, Pa: Judson Press, 1979).

26. The following are possible resources related to divorce and remarriage: Roger L. Crook, *An Open Book to the Christian Divorcee* (Nashville: Broadman Press, 1974). R. Lofton Hudson, *'Til Divorce Do Us Part* (Nashville: Thomas Nelson, Inc., 1974). Earl Joiner, *A Christian Considers Divorce and Remarriage* (Nashville: Broadman Press, 1983). Dwight Hervey Small, *The Right to Remarry* (Old Tappan, N.J.: Fleming H. Revell, 1975).

13

Adults and Music

S. Alfred Washburn

Because of the diversity of musical styles and tastes, and because of the culture in which one was raised, the church must take a closer look at adults and church music. Step into a church of any size in our land on a Sunday morning and more than likely you will find anywhere from two to two thousand adults involved in some way with church music. In the small rural church two adults may be church music leaders: a song leader and a church pianist. In a large metropolitan church two thousand adults may be a choir, orchestra, organist, minister of music, and a congregation singing "Crown Him with Many Crowns."

Adults involved in church music may be those in leadership positions. But a ministry of music would not need leaders if it were not for laypersons—that single adult singing hymns at morning worship, that older adult who is a member of a senior adult choir, that middle-aged adult couple who play in a church's instrumental ensemble. Churches should provide opportunities for *all* adults to be involved in church music.

The Book of Psalms was the songbook of the Hebrew people. Many of the psalms were sung. They were expressions of praise to God, or in some instances prayers of intercession, confession, or despair. Some were jubilant songs of victory. One will find numerous references to singing and making music: Psalm 95:1; 96:1; 98:1; 100:2; 89:1; 81:1; 105:2; 135:3; 146:2; 149:1; 92:1-3; 81:1-2; 33:2-3.

These references are injunctions and are not to be taken lightly. Many are commands, not options. As believers we should have a song in our hearts. We need to make that "joyful noise" (95:1) with as much enthusiasm as we can. And what better place to do it than in corporate worship? Every church can become a "musical church" when we begin to take seriously the psalmist's pleas. What a thrilling sound when instruments and voices blend in offering to God our music making! Read again and again Psalm 150:

207

Hallelujah! Yes, praise the Lord!

Praise him in his Temple, and in the heavens he made with mighty power. Praise him for his mighty works. Praise his unequaled greatness. Praise him with the trumpet and with lute and harp. Praise him with the tambourines and processional. Praise him with stringed instruments and horns. Praise him with the cymbals, yes, loud clanging cymbals.

Let everything alive give praises to the Lord! *You* praise him! Hallelujah! (TLB).

Adults and church music go together. Adults in music leadership positions are part of a church music ministry. Yes, it is a ministry, for it is an actual service—people serving people—people ministering to others. We often hear the obsolete terminology used: a music department. But no church has a music department. Church music cannot and should not attempt to be compartmentalized or departmentalized. Church music is for all!

Let us look at adults in church music in three areas: worship, education, and outreach. In fact, are not these three functions of a church?

Worship

Worship involves more adults than any other age group. The worshiping congregation should be the most important facet of a church music ministry. Too often it is not the case. Church leaders should restructure priorities and give more emphasis to planning and implementing services of worship. Music is a vital element in worship. It must receive adequate planning from all worship leaders: pastor, minister of music, organist, pianist, choir, and others. As preparation is made, orders of service must be prepared. Examine the following two orders of service. Take a close look at all musical ingredients.

MORNING WORSHIP

March 10, 1985

Sing We to Our God Above
Organ Prelude: "Come, Thou Fount of Every Blessing" arr. Hutson
Call to Worship** "Where Two or Three Are Gathered" Purifoy

Sanctuary Choir

Invocation
Hymn 10: "Praise to the Lord, the Almighty"LOBE DEN HERREN
Welcome to Our Guests/Opportunities for Service

Praise Eternal as His Love
  Hymn 70** "In the Cross of Christ I Glory"   RATHBUN
  Scripture Reading
  Morning Prayer
  Offertory Hymn 420: "Lead On, O King Eternal"   LANCASHIRE
Praise Him, All Ye Heavenly Host
  Offertory Prayer
  Organ Offertory "My Jesus, I Love Thee"   arr. Hutson
  Solo*
  Anthem** "Now Sing We Joyfully unto God"   Young

Sanctuary Choir

Father, Son, and Holy Ghost
  Message "Living The Transformed Life"
  Hymn of Decision 191:
  "I Have Decided to Follow Jesus"   ASSAM
  Benediction
  Organ Postlude "A Joyful Song"   Wihla Hutson
        *8:30 Service - **10:45 Service[1]

MORNING WORSHIP SERVICE

February 17, 1985	8:45 and 11:00 A.M.
Organists: 8:45—(Name)	11:00—(name)

Preparation for Worship—The Organ Prelude
  "God of Grace and God of Glory"   Held
The Church at Work
The Ministry of Hospitality
  Welcome and Christian Greeting
  The Doxology and Invocation
Ministry of Praise and Instruction
  Hymn No. 292: "Ye Servants of God"
  Choral Worship: 8:45—"In the Quietness of My Life"
    11:00 - "Turn Thy Face from My Sins"
  Learning with Little Friends
  The Scripture Lesson   Mark 2:1-12
  The Church at Prayer
The Ministry of Thankful Commitment
  Hymn No. 369: "O Master, Let Me Walk with Thee"
  The Offering and Deacon Shepherd Prayer
The Ministry of Proclamation
  Choral Worship: 8:45

"Come, Thou Fount of Every Blessing" arr. Hopson
11:00 "God of Grace and God of Glory" Langston
Sermon: "It Takes Compassion to Reach People" Pastor
Hymn of Invitation No. 325: "Footsteps of Jesus"
Postlude "Fantasia in D minor" Pachelbel[2]

A Brief Evaluation

1. Was there a variety of hymns?
2. Was the listing of all musical items complete?
3. Was there any correlation of hymns/Scripture/sermon?
4. Was adequate planning given to the printed order of
   service?
5. Was the order of service listings attractive? Logical?
   Progressive?
6. What were the strengths? Weaknesses?
7. Was there involvement of the congregation other than in
   hymn singing?

Let us reexamine our church's worship practices, always looking for ways in which we might meet the spiritual needs of the worshiping congregation. Emphasis on congregational singing may be the first step. Music leaders should encourage participation in positive ways. A sensitive hymn leader and trained organist and/or pianist working together are needed. Adequate hymnals provided in the pew racks are also necessary. And how important it is to see the worship leaders singing on all hymns! The choir's major responsibility is to offer leadership in the hymn singing. The choir and worship leaders are "up front" and should be examples and role models for the people in the pews.

Education

Education of adults involved in church music is a continual process. It is exciting to look at the many educational and service opportunities that are available in the area of church music.

1. *Adult Choir.* It is thrilling and helpful to read of the Levitical choir in 1 Chronicles 23 and 25. In addition to these biblical references, Robert Mitchell discusses in a most enlightening way the purpose and function of a choir in *Ministry and Music.*[3]

The adult choir should be an active, functioning group of singers whose purpose is to lead in the musical portions of worship. Choir members are "ministers of song" and should find spiritual and musical growth by regular attendance at rehearsals and services of worship. A choir never performs "special music." I wish this term could be deleted from our conversation and from our printed orders of service. What is so special about any musical ingredient in worship? Or we could conclude that every item in worship is *special.* If we continue to use "special music," let us also describe other items as special: special Scripture, special prayer, special sermon. Let us replace "special music" when we refer to the choir's musical offering as *anthem, choral worship,* or *message in music.*

Don Hustad spoke of the importance of the adult choir:

> There is obviously much yet to be learned by the adults in the church choir. Vocal development—good tone produced by proper phonation and support—goes on. Musicianship—intonation, rhythmics, articulation vs. legato singing, dynamic control, diction, phrasing—is the constant goal of the older choir. . . .
>
> Many young adults drop out of the choir program, even though they were active as children and teenagers. Some who continue to participate have forgotten, or possibly never learned, the spiritual significance of their service to the church, and sing simply because they enjoy doing so. The call to give our musical gifts back to God who gave them to us—not in the rough form in which we receive them, but developed and refined—is one that needs to be constantly reviewed in the adult choir.[4]

2. *Adult Ensemble.* Many churches provide opportunities for interested adults to participate in a small, selected group of singers. An ensemble may be organized by the minister of music as resources and talent become available. The group itself may decide upon a name: JOY Singers, B.A.S.E. Hits (Baptist Adult Singles' Ensemble), or any other appropriate appellation. A variety of music may be used. Regular rehearsals are necessary to maintain musical excellence. The ensemble may build a broad repertoire and sing for special occasions. An ensemble is often a manageable-sized group to sing for various community functions and can be an outreach arm of the church.

3. *Senior Adult Choir.* This group of singers continues to grow in number of choirs organized and also in popularity. It is often the most active choir in a church music ministry; for in addition to singing for worship, senior adults love to travel, and trips are planned where they can sightsee as well as sing in various churches. Recently I saw in a church bulletin where senior adults and children were combining to sing

a musical.[5] Vast opportunities are possible in ministering to senior adults by their participation in a senior adult choir.

4. *Ladies' Ensemble.* A selected group of singers who enjoy singing both sacred and secular music could be organized. Many arrangements are available for treble voices. I am aware of a group such as this that rehearses for an hour each Wednesday evening under the direction of the minister of music. On occasions, the ensemble sings for the church's early morning worship service. Recently, they sang for a stewardship banquet and a Christmas fellowship. At the latter event they were able to do some secular, fun-type pieces.

5. *Male Quartet.* What church does not enjoy hearing a well-trained, well-balanced group of four men singing the great hymns, gospel songs, and spirituals of our faith? Using a male quartet on occasion can enhance the worship experience of believers and at the same time be a witness to unbelievers. Participation in a small group such as this can "fine tune" one's musical expertise and add another dimension to spiritual nourishment.

6. *Women's Chorus.* A group such as this can function as a service choir and sing once a month or on some kind of regularly scheduled basis. In some churches a female director and female accompanist will be enlisted to provide leadership for a women's chorus. Additional groups such as this may find appropriate rehearsal times that would enable adult women to sing who might not otherwise be able to do so. Having a women's chorus to sing at special mission meetings and services would enhance these times.

7. *Men's Chorus.* Men are sometimes hesitant about singing in a choir. Some feel that they must have beautiful voices and be able to read music. But on various occasions through the years, I have promoted and used a group of men to sing for worship. I have done it in a positive and encouraging way—"Come, make a joyful noise unto the Lord. Let's fill the choir loft with men." I usually rehearse them just preceding the service, and I'll begin with a simple arrangement from the hymnal (a stanza in unison, another with a solo, and a final one in parts). Many variations can be made after a beginning such as this. After the men realize that they can produce a rather pleasing sound, they gain confidence, and their next attempt will be even better. And who knows, the choir loft may become completely filled! Let the men help "sell" other men on the idea of singing. And joyful praise to God can be the satisfying results of service "Serve by singing."

8. *Handbell Choirs.* In many churches the instrumental program is growing. And why does church music enrollment continue to rise? Because of new groups that continue to be organized. When new groups are formed, more people become involved. We are speaking specifically of adults involved in church music. Adults enjoy handbell ringing. Congregations enjoy hearing handbells. The sound is unique. Here is yet another vehicle to worship. Here is another group in which adults may serve. Being able to read music is imperative in being a ringer. As a handbell choir becomes more experienced and as the music becomes more difficult, intense concentration and control are necessary. But being a handbell ringer can be fun and a good experience for one to grow musically, socially, spiritually—and to develop arm muscles you never knew you had!

9. *Instrumental Ensembles.* An instrumental program in a church may begin with an adult playing a trumpet solo for a Sunday morning offertory. After a survey has been taken to determine who plays what instrument, results are compiled. The minister of music determines who will direct the instrumental ensemble, and promotion is underway. Prospects are contacted, the number of available instruments are found, and the first rehearsal time is set. A wind ensemble, after adequate rehearsals, can be a tremendous asset in a service of worship. Hymn singing will become more meaningful when accompanied by organ and brass. An instrumental prelude or postlude will become another means of involving adults in church music.

10. *Adults Working in Children's Choirs.* The aforementioned headings have referred to performing musical groups in which adults may participate in a church music ministry. Preschool, younger, and older children's choirs are another facet of a music ministry where adult workers are needed. And these workers should not be limited to women only! In children's choir workshops that I lead and in seminary classes that I teach, I strongly emphasize the need for men to work with these age groups. Ideally, there should be a man in a leadership position in every preschool and children's choir. A church's minister of music should schedule himself or herself to direct one preschool or children's choir every year. Leadership positions include a director, a pianist-teacher, and several assistants (teachers); the number of adult workers depends upon the size of the group. Adults find working with children's choirs to be challenging, yet rewarding, as the weekly sessions of the teaching-learning experiences are further ways of growth for both the

child and adult. How exciting it can be to teach children more about God through music at church!

11. *Solo singing/ Playing piano/ Accompanying.* Many adults in a music ministry study voice and piano privately. Why not take advantage of such talent and use them in Sunday School departments, Church Training events, WMU meetings, prayer service, and worship times? Adults should be encouraged to develop and refine their personal music skills and to become more proficient.

12. *Church Organists and Pianists.* Some larger churches employ more than one organist and pianist. Opportunities for attending training events and for participating in continuing education events should be afforded these keyboardists. Perhaps a budgeted item could help cover expenses that would be incentive for these church leaders to become more competent in their fields.

13. *Adults Teaching Adults.* How helpful it would be if churches would schedule church training events in areas such as class piano, class guitar, class voice, music theory, hymnology, and conducting. Adults are willing to serve in various areas of a church music ministry, but many feel unqualified or insecure, or just plain "rusty." Ongoing classes in these areas, and others, will help adults grow and serve in a more effective way.

14. *Media Technicians.* In our day of broadcasting and televising church services, many adults trained in the area of communications find a place of service in the church. Music leaders often delegate responsibilities of a musical production to laypersons trained as sound and lighting technicians.

15. *Music and Missions.* Seminaries offer training in the area of music missions as well as studies to become a minister of music or a denominational worker. A few students feel a definite call to missions and specifically music missions. Areas of interest include associational, home, and foreign mission fields. Churches should offer encouragement to youth as well as young adults that may have an interest in this area.

16. *Creative Experiences.* Adults can be guided and encouraged by church music leaders to develop innate gifts in composing and/or arranging music. There is a great need for worthy hymn texts and tunes. A special committee, possibly a worship committee, could plan and implement a church arts festival incorporating creative crafts from members. Paintings, drawings, and music could be included. Don Hustad eloquently captured the idea of creativity.

Every believer is expected to offer to God his *best* creativity, in all of life. This is good stewardship of our talents—"a worthy sacrifice"—whether we are playing (or hearing) a recital, singing in the church choir or worshiping through its music, writing a business report, making a dress, or cooking a meal. In music, God expects J. S. Bach's best, John Stainer's best, John Peterson's best, the Auca Indians' best, each Christian's best. Nothing less is acceptable, but our best is good enough![6]

Outreach

Outreach with adults may be thought of as a result of the first two areas we have discussed, that is worship and education. After adults have worshiped and have been engaged in educational/organizational pursuits, church music leaders need to externalize music making. Too often, we become so wrapped up in what we are doing within the four walls of the church that this area is neglected. And this should not happen! Let us become involved in going out into the community wherever we are and taking our groups to minister to a needy world.

That world may be down the street, around the corner, or at the local hospital. Individual choir members, a male quartet, a handbell choir, a song leader, and pianist may minister in a nursing home or a retirement center. A small children's choir, along with adult leaders, would be welcome to sing some songs and share Scripture at a homebound church member's house. An adult ensemble may schedule a time to sing a program at a shopping mall at Christmastime. An instrumental ensemble and a vocalist could offer to present a program for a civic club luncheon meeting. And on and on we could go! The opportunities are limitless for adults to be involved in making music in the community. In doing so, we are obeying Christ's command: "Go ye."

As we go into the community with a song in our hearts of God's great love, let us be prepared before we go. That preparation should have taken place at church (rehearsals, practice, and so forth). But even before we prepare at church, preparation must be made in the home. Sometimes we are so fatigued from work and church responsibilities that we forget our own and our families' musical and spiritual growth. Is the church hymnal a companion to the Bible in our homes? Instead of rock music blaring from our stereos, do we ever listen to quality church music from different periods of music history? Singing as a family is almost an obsolete activity. Will you help me to restore it?

Conclusion

Churches, church music leaders, pastors, adults in service for our Lord—are we willing to be challenged by the opportunities available for us in church music?

Churches function in at least three areas we discussed: worship, education, and outreach. How are we doing in each of these? What are our (my) strengths and weaknesses in these areas? What can we (I) do to improve each area?

Within our churches a music ministry provides educational opportunities for spiritual and musical growth for adults. Can we as music leaders make such opportunities as attractive and Christ-centered that more adults will want to become involved?

As adults become more involved in musical activities and as they mature in the faith, they may be led to share their gifts within the community.

Church music leaders are in the equipping business. We would find it helpful to read and practice the apostle Paul's advice found in Ephesians 4.

Church music can be worship for many worshipers. Church music can be a means of winning souls into the Kingdom. Church music can be a means of spiritual growth for the believer. Adults, pray with me that we can have a part in these areas of church music.

Notes

1. *The Vision,* Oak Park Baptist Church, New Orleans, Louisiana, 10 Mar. 1985.
2. *First Baptist Newsletter,* First Baptist Church, Kingsport, Tennessee, 13 Feb., 1985.
3. Robert H. Mitchell, *Ministry and Music* (Philadelphia: The Westminster Press, 1978), pp. 48-63.
4. Donald Hustad, *Jubilate!* (Carol Stream, Ill.: Hope Publishing Co., 1981), p. 302.
5. Sheldon Curry, *Side by Side* (Nashville: Laurel Press, 1984).
6. Hustad, p. 11.

Suggested Resources

Allen, Ronald and Borror, Gordon. *Worship: Rediscovering the Missing Jewel.* Portland, Ore.: Multnomah Press, 1982.

Eskew, Harry and McElrath, Hugh T. *Sing with Understanding.* Nashville: Broadman Press, 1980.

Hustad, Donald. *Jubilate!* Carol Stream, Illinois: Hope Publishing Co., 1981.

Mitchell, Robert H. *Ministry and Music.* Philadelphia: The Westminster Press, 1978.

Posey, Phillip C. *Strings and Things: Building a Successful Instrumental Program.* Nashville: Convention Press, 1974.

Reynolds, William J., ed. *Baptist Hymnal.* Nashville: Convention Press, 1975.

Reynolds, William J. *Companion to Baptist Hymnal.* Nashville: Broadman Press, 1976.

Reynolds, William J. *Building an Effective Music Ministry.* Nashville: Convention Press, 1980.

Wohlgemuth, Paul W. *Rethinking Church Music.* Carol Stream, Illinios: Hope Publishing Co., 1973.

14

Adults Continuing to Learn
Bruce P. Powers

One of the joys of adulthood is that you can quit studying! Really? Or, perhaps, the approach to study changes, for adults are reading more, studying more, and doing more with their minds and hands than ever before. The only difference is that adults now are learning what will help them in their jobs, homes, churches, clubs, and hobbies. They are soaking up things that teachers never could have taught them through lecturing and testing. What is the difference? The desire to know, to do, and to appreciate.

Whereas earlier periods of life focus on deductive learning, adults tend to focus more on inductive learning. Do you know the difference?

Deductive Learning

Learning that comes from deduction is the result of mastering general statements, then determining ways in which those statements apply to specific instances. For example, income tax laws represent a body of general statements. You learn them, then determine ways in which they apply to your situation. Of course, you are aware that many people make their living interpreting the application of those laws for others.

In Christian education, we most often use this approach when we are studying a passage of Scripture or a doctrinal belief. A teacher lectures on the topic being covered, or the learner reads the assigned material. The goal is to master the material so that you can recall it, discuss it, and tell how it relates to life. The test of whether learning has occured is, Do you *know* it?

Inductive Learning

Learning by the inductive method begins with activity. The ways in which a person *experiences* something causes the learner to focus on a general truth or principle as a way of interpreting meaning and general application to life.

218

The activity that encourages this type of learning usually is life centered. That is, it relates to the problems, needs, and day-to-day activities in which adults find themselves. When there is sufficient interest or need, a person seeks general guidelines that will help resolve the problem.

You often see this approach in your church when people become aware of a particular problem. For example, a number of parents in my church became interested in having a marriage enrichment workshop. The activities in their homes led them to look for ways to improve communication with their children and to increase their enjoyment of family evenings at home. Persons who came to this study group brought their experiences with them and wanted to talk and discuss. They sought ways to understand and improve their current experience. The test of their learning was not how much they knew, but what they felt about their families and the actions they were prepared to take for improvement.

A Comparison

The difference in the two is not just in the primary learning outcome, that is, knowledge vs. skill or attitude. It also is in the teaching-learning methods used, the design of the curriculum used, and in the planning and administration of your education program.

Here is how I visualize the two approaches:

Deductive	*Inductive*
Select Content	Examine Experiences
Determine Method	Determine needs
Involve People	Select Learning Approach
Transmit Content	Secure Resources
Tell Application	Match Needs and Resources
Test Recall	Test Application
Encourage Use	Use as Appropriate

Primary Learning Focus

Knowing	Doing	Feeling
	(relates to both)	

These two approaches usually are not used separately, rather they are used in combination. For example, a teacher might lecture for a while to convey information, then lead the class in a discussion to consider practical responses.

Learning during school years focuses primarily on the deductive approach. By adolescence, there should be a mixture of approaches as youth are led to develop skills and clarify values. As a person moves into adulthood, there is a strong preference for inductive learning—involvement in self-chosen activities that are related to life needs.

Of course, even the *deductive* approach to adult learning may be preferred by some people who feel the need of close direction in their educational activities. The key then is not the same style by everyone, but self-choice and self-direction in areas of learning that are important to the adult.

The involvement of adults in local-church educational activities is the largest single form of continuing education in America. And adults do it by *choice*. The reason relates to the approach to learning. Let me review a few points about adult learning that relate to keeping adults actively involved.

Pedagogy is the art and science of teaching children. It is oriented toward deductive learning. This is the image of teaching that most adults have imprinted in their minds from childhood. Learning is content centered and teacher directed.

Andragogy is the art and science of helping adults learn. Andragogy, a word coined by Malcolm Knowles, describes an approach to teaching that is uniquely adult.[1] It is based on the assumption that learning should be self-directed, utilizing whatever resources that are available to the learner. The role of the teacher is to be a facilatator or helper. Content is not the issue; rather the question is: What effect will the activity have on the learner?[2]

Programming for Adults

Due to rather basic objectives among most churches—making disciples, enabling members to grow and mature, and developing spiritual awareness and power in the lives of believers—similar structures have evolved among denominations to enable churches to do their work. For example, most churches have organizations to facilitate Bible study, discipleship development, mission activities, and worship experiences. Although names of these may vary such as Sunday School, Bible school, and church school, the functions and general organizational principles for educational organizations are remarkably similar from denomination to denomination and from church to church.

Figure 1

A Comparison of Pedagogical and Andragogical Learning[3]

Assumptions

Pedagogy		Andragogy
Learner is generally dependent on others	About the Learner	Learner is increasingly self-directed
Depends on maturation	Readiness to Learn	Develops from life concerns
Subject centered	Learning Focus	Task or problem centered
External rewards and punishment	Motivation	Internal incentives and personal satisfaction

Learning Approach

Pedagogy		Andragogy
Formal	Environment	Informal
Competitive		Mutually respectful
Judgmental		Collaborative
Primarily by teacher	Planning	Participative decision making
Primarily teacher	Determines Needs	Mutual assessment
Primarily teacher	Sets Goals	Mutual negotiation
Units of study	Learning Plan	Learning projects
Logical sequence		Content based on need
Lecture/presentation	Learning Activities	Projects/workshops
Assigned study		Independent study
By teacher based on learner's performance	Evaluation of Effectiveness	Mutual assessment of self-collected evidence

The Formal Structures

Most churches provide within these organizations regular, ongoing opportunities for adults. These established structures are the primary channels for a congregation's continuing education program. Activities are designed to help a church achieve its objective and, at the same time, to meet the general needs of participants.

Most ongoing organizations have an administrative plan, such as described in the preceding chapters, and follow an established curriculum published by the church's denomination or planned and secured by local church leaders. Publishers of curriculum materials will share information about product lines and often will provide samples copies of literature so that churches can make wise choices when selecting study materials.[4]

These organizations faithfully seek to combine a wide range of deductive and inductive learning experiences. The usual response from adults is, "I joined the group because I was interested in the subject, but I stay because of my commitment to the people and the purpose of our organization." Those who fail to enlarge their appreciation of learning to include the inductive approach usually drift in and out based on whether or not they like the topic and/or teacher. Those who become self-directed and appreciate the cohesive interdependency of such learning opportunities usually become the stalwart participants in Christian growth and service.[5]

Short-term Learning Opportunities

In addition to the ongoing learning opportunities available in most churches, there often is need for specialized or short-term courses. These usually are designed to provide a level of intensive study or training not usually available in the regular curriculum.

Administratively, these learning opportunities may be planned by a church staff member, by a general officer in one of the existing program organizations, or may be handled on an ad hoc basis with a temporary leader enlisted for the duration of the activity.

The process of implementing short-term learning opportunities follows these steps:
1. Discover needs and/or interests.
2. Define objectives for program.
3. Design program.
4. Determine leadership and curriculum resources.
5. Provide learning experiences.
6. Evaluate results.

In this way, leaders can develop specific learning opportunities to meet the particular needs of adults in any congregation or church community. Obviously, those who would be involved in such activities should be consulted, and short-term activities should be considered as a regular part of a church's overall program planning.

An example of an administrative structure and curriculum resources for short-term studies is the Church Study Course offered by Southern Baptists.[6] This educational plan consists of short courses with a record-keeping and recognition system. Courses are promoted for use in addition to the ongoing study curricula made available to churches by the denomination.

There are more than five hundred courses in twenty-three subject areas. Study may be done individually or in organized groups, on a regularly scheduled basis or as needed, and in any location convenient for participants.

Diplomas may be earned in leadership categories related to church responsibilities, in subject areas, and for participation in Christian development courses. A *leadership* diploma indicates that a church worker has secured the basic training needed to serve effectively in the area represented by the award. A *subject area* diploma represents intensive study in one of eight subject areas, such as Bible Survey, Missions, and Christian Family Life.

A *Christian development* diploma is a symbol of continuing education for the Christian. All courses, whether counted elsewhere or not, apply toward this recognition. The initial award, a diploma, is given at the completion of five courses. For every additional five courses, the participant earns an additional seal, and after twenty courses, an advanced diploma.

Another example of a way to provide short-term study is the Equipping Center approach.[7] This is a series of modules—or learning kits—that come in boxes. Every module contains study materials, teaching-learning aids, and instructions for the leader. The kit is carefully designed so that everything a leader will need from beginning to end—promotion to evaluation—is covered and resources provided. It is not unusual to find promotion and teaching posters, learning games, discussion sheets, filmstrips, and other helpful items, along with full details on how to plan, organize, and lead the study.

Equipping Centers may be used in a variety of approaches:

Seminar   A leader-centered approach to learning, with primary emphasis on presentations by the teacher.

Small Group A group-oriented approach, with primary emphasis on informal discussion and the free exchange of ideas and information.

Individual A self-directed approach, with primary emphasis on the completion of individualized learning activities related to the study materials.

Courses are published in six study areas. Churches are entirely free to choose any course from any area, and custom-design their curriculum. Here are the study areas and representative courses:

- Evangelism and Mission
   How to Witness
   Preparing Your Church for Revival

    Helping a Child Understand Salvation
- Family Life
  - Parent-Teen Relationships
  - Strengthening Family Relationships
  - The Christian and Divorce
- Christian Doctrine
  - Discovering Your Spiritual Gifts
  - The Priesthood of Believers
  - The Bible Speaks on Stewardship
- Leadership
  - How to Train Church Committees
  - Becoming a Christian Leader
  - Equipping Teachers to Teach
- Church and Community
  - The Bible Speaks to Current Issues
  - How Spiritual Awakenings Happens
  - Acts Alive: How Your Church Can Grow
- Christian Growth
  - How to Know the Will of God
  - How to Pray for Others
  - How to Deal With Your Feelings

Keeping on Learning

At the beginning I suggested that one of the joys of adulthood is that you can quit studying. What do you say now? The focus of my question perhaps is off target, for now you surely are aware that adults may shy away from traditional teacher-directed study (pedagogy), but self-directed *learning* (andragogy) is a major part of an adult's life.

Adults need to keep growing and maturing as Christian disciples, and they will if leaders and churches will provide meaningful and challenging opportunities.

To keep adults learning:
- Provide a balanced program of continuing and short-term opportunities.
- Arrange for different learning approaches: small-group, seminar, and individual.
- Treat participants with respect, as intelligent self-directing persons; involve them in setting goals and making plans related to their program/study.

- Provide ways for participants to see progress and receive recognition for their study.
- Involve persons in evaluating what they have achieved and in determining ways to enhance future study for themselves and for new participants.
- Focus on enabling adults to identify the gifts God has given them, developing these gifts, and using them in Christian service.

Notes

1. Malcolm Knowles is Emeritus Professor of Adult Education, North Carolina State University. He is author of *The Modern Practice of Adult Education, Self-Directed Learning* (p. 40 *ff*), and numerous other books and articles advocating andragogy.

2. Due to their significance, a comparison of these two teaching philosophies is given in figure 1. Although rarely seen in a pure form, these two stances are the most widely discussed approaches to influencing the lifelong learning of adults.

3. Adapted from Malcolm S. Knowles, *Self-Directed Learning* (New York: Association Press, 1975), p. 60.

4. For example see *Church Materials Catalog, 1985-1986,* (Nashville: The Sunday School Board, SBC), p. 10.

5. See Chapter 4, *Bible Teaching for Adults Through the Sunday School,* by C. Ferris Jordan. (Nashville: Convention Press, 1984.)

6. This plan is designed and promoted by the Sunday School Board, the Woman's Missionary Union, and the Brotherhood Commission, educational agencies related to the Southern Baptist Convention, and by the respective departments of the state conventions associated with the Southern Baptist Convention. For information write Church Study Course, 127 Ninth Avenue, North, Nashville, TN 37234.

7. This educational design was developed by the Church Training Department, Sunday School Board, SBC, 127 Ninth Avenue, North, Nashville, TN 37234.

Bibliography

Cooper, Polly, *How to Guide Adults.* Nashville, Convention Press, 1982.

DeBoy, James J., Jr. *Getting Started in Adult Religious Education.* New York: Paulist Press, 1979.

Erikson, Erik, ed. *Adulthood.* New York: W. W. Norton, 1978.

Gould, Roger L. *Transformations: Growth and Change in Adult Life.* New York: Simon and Schuster, 1978.

Gray, Robert M. and David Moberg. *The Church and the Older Person,* rev. ed., Grand Rapids: William B. Eerdmans, 1977.

Jordan, C. Ferris. *Bible Teaching for Adults Through the Sunday School.* Nashville: Convention Press, 1984.

Knowles, Malcolm. *The Modern Practice of Adult Education.* Chicago: Association Press/Follette Publishing, 1980.

_____. *Self-Directed Learning.* New York: Association Press, 1975

Knox, Alan B. *Adult Development and Learning.* San Francisco: Jossey-Bass, 1977

Peterson, Richard E., et. al. *Lifelong Learning in America.* San Francisco: Jossey-Bass, 1979.

Powers, Bruce P. *Growing Faith.* Nashville: Broadman Press, 1982.

Tough, Allen. *The Adult's Learning Projects.* Toronto: Ontario Institute for Studies in Education. 1979.

PART III:

Is Adult Learning Different?

Does an adult learn differently than a child? How do adults learn? Knowing the uniqueness of adult learning can be advantageous in designing, scheduling, and leading adult learning experiences. Part III examines adult learning.

Chapter 15 explores learning differences in adulthood. Adults learn through experience and discovery. Learning involves activity on the part of the adult learner. A comparison is made between pedagogy and andragogy. The uniqueness of adult learning is described.

Are there adult teachable moments? The adult developmental tasks offer a multitude of teachable moments. Adult readiness for learning is reviewed in chapter 16.

Chapter 17 focuses on examining the myths that exist concerning how and what adults learn. Adult Christian education programs should be based on facts and truths, not on misconceptions or half-truths.

15

Learning Differences in Adulthood
Jerry M. Stubblefield

Introduction

Until recently, it was assumed that an adult learns the way a child learns. The method of learning is basically the same—a person learns through experience and discovery. The biggest differences between adult and child learning are the context and the motivation for learning. A child is placed in a formal setting where learning is intended to take place—a school. Adult learning may take place in a formal setting, such as a school, but the motivation for learning is different. The child learns in order to complete school and because he may use the information gained later—as preparation for life. An adult is learning for present and possibly future tasks that will be faced, but it is more present and need oriented.

All teaching has been called pedagogy. The word *pedagogy* comes from the Greek word *Paidagogas* who was a Greek slave and who escorted children to school. It has been seen as the art and science of teaching children. Now "pedagogy" is descriptive of the art and science of teaching. Recently, European educators began using a new term *andragogy* which Malcolm S. Knowles has popularized in America. He defines "andragogy as the art and science of helping adults learn."[1] The distinction is that it is education related to adults, not to a child.

Part of the reaction to *pedagogy* as a descriptive term for adult learning comes from what some see as the presuppositions, such as the contexts and goals of pedagogy. Knowles has reacted to pedagogy in four main areas—the concept of the learner, the role of the learners' experience, readiness to learn, and orientation to learning. Before examining these concepts as they relate to learning differences in adulthood, let's examine what learning is.

228

What Is Learning?

Webster's Ninth New Collegiate Dictionary defines learning as "the act or experience of one that learns; knowledge or skill acquired by instruction or study; modification of a behaviorial tendency by experience."[2] This definition means learning includes more than teacher instruction or classroom instruction which is usually identified with learning.

Martha M. Leypoldt[3] has described Learning Is. . . .

Since we define learning as changing, we can attribute the following characteristics to learning:

Learning is active.	It involves movement. Movement may be in the same or the reverse direction of present movement or goals.
Learning is experiencing.	It involves the entire being.
Learning is dynamic.	It has forceful motion.
Learning is discovery.	It is a discovery of self, persons, feelings, knowledge, and new ways of behaving.
Learning is vital.	Life cannot exist without it.
Learning is growth.	It is directed toward some desired end.
Learning is self-realization.	It involves self-fulfillment.
Learning is creative tension.	Tensions bring possibilities of choices.
Learning is meaning.	Life has value.
Learning is insight.	It brings the "aha" feeling.
Learning is involvement.	It includes both giving of oneself and receiving the giving of others.
Learning is self-revolution.	We are changed persons.
Learning is meeting of meanings.	We understand the meanings of others and they understand our meanings.
Learning is unfreezing.	From a frozen state we become fluid so we can change.
Learning is ecstatic.	The time of learning is a moment of delight.

Learning is what is happening now.	The change is now, not in the past or in the future. The past will have had a significant part in the learning experiences, and the consequences of learning will affect the future.
Learning is becoming.	The new person has the potential for future newness.

Learning has been described by eighteen different concepts, all of them active. For Leypoldt, learning is not ingathering facts or information, but what happens to the person while learning. If one has learned, then the person is changing. She wrote:

> Learning is making me a new person. Since learning involves change, we are different persons when we have learned. We are different persons when we have added new information; we are different persons when we have changed our attitudes, and we are different persons when we have changed our actions.[4]

Is Adult Learning Different?

Knowles has made a comparative study of what he perceives as the assumptions of pedagogy and andragogy. His ideas have many implications for the practice of adult Christian education as well as for secular adult education. His analysis is:[5]

Regarding:	Pedagogy	Andragogy
Concept of the learner	The role of the learner is, by definition, a dependent one. The teacher is expected by society to take full responsibility for determining what is to be learned, when it is to be learned, how it is to be learned, and if it has been learned.	It is a normal aspect of the process of maturation for a person to move from dependency toward increasing self-directedness, but at different rates for different people and in different dimensions of life. Teachers have a responsibility to encourage and nurture this movement. Adults have a deep psychological need to

be generally self-directing, although they may be dependent in particular temporary situations.

Role of learners' experience

The experience learners bring to a learning situation is of little worth. It may be used as a starting point, but the experience from which learners will gain the most is that of the teacher, the textbook writer, the audio-visual aid producer, and other experts. Accordingly, the primary techniques in education are transmittal techniques — lecture, assigned reading, AV presentations.

As people grow and develop they acumulate an increasing reservoir of experience that becomes an increasingly rich resource for learning — for themselves and for others. Furthermore, people attach more meaning to learnings they gain from experience than those they acquire passively. Accordingly, the primary techniques in education are experiential techniques — laboratory experiments, discussion, problem-solving cases, simulation exercises, field experience, and the like.

Readiness to learn

People are ready to learn whatever society (especially the school) says they ought to learn . . . provided the pressures on them (like fear of failure) are great enough. Most people of the same age are ready to learn the same things.

People become ready to learn something when they experience a need to learn it in order to cope more satisfyingly with real-life tasks or problems. The educator has a responsibility to create conditions and provide tools and proce-

	Therefore, learning should be organized into a fairly standardized curriculum, with a uniform step-by-step progression for all learners.	dures for helping learners discover their "needs to know." And learning programs should be organized around life-application categories and sequenced according to the learners' readiness to learn.
Orientation to learning	Learners see education as a process of acquiring subject-matter content, most of whom understand will be useful only at a later time in life. Accordingly, the curriculum should be organized into subject-matter units (e.g., courses) which follow the logic of the subject (e.g., from ancient to modern history, from simple to complex mathematics or science). People are subject-centered in their orientation to learning.	Learners see education as a process of developing increased competence to achieve their full potential in life. They want to be able to apply whatever knowledge and skill they gain today to living more effectively tomorrow. Accordingly, learning experiences should be organized around competency-development categories. People are performance centered in their orientation to learning.

How does andragogy differ from pedagogy? What are the practical implications if andragogy should be adopted as the method of adult education? If andragogy were practiced, what changes would occur in adult Christian education? What effect would these changes have on the church's program of adult Christian education? In an effort to answer these questions the following ideas are presented.

Concept of the Learner

Teachers have traditionally perceived students as dependent persons whose lives need to be managed. The young student's entire world revolves around the role of learner—at school, home, church, playground, and so forth. In the posture of a learner she receives rewards and whatever self-fulfillment is achieved. She is expected to be passive as she is in the process of receiving and storing up information or data which adults have decided that children either should know or have. These concepts of the learner persist into late adolescence and sometimes even into early adulthood. The person is expected to take charge of other areas of life but not as a learner. The basic attitude is that those who are responsible for learning—teachers, curriculum planners, and so forth—know what the person needs to learn and thus prescribe the course of study. The learner sees herself as dependent for educational endeavors.

Adults see themselves differently from the time when they were students. An adult has many roles other than that of learner. Satisfaction and fulfillment are now based on performances as producers or doers. Adults are heavily involved in work, family relationships, community activities, and so forth. Adults see themselves as self-directing personalities. They make their own decisions and assume responsibility for running their own lives. Not only are adults self-directing but they are perceived by others as being self-directing.

When adults are placed in teaching-learning situations, it is difficult to break the old dependency attitude of "Teach me." Adults are influenced by their experience in previous learning environments. Few of them have had the opportunity to be involved in planning their learning activities. I have worked with seminary classes as they try to design their own courses in adult Christian education. It takes several class sessions before the students feel comfortable in assuming responsibility for their own learning. Once it has been accomplished, the learners are very excited and feel a sense of achievement and satisfaction.

The learning climate must be different from that experienced earlier. Furnishings and equipment should be designed with the comfort of adults in mind. More is involved than just the physical climate. Knowles feels:

> The psychological climate should be one which causes adults to feel accepted, respected, and supported; . . . there exists a spirit of mutuality

between teachers and students as joint inquirers; . . . there is freedom of expression without fear of punishment or ridicule.[6]

The adult learning environment should be characterized as friendly and informal.

Adults may have negative feelings and reactions to what they have associated with earlier learning experiences—chalkboards, student desks, and so forth. However, the single most significant influence on the character of the learning climate is the teacher's behavior. The attribute most appreciated by learners is the ability of a teacher to really listen to what is being said. What has been said about the facilities and the teacher are applicable for educational institutions and administrators. Adults want adult educational institutions to be equipped for adults and for educational administrators to consider them as adults, involving them in appropriate decision-making endeavors.

If adults have the self-concept of self-directivity, then they will be more deeply motivated to learn what they see a need to learn. Adults must be engaged in the process of self-diagnosis of needs for learning.

Much has been said about involving adult learners in planning what and how they want to learn. Adults make decisions about every facet of life—this should include the learning process. Through planning, adults can translate diagnosed needs into specific educational objectives or personal growth goals.

The role of the teacher shifts in andragogy from what it was in pedagogy. In andragogy the teaching-learning process is the mutual responsibility of learners and teachers. The teacher shifts from an authority figure to that of a facilitator, guide, director of learning. Each person—learner and teacher—helps one another learn[7]

The andragogical concept of learning has several implications for adult Christian education. Responsibility for the teaching-learning experience is one shared by teacher and the learner. This shared responsibility means that both teacher and learner must be equally involved in planning the learning activities and curriculum. Much of adult Christian education has been subject or content centered.[8] Adult Christian education seeks to teach religion and religious ideas, yet it must be aware of the developmental needs of its participants. Emphasis must be upon helping people cope and deal with the issues of life. The biblical message must be shared and will be as the teaching-learning process seeks to help participants live more effective lives. It is not an either/or proposition but involves both—the message of the Bible and the needs of persons.

This approach will cause many churches to alter the climate in which adult Christian education takes place. More informal settings and approaches to the teaching-learning situation will be called for. Teachers must understand and know the life needs of class members. Classrooms will take on a more adult look—chairs, tables, easels rather than chalkboards, and so forth.

The teaching-learning experience will be seen as one that is shared by the learners with the teacher. The class will not belong to the teacher but will be seen as "ours."

The Role of Experience

Obviously, the adult has had many more experiences than youth. Experience is viewed differently by children and by adults. For children experience is something that happens to them; it is not an integral part of them, but it is an external event that affects them. An adult's self-identity comes from personal experiences. Adult self-identity comes from where and what a person's work is, what the person has done—travels, education and experiences, and achievements.

Adult experience can be a great asset to learning in that such experiences can be a rich resource for learning. It may also provide a foundation of experience to which new learning can be related. It should be observed that adults are more fixed in habits and patterns of thought and tend to be less open-minded.

With the added experience of adults, more experiential techniques can be used in the teaching-learning process. It is assumed that "the more active the learner's role in the process, the more they are probably learning." Wise adult educators use life experiences drawn from the learners to illustrate or explain new concepts or ideas.[9]

Good teaching seeks to relate what is being learned to the life experiences of the learners. Helping adults see how a biblical truth or idea relates to a life situation can help adult learners become more involved in Bible study and ultimately help them live a more effective Christian life.

Readiness to Learn

The next chapter examines "readiness to learn" in detail. As a person moves through the three phases of adult life, one must continue to deal with different developmental tasks and thus change readiness to learn. A person's readiness to learn is dynamic in that one must change to meet different circumstances or issues in life. One may be ready to learn certain skills as needed but not before he really feels confronted to do so.

Readiness to learn determines the timing of learnings. For instance, an older person will have little interest in learning about getting started in an occupation, having already spent a lifetime in the work world. However, a young adult will be most interested. On the other hand, the young adult will not see the need to learn about retirement or tasks confronting the older adult. Curriculum planning and development should take into consideration where a person is in the adult life cycle and what developmental tasks the person is facing and will soon encounter.

Grouping of adults follows one of two patterns—homogenous or heterogeneous. When considering developmental tasks, homogeneous groups are preferable. Persons in the group will be experiencing similar tasks or needs. Each can profit from the experiences of others and how others are handling a similar task. One may also find a support group which will provide encouragement and strength. Homogeneous groups are usually found in adult Bible study groups which are formed according to age, sex, marital status, and so forth. Other homogeneous groups would be marriage enrichment, parenting, or other special interests.

Heterogeneous groupings would be utilized when the learning objective is not related to a developmental task. Most discipleship training programs would utilize heterogeneous groups since this is not a developmental task, but rather an attempt to help adults develop skills and attitudes for more effective Christian living.[10]

Orientation to Learning

Children view educational activities as subject centered and futuristic. Adults think of learning as being immediately applicable. Adults are motivated to engage in educational activities to improve their ability to cope with current life problems. Education is seen by an adult as problem centered or performance centered.

Learning experiences need to be planned around the life concerns of the individuals. Adult learning needs to be organized around problem areas (not subjects) since adult learners are problem centered in their approach to learning.

Adult education courses should be designed around the current problems and issues that the adult learners are experiencing. Initially, inquiry should be made about what the adult learner wants to get out of a particular study. Then the starting point is the problems the learners are aware of and how to help them discover potential solutions to the problems.[11]

Adult Christian education programs should consider the different orientation the adult learner has. It is assumed that an adult is interested in the Bible, so she will attend a Bible study group. The Bible is a book about life that was written by adults for adults. The Bible describes life needs experienced by all adults. Adult Christian educators must be aware of needs and problems encountered by the adult in her everyday life. Through approaching the religious needs of adults in this way, the teacher can assist the adult learner in discovering spiritual resources to help her meet the life challenges being dealt with.

Uniqueness of Adult Learning

Adult learning is unique in that the adult assumes major responsibility for his own learning. He chooses whether or not to participate in a particular educational opportunity. This means that the educational activity must be perceived by the adult as being relevant to his own needs. The adult must feel that it is beneficial, offers either help in meeting needs or issues, or will contribute to his own personal growth.

One reason adults give for participating in teaching-learning activities is the fellowship/contact with other adults. This provides a group with which one can identify and find support.

Adult learning is unique in that the learner is living life. What the person learns has an immediate application. This is not preparation for the future. Adult Christian education must strive to equip and enable adults to live full and meaningful lives now.

Notes

1. Malcolm S. Knowles, *The Modern Practice of Adult Education* (Chicago: Follett Publishing Company, 1980), p. 43.

2. *Webster's Ninth New Collegiate Dictionary* (Springfield: Mass.: Merriam-Webster Inc., 1983), p. 681.

3. Martha M. Leypoldt, *Learning Is Change* (Valley Forge, Pa.: Judson Press, 1971), pp. 29-30. Used by permission.

4. Ibid., p. 30.
5. Knowles, pp. 43-44.
6. Ibid., p. 47. Used by permission.
7. Ibid., pp. 45-49.
8. Ibid.
9. Ibid., pp. 49-50.
10. Ibid., pp. 51-53.
11. Ibid., pp. 53-54.

16

An Adult Teachable Moment
Jerry M. Stubblefield

Introduction

Is there an adult "teachable moment?" Is there an adult readiness for learning? *Yes!* As an adult moves through the adult life structure he is confronted many times with the need and the desire to learn new skills, new attitudes, new behaviors, and new knowledge. *Learning Is for Life*[1] affirms that adults need to continue to learn throughout life.

If education received through the individual's first eighteen years is preparation for life, how much more do the adult years require that one continue that education. The adult years are life, not preparation for life. Concerning this need Havighurst wrote:

> Of all the periods of life, early adulthood is the fullest of teachable moments and the emptiest of efforts to teach. It is a time of special sensitivity and unusual readiness of the person to learn. Early adulthood, the period from eighteen to thirty, usually contain marriage, the first pregnancy, the first serious full-time job, the first illnesses of children, the first experience of furnishing or buying or building a house, and the first venturing of the child off to school. If ever people are motivated to learn and to learn quickly, it is at times such as these.[2]

As individuals become oriented increasingly to the developmental tasks of their social roles, their readiness to learn is heightened.

Much of formal schooling should have prepared the young adult to deal with these life issues. The person might not have seen the relevance since these matters were not currently being lived—the application was to come later. Previously their learning was related to a subject being studied, now the learning shifts to performance—tasks that must be done now.

In a recent course I taught on Church Administration, this principle was demonstrated. Usually, the course is taken in a student's second or third year. Several first-semester students were admitted. All the first-

239

semester students were on the same group to work on a term project. This group had great difficulty in deciding *what* to do for the project while the second and third year students moved through it quickly. The older students, not in age but in seminary experience, had enough experience in church work to see the immediacy of application.

A pastor friend does his premarital counseling three months *after* the wedding. His experience has been that *prior to* the wedding the couple is interested primarily in the wedding ceremony. He has learned that they are more attentive and open to his counseling after they have lived together for three months. There are some things that people must experience for themselves; it cannot be done by others and passed on to them. In an unforgetable television commercial, a young woman said, "Mother, *please,* I'd rather do it *myself!*" Some things must be learned experientially rather than through the transmission of experience or knowledge learned by others.

What Is a Teachable Moment?

There are many "teachable moments" in the life of an adult. Whenever an adult encounters a new situation for which she does not have an "answer," that is a teachable moment. A teachable moment occurs when an adult has a "crisis" experience—a new job, marriage, birth of a child, moving to a new home—those events which require a heavy outlay of emotional energy, particularly when it is experienced for the first time.

A teachable moment occurs when an event or action happens in the life of an adult for which the person does not feel prepared or does not have an answer or potential solution at hand. It is a time when one has to admit, "I am not in charge; neither do I have the internal resources to deal adequately with the events at hand." It means that a person is vulnerable, feels helpless or powerless. Usually at such a teachable moment, major breakthroughs have occurred in terms of direction for the person's life or in relationship to others or to God. One of the hardest tasks for someone is to admit that he is not the captain of his own ship, but is dependent upon others for safety and well-being. This event may signal a deeper spiritual life as the person turns to God during this teachable moment. Many have told how they have wrestled with major decisions and issues in their lives which have been answered when they admitted to God that they could not cope in their own strength.

Not everyone handles a teachable moment successfully. Sometimes an adult is unable or unwilling to acknowledge that he cannot meet his own needs. The task is too great for the person, but he will not admit it. A teachable moment may pass by if the resources, such as people, are not immediately available. For a person to move forward at a teachable moment requires a support system. This may be found in a newly established relationship with God and/or encouragement and support from family and friends.

Some Teachable Moments

Adulthood is filled with many potential teachable moments. We will focus on some of the major ones.

Establishing Independent Living Arrangements

At whatever the age, moving from the security and dependability of living with family can be very exciting but an equally frightening experience. Making the transition from living with family to going to college, joining the military, or getting an apartment can be teachable moments for both the young adult and for the parent. The young person will quickly learn the costs of food, utilities, and so forth. He will also learn to take responsibility for laundry, food purchase and preparation, cleaning of the living quarters, much of which has previously been done by the parent.

Parents will either let the young person be responsible for this segment of life, continue the pattern established in the home, or will share some of the responsibilities with the young person. Parents may discover that they are able to do many things with time and energy which had been given to the adult child. Parents probably will have mixed emotions about this new event much as one father described his feelings about his oldest child learning to ride a bicycle on a busy street, "I was thrilled beyond words and scared to death, all at the same time."

Upon completion of high school, the young adult may feel that the world is at her feet. However, it will not be long before Mom, Dad, older brothers and sisters, or friends will be asked, "What do you think about . . .?" The young adult may not be asking what you think about the subject at hand but may be wanting confirmation for a decision already made. As one begins to sample the adult world, it may be a teachable moment.

Entering the Work World

Most of us had no real concept of what our first full-time job would be like. We tend to glamorize it. Finding that first job may not have been as easy as we had imagined. We may even accept a job that we didn't really think we wanted. The first job may be seen as either temporary or permanent. If the person is single and living at home, the first job may not be considered a first step toward independence. It might be a means to pay for a car or to support the life-style of the individual. Most jobs lose their glamor as they become more and more monotonous.

As the young adult begins to have second thoughts about the job, the person may seek advice about whether or not to keep the job. Unless the young person has acquired debts for a car, stereo, and so forth, he may just quit the job without having another. If there are debts to be paid, one may feel trapped or forced to remain with a job that may not be fulfilling. This may especially be true if the young adult has married. With the high rate of unemployment, new jobs may not be found easily. Both entering and deciding whether or not to stay with a particular job may be a teachable moment.

To Marry or Not to Marry

The decision to marry or to remain single is a significant question faced by young adults. There is peer pressure as friends are marrying. There is also pressure from one's family. Many young adults are choosing to delay marriage until they are better established in the work world or in order to complete graduate or professional training.

Young adults now feel that they have an option to marry or to remain single. Their parents probably did not feel this was an option as society expected they would marry. The rising divorce rate suggests that young adults may not perceive that marriage is a permanent relationship. One of the best helps for young adults in preparing for a happy, successful marriage is the observation of a good relationship between their parents. Many teachable moments should have been observed as young adults have "watched" their parents in their homes.

Many young adults enter into marriage with unrealistic expectations feeling that they will be eternally happy. The traditional wedding vows have some interesting contrasts—for better or worse, for richer or poorer, in sickness and in health. Marriage should be seen realistically rather than as a fantasy.

Trying to decide to marry or not to marry and choosing the proper marriage partners are teaching moments. Unfortunately, one is usually so emotionally involved that one might not be very teachable at this time. True teachable moments cannot be contrived or preplanned. They must be serendipitous experiences—they just happen. One should be alert to a teachable moment.

To Be Parents or Not to Be Parents

Many married couples have decided that they do want to have children. This decision should have been basically agreed upon before marriage. A great deal of stress can be placed upon the couple if one of them wants to have children and the other doesn't.

Assuming that the couple have decided that they want children, the next questions are, *When* do we want children? and *How many* children do we want? Family planning is available to the couple with modern birth control methods readily accessible.

The decision to become parents is a decision that should be made by the couple. Sometimes pressure has been placed on married children by their parents—almost demanding that they have children. The couple knows best whether and when they want children.

There are many teachable moments for the couple who desire children, both before the birth of the child and after. Every couple anticipating the birth of their first child has a good bit of anxiety and apprehension prior to and after the birth. The need for encouragement, accurate information, and friendly support is education at its best during this teachable moment prior to birth and the first few months of infancy.

Being a Good Citizen

Young men tend to become overextended in carrying out civic responsibilities—whether it be to a church, a civic, community, or political organization. Women tend to overextend in commitments to church and schools. In young adulthood, there are heavy demands upon both men and women from work, family, civic, and community groups. The young adult wants to be responsible, sometimes so much that the person becomes too heavily involved and cannot meet the various time demands. When these pressures come, and they will, the young adult is at a teachable moment.

Choosing the Right Kind of Friends

Young adulthood demands the formation a new core of friends. Friendships began in one's community and school are seldom kept into the adult years. Getting established as an adult forces one to seek new friends. Moving to new places, starting new jobs, getting married, or remaining single—all compel the young adult to find persons who have similar interests, people near one's own age, and those whose social life is similar.

Making choices between which club or social group to join, what church to belong to, which political party to participate in, or how to find persons whose interests, values, and life-style are similar—these present many opportunities for teachable moments.

Being a Community Leader

As one moves into the middle adult years, demands upon one's time and influence increase sharply. The person is recognized as a leader in the civic life of the community.

With the increased demands of family, work responsibility, civic and community obligations, and church responsibilities, the individual is pulled between conflicting demands upon time and influence. Any one of these tasks could easily require one's full time, but these are to be juggled in one's leisure time. Achieving civic and social responsibility provides a teachable moment.

Living with Teenagers

Many parents have great anxiety just thinking about their children's entering the teen years. There are so many things to do to assist adolescent children to begin to move toward adulthood. Adults are aware of the manifold pressures upon the teenagers—how to handle the issues of drugs, alcohol, sex, new freedoms, and so forth.

Freedom of mobility creates many anxious moments for the parents. Questions abound at this juncture in life: When should dating begin? What time should they be in on week nights, on weekends? What are their friends like? Do I know the families of their friends? Are the teenagers mature enough to handle the different kinds of situations they will encounter? Will they tell me where they are going, whom they are with? Will they be home at the agreed-upon time? Will they be honest with me about all things? How much money should be given for an allowance? How much supervision is needed in buying clothes, getting haircuts, and so forth? Why do they do such crazy things? The list goes on and on.

Parents frequently try to deal with their own teenagers as their parents dealt with them. It is hard for parents to accept that changing circumstances require new patterns, new approaches to dealing with problems experienced by teenagers of every generation. Parents must recognize that what works with one teenager may be completely ineffective with another.

Parents do not like to scold or complain about routine things, but it seems that some teenagers rarely remember to hang up clothes, clean up the bathroom, clean their rooms, or clean the kitchen after school or late evening snacks.

Establishment of family rules can be an exasperating time especially when your teenager keeps saying, "Everybody else is doing it. Why can't I? If you don't let me do . . . I'll be the laughingstock of my school?" Parents would like to be able to influence the teenager as much as the teenager's peers. Teenagers want to know what the boundaries are and will "lean" on the parent to see if the rules can be bent—even if just a little.

The issues of driving a car, getting a driver's license, or having a car of one's own are common experiences in most families. After getting the license, the issue comes up frequently about whose use of the family car has priority. Teenage drivers add significantly to the cost of automobile insurance as well as to the costs of operating the vehicle.

Helping adolescent children grow into adulthood is a task faced by every family. Parents want to know how to teach their teenager to be responsible for his personal belongings and to act in ways that assist the family in its routine, daily functioning. Helping the teenager handle financial matters in a mature and responsible way is a task parents must work at.

Working with adolescents in making the choice of a college, or the decision not to attend one, is time consuming for parents, particularly if the high school graduate is not sure what vocation to pursue. Assisting the teenager to realistically consider what his capabilities are may cause parents to have to examine honestly and frankly the various options with the young person.

Knowing what to do with a high school graduate who does not want to go to college and who will not get a job will try the patience of parents.

Deciding, for example, what responsibilities for household chores should be assigned to the young adult living at home is typical of the concerns which parents must explore.

Living with teenagers provides many teachable moments. Helping the adolescent develop skills and begin to move into adulthood offers many teachable moments.

Living Within Your Income

Earning power is probably at its height during the middle-adult years. As one enters middle adulthood, income will not be as great as it will be during the middle and later years of middle adulthood. Many American families have become two-income families with both husband and wife working. Many families have found two incomes are necessary to survive financially.

It seems as if every time you feel that you may be getting ahead financially, an unexpected expense comes along. As family members grow up, the money necessary to meet ongoing needs increases. Many needs cost significantly more than when the children were younger.

The idea of a second car now seems more like a necessity. As teenagers begin to drive, some consider a third car, which means that insurance, maintenance, and gasoline costs are being added to an already tight budget.

The comfortable nest egg or insurance policy that has been saved for the children's college education appears now to meet half or less of current college costs. The fact is, what you had felt was going to be adequate for retirement years has been eroded by the high rate of inflation.

The home that was going to last a lifetime now needs major repairs. As the family has grown and the children have entered the teen years, a room needs to be added, or you must look for a larger house.

Trying to meet the financial needs of a growing family provides many teachable moments.

What to Do with Leisure

Leisure activities that were satisfying and pleasurable during young adulthood often lose their attractiveness as one moves through middle adulthood. Young adult leisuretime activities need to be replaced by less strenuous ones. Very physical leisure activities are being gradually replaced by less-physical ones.

Leisuretime activities should give a measure of pleasure and satisfaction. Leisuretime activities tend to move in the direction of hobbies, skill development, personal growth, and enrichment interests.

This period of life may cause a person to want to fulfill lifelong dreams or goals—a trip to another land, a visit to that romantic place, a special wedding anniversary trip, all of these interest the middle adult.

As the person moves through the middle adult years, that fleeting thought about what will I do when I retire seems more important now. Leisure-time activities must have a certain challenge to the person as well as a sense of achievement and satisfaction.

Developing appropriate leisure-time activities provide many teachable moments.

Living with One's Spouse

One of the couple looks at the other and says, "You are not the same person I married." Of course, twenty-plus years do bring many changes —looks, attitudes, ways of doing things, and so forth. Many changes have occurred in each person during the time of the marriage—some visible, some hidden. Each partner must recognize and accept that the other has changed in many ways.

One significant change is that each of the marriage partners has developed significant interests other than in each other. Both have been heavily involved in roles other than being a husband or a wife. If there are children, she devoted much of her time and energy to bearing and raising the children. Even if she has worked, children have consumed much of her interests. The man has been equally involved in getting ahead in his chosen work. His interest has been in his work but also in trying to provide the material necessities—a home, clothes, medical care, recreational advantages, and so forth.

The postparental family can be a crisis time for many families. The couple may realize that they have drifted apart even though they have lived in the same house and have been working for the same objectives and goals. The problem might be that they have not taken time for themselves. Time and energy have been consumed in being parents, wage earners, civic and community leaders, or even in the pursuit of leisure-time activities.

With the nest empty, the couple may discover that they are strangers. Many couples begin "courting" each other again in an effort to recapture that spark that first brought them together. It is impossible for the couple to resume their relationship as it was prior to the birth of their children. There must be a "bridge" that unites them which has also sustained them during periods of stress in the marital relationship.

Each of the couple has unique, special needs that were not present at the time of the marriage. Their needs are no longer the expressed needs of young adulthood. The man must understand the special needs of his wife. She will need more of his time and attention. He will need to be sensitive to her psychological and physiological needs associated with menopause. Neither should take the other for granted. Attention should be paid to grooming, courtesies, and consideration by both husband and wife. The wife needs to be aware that he may be experiencing some of the same psychological and physiological needs that she has. Both need encouragement and appreciation that they received in the early days of the marriage.

Both may have unfulfilled dreams and ambitions related to what has been achieved or not achieved and what can yet be accomplished in the days ahead. This may be a time for educational pursuits either to complete what was begun earlier or to gain skills and information deemed necessary to reach personal goals.

Learning to live with one's spouse was begun in early adulthood and will continue into later adulthood. Clearly, relating to one's spouse as a person presents a multitude of teachable moments.

Accepting Physiological Changes

Physiological changes that occur in middle adulthood cause middle adults to begin to look and act differently. Many middle adults cannot accept the physiological changes that occur in their bodies. A person may try to hide the loss of hair by wearing a hairpiece or use artificial hair coloring to cover grayness. Advertising appeals are made to middle adults to stay younger or, at least, to look younger.

Psychologically, the image of both men and women change in middle adulthood. There may be denial that one needs glasses, cannot hear as well, or does not have the physical energy previously possessed. One begins to see oneself differently. Many compensate by taking up new activities to prove that they are still young or can act young.

Many middle adults engage in a flurry of activity to make up for lost time or to achieve unfulfilled dreams or goals. One becomes aware that time is running out. Major physical problems (for example, heart attack) may result as one works beyond his capacity or potential in order to make a "niche" or name for himself.

Middle adults need adequate, accurate information about their physical bodies, so they can behave in an appropriate manner. A person is challenged to develop new interests and activities that are appropriate to biological and psychological capacities. The ability to accept and adjust to the physiological changes of middle adulthood will have a major effect on how the individual will accept and adjust to retirement.

Accepting and adjusting to physiological changes in one's body offers many teachable moments.

Adjusting to Aging Parents

Most middle adults have parents who are in their late sixties or early seventies. During middle adulthood, one might be involved in a three-generation family. Often as children become adults and establish families of their own, the middle adult becomes more involved in the life and care of aging parents.

Assisting aging parents requires much financially and psychologically. One may have to help parents, possibly even giving financial help. Aging parents may need assistance in moving to more appropriate housing arrangements. Depending upon the size and geographical location of one's family, someone must help aging parents get the necessary medical attention and so forth.

A source of great anxiety comes when the adult child has to assume the parent role for his own parents. This is doubly hard if the parent does not realize or recognize that this is best. Whether or not the aged parent should continue to drive an automobile, live alone, continue in previous residence—these and countless other issues are perplexing and without easy answers.

The death of a parent stirs many emotions. Much depends upon the quality of the relationship that one has had with the parent. Unresolved issues may cause feelings of guilt or regret. If the parent has had a lingering, debilitating illness, death may be seen as a relief. There may be heavy medical or convalescent home expenses above those covered by insurance.

Many teachable moments occur as one adjusts to aging parents.

Am I Getting Older?

An older man bends over to tie his shoes. While bent, he surveys the territory around him and asks, "Is there anything else I can do while I'm down here?" This "incident" epitomizes the loss of physical energy. As one gets older, one has less physical energy. The person may be able to do what one did previously but may not be able to do it for as long or as often. Several retired men played golf three times a week. They always played fourteen holes rather than eighteen. The fourteenth green was located in back of the clubhouse. Instead of heading to the fifteenth tee, they headed for the clubhouse. They said that they had had *enough* exercise for one day.

Not only does one not have as much strength or energy, but physical ailments seem to multiply. While one's health may be precarious, the older person has great concern about the rising costs of medical care not covered by insurance.

A deep concern older people have is the fear of not having sufficient sources of money to care for themselves either through an extended hospitalization or convalescent home care. If the person's spouse has died, she may worry about who will take care of her during illness or should she become unable to care for herself. The older person does not want to be a burden or in the way of children or others who become caregivers.

The older person realizes that he is not as strong as he once was when illness occurs. These are very teachable moments for the older person and also for the person's children or the caregivers.

Where Has All the Money Gone?

With retirement there usually comes a reduction in income. It is also a time when expenses can accelerate. Being on a fixed income, persons may feel that they must be extremely cautious in what is purchased. Most older people do not make major expenditures and may try to conserve money by moving into smaller houses or apartments.

Retirement may be a period of great financial anxiety as inflation has reduced what was available for retirement. Due to tight budgets, older persons sometimes will not buy foods which will provide a balanced diet, thus compounding health problems.

The older person may resent retirement because financial resources are not adequate to do the things anticipated during retirement.

For many, particularly men, retirement brings boredom and a loss of meaning. A man has devoted much of his emotional and physical energy to earning a living. Without hobbies, friends, and interesting activities, retirement becomes something to resent rather than enjoy. Additional time together can help the couple enjoy and enrich their marital relationship. For other older couples, retirement time can magnify problems or difficulties. There is an alarming number of older persons who are divorcing.

Retirement and reduced income can be times of stress and adjustment for the couple. Both experiences provide opportunities for teachable moments.

Now I Am Alone

During older adulthood, one has to adjust to the death of a spouse. The couple might have had many years together. Often there are children, grandchildren, many shared activities, and significant events. When death occurs, the surviving spouse feels the grief and loss of a marriage partner of many years and also the loss of a "best friend." Because of the nature of the marital relationship, each has begun to depend more and more on the other for intimacy needs.

As the person adjusts to the death of a spouse, she must begin to perform those duties and tasks which the spouse has done. Usually the house is filled with mementos and reminders of major events in the couple's lives. After one has been married thirty, forty, fifty or more years, the sense of loss and aloneness may seem overwhelming.

Working through the death of a spouse can be a most teachable moment.

Living with One's Peers

With the exception of the adeolescent years, older adulthood causes one to be most dependent upon and be closer to one's peers. With retirement, the older person has fewer opportunities for intergenerational friends. Work, church, civic, and community activities have the possibilities of providing friends of all ages. As people grow older, they need to identify and have friends near their own age.

An older woman in good health began to live in a convalescent home. Her family and friends were puzzled and confused by this. She simply explained, "I want to be with people who want to talk about what I want to." She wanted to be with persons her own age.

It can be frustrating to children of older persons when the parents insist on having the same friends as their children. It is important that an older person identify with persons of the same age. We usually do not see ourselves accurately through the eyes of people around us. A man in his eighties always referred to an acquaintance in his seventies as "Old man Light." It never occurred to him that he was the older of the two.

An issue that older persons must continue to deal with is the cultivation and discovery of new friends. A minister observed at the memorial service for a sixty-two-year-old man that both he and the deceased had more friends in heaven than on earth. As one gets older many of one's friends are no longer around.

Identifying with one's own age group has the potential of offering teachable moments.

Being a Good Friend and a Good Citizen

Trying to meet social and civic obligations can be a source of great joy and of great frustration for the older person. Entertaining people in one's home may not be as easily done as previously. A person's energy level is not what it used to be. Another problem is that couples or special groups of friends have changed through death of one of the couple, retirement, and so forth. One's income may not be adequate to entertain on the level or frequency to which one was accustomed.

Health problems such as weak eyes or hearing may make the old games or activities not as much fun or as easy to participate in. Most older people want to be around other people—to enjoy relationships, friendships, and interests. The problem may be that entertaining is more physically exhausting and therefore not as enjoyable.

Meeting civic and community responsibilities will normally change as one gets older. Instead of serving as chairperson or leader of community and civic activities, the older person may assume the role of encourager or supporter. Even in retirement, one wants to feel that one is carrying one's share of the load. As one gets older, the person becomes more selective of the activities and events to become involved with.

Being a good friend and a good citizen are teachable moments for older adults.

Where Shall I Live?

As a person gets older, adjustments must be made in living arrangements. A house large enough for a growing family may become too much house. Depending upon the physical arrangement, the home may be unsafe for continued occupancy by the older person—steps, bedroom location, kitchen stove, entrance ways, and so forth.

If the older person has to move to another house, the issue of what to keep, what to sell or give away, what to take to the new home, and so forth, is extremely hard on the older person. Usually more difficult is when the older person must go to live with other family members or to a convalescent home. One feels that much of one's life is being left behind—which it is. No one wants to give up one's home. The person usually experiences grief when this occurs.

Getting used to new appliances and the location of everything in the new home can be frightening, frustrating, and threatening to the older person. Usually something familiar and cherished from the former residence helps the older person adjust.

The trauma of moving to new living quarters can be compounded, particularly if the person has not wanted to move or does not understand why he must do so.

The older person has mountains of stored memories concerning the old residence. It may be the last vestige of independence the person has. He may feel if the house is no longer his, that he will soon die. The place of abode may be the person's security blanket—in the house he feels protected.

Adjusting to living arrangements can be teachable moments for the older adult and for the caregiver.

Adult Readiness for Learning

I have described *some* of the teachable moments for an adult. Others that could have been listed include losing a job because of obsolescence, learning to live with a second or third spouse as a result of widowhood or divorce, learning to live with stepchildren, and disillusionment from many different sources.

The desire for self-fulfillment—to be all that one is capable of becoming—should create many teachable moments in the life of an adult. When one considers all the changes that have occurred during one's lifetime, a person becomes conscious of the great challenge to continue to learn, to be able to keep living successfully in today's world.

Each adult should have goals that include reaching out beyond oneself —goals which call for personal growth, stretching the person far beyond the imagined limits. These goals may be personal goals or dreams. They may involve knowing that someone has faith in you—they believe you can do things you never dreamed possible.

Throughout the normal life span, there must be the desire for continuing personal growth. Human nature looks to the future, believes that things are going to be better. For the Christian, this is hope—belief that you can make a difference because Jesus Christ has made a difference in your own life. Without a vision of the future, life becomes tedious, even meaningless.

Even as one moves into later adulthood, the need for continued growth is evident, for one must continue to make adjustments—to grow, to change.

An adult is ready to learn because throughout life there are issues, problems, people who confront a person for which there may be no ready answer. Havighurst's developmental tasks apply to adults as well as children. Each developmental task produces a "readiness to learn" or a "teachable moment."

Knowles suggested two implications related to readiness to learn. One is the timing of learning. Planning adult learning activities should not be organized around subjects or courses to be studied but around events or activities being experienced by the adult during the particular phase of life. The second implication is the way in which learners are grouped. The key idea is organizing homogeneous groups according to the developmental tasks being experienced. This is what churches seek to do in grouping adults according to age and sex in Bible study groups.

Structuring the Adult Teachable Moment

Bible study groups have been organized along developmental lines—age, sex, marital status, and so forth. A church cannot take advantage of the multitude of adult teachable moments in one hour a week through the Bible teaching program. Bible study lays the foundation upon which a person can build a life. Bible study related to the needs of adults should be provided for every adult in what churches call Sunday School or church school.

A church also needs to have programs that consider the various needs and tasks confronted by an adult during the person's entire life cycle. The Bible speaks to the totality of needs and must be offered as a source of instruction, direction, and guidance for one's life. Most churches have persons within them who have experienced or are experiencing the issues resulting from the various developmental tasks. These persons can offer encouragement and can assist persons to effectively consider and develop some life goals to meet these challenges. Those who have successfully dealt with the issues being experienced can offer guidance, encouragement, and support. Those who are struggling with the task will be strengthened by knowing that they are not alone.

Life is filled with many teachable moments. The church must assist its adults in being complete, whole beings following the apostle Paul's affirmation, "I press on toward the goal for the prize of the upward call of God in Christ Jesus" (Phil. 3:14, NASB).

Notes

1. Raymond M. Rigdon. *Learning Is for Life.* (Nashville: Broadman Press, 1971).

2. Robert J. Havighurst. *Human Development and Education* (New York: Longman, Green and Co., 1953), p. 257.

17

Demythologizing Adult Ministry in the Church

C. Ferris Jordan

Significant progress in reaching the adult religious education challenge is hindered by the existence of myths about adult ministry. In this chapter, myth is used in the sense of inaccurate statements assumed to be true by certain persons but actually false. The myths are perpetuated sometimes by church staff ministers, sometimes by denominational leaders, and sometimes by laypersons. These false beliefs are barriers to innovation, and they interfere with the search for viable alternatives in the effort to upgrade the quality of adult ministry.

The purpose of this chapter is to present some of the more commonly held myths, to offer data that may provide a basis on which to identify the falsehood in each statement, and to stimulate renewed efforts in adult ministry in areas that may have been hindered by the erroneous concepts. The myths will be presented in three categories: myths about adults, myths about adults as learners, and myths about adult ministry and organization.

Myths About Adults

Misconceptions about the adult years and the persons living in that segment of life are widely held. The erroneous ideas are rooted partially in the ignorance created by the long delay in studying adulthood. The false beliefs became more entrenched with the passing of time. Current investigation is focusing the light of truth on the myths. Five myths will be considered here.

Adulthood Is a Plateau Period

Growth and development are strikingly obvious in childhood and youth. From one year to another, one can see progress in physical development, and stages in cognitive development are readily identified. By contrast, change in adulthood appears to occur more slowly and subtly. For these reasons, both trained and untrained observers gave birth to the myth that the most dynamic years in life are the first seventeen. They are followed by a longer, less-eventful span called adulthood, according to the myth. The relative calm of the adult years is interrupted only by the onset of the deterioration produced by old age.

Recent findings in life-span studies have revealed the error of the plateau theory of the adult years. To be sure, preschool, childhood, and youth years are filled with changes. Mental, physical, emotional, and social development do occur at a rapid pace during the first seventeen years. However, the coming of the eighteenth year does not mark the arrival of a plateau of maturity on which change is either inconsequential or nonexistent. Researchers now know that adulthood, including the late years, offers potential for growth and development. It is marked by stages, crises, challenges, disasters, and triumphs. The crises faced and the solutions discovered in adulthood often produce progress as dramatic and far-reaching as some of the advance made in the younger years.

Daniel Levinson suggested that the adult years are marked by alternating periods of stability and instability. In the less-stable years, the life structure is reexamined, goals are evaluated, and values are reconsidered. On the basis of such investigations, an adult builds a new life structure and pursues new goals. According to Levinson's theory, the five-to-seven-year periods of stability are alternating with three-to-four-year transitions.[1] Havighurst's developmental tasks, Erikson's ego stages, Levinson's life-structure theories, and all the other developmental views represented in Part I, chapter 1, contradict the myth that adulthood is a level plateau with few ups and downs and with minimal challenge.

To accept the plateau myth is to fail to take ministry to adults seriously. It is to conclude that the adult years made fewer demands upon a person and offer little opportunity for the church. On the other hand, to understand that adulthood is synonymous with flux, challenge, and potential for growth or decline, is to find stimulation to provide an adult ministry that seeks to meet personal needs and offers resources to help adults enjoy the quality of life Jesus offers.

Adults Have Had Their Day

A second myth is closely aligned with the first. This false belief postulates that adults have already had their day. With life's greatest challenge behind them, adults are set to move through life with little difficulty, according to this view. It is falsely assumed that the religious education experiences of childhood have equipped persons adequately for the adult years. They have little pressing need to continue in Bible study, and they make few demands upon the church's limited resources.

The false claims of this position have contributed to the death of adult education programs in most mainline denominations through the years. In many quarters, Sunday School has been a children's movement. The information and insights acquired in catechetical instruction have been relied upon to sustain adults through the more mature years. Even in those quarters where adult religious education provision has been made, the effort has been minimal and the organization inadequate when compared with the offerings for younger persons.

A very interesting stance taken by Mortimer Adler undercuts the myth that adults have had their day and magnifies the need for quality education for adults. Adler contended that true education, in contrast to schooling, is impossible during childhood and youth. Only adults, with their maturity, experience, and superior capacity to think, can grapple with the complex ideas and achieve the deepest understandings associated with advanced learning, Adler believed. Insisting that the real goal of learning is wisdom, Adler asserted that it takes a lifetime to become wise.[2] Adler's position certainly enhances the view that Christian education programs for adults are absolutely essential as long as adults live. His view about the goal of learning is especially significant for the church, since "The fear of the Lord is the beginning of knowledge" (Prov. 1:7).

Wherever adulthood is perceived to be the dynamic segment of life that it really is, adult programs are vital and are sustained by an appropriate proportion of the church's resources. Adults are considered to be a viable part of the outreach, teaching, and worship ministries of the congregation. When adulthood is properly understood adults will be viewed as persons in life's prime time, not as individuals whose opportunity has passed.

Adults Are All Alike

A third myth about adults assumes that they are a homogeneous group that does not require grouping grading decisions. From this point of view, a closely graded grouping plan is necessary for preschoolers, children, and youth to accomodate their very distinct life stages. Their motor and cognitive skills are changing, and their interests vary with their life stages. Therefore, distinct groupings that acknowledge these changes are desirable to facilitate outreach and teaching with children and youth.

However, all adults are alike and can be grouped without regard to age, sex, or other factors with only negligible negative impact upon religious education efforts, according to proponents of this third myth.

The truth is that adults' interests and circumstances vary widely. With regard to circumstances, some are married, but many are single; some are parents and/or grandparents, others are childless; some are quite affluent, others are poverty-stricken, and most are somewhere between those extremes on the socioeconomic scale; some are employed in the professions, many are clerical employees, some are in various management-level positions, and not a few are engaged in jobs regarded as necessary but menial by the world's standards. Educationally, adults range from the illiterate to those who hold terminal degrees. A great variety of circumstances does indeed exist in the adult population.

Adult interests are also varied. They are closely correlated with adults' ages and developmental stages. Since adulthood encompasses such a broad age and numerous developmental periods, it follows that a wide variety of interests are included. "A particular life situation or a complexus of events related to stage of human development sets up learning requirements, expectations, needs, interests, and aspirations that may not be present in other life situations or at other stages of development," according to adult education specialist Leon McKenzie.[3] The most effective religious education efforts are directed toward adults' interests, needs, and problems. A learning leader will be in best position to capture the interest and need-related teachable moments[4] when adults are grouped so that the persons present are in similar life stages.

Adult differences continue throughout the adult years. In fact, in the latter years individuation becomes even more pronounced.[5]

Linking adults' readiness to learn with the needs of the various developmental stages does not eliminate the possibility of and need for intergenerational experiences in adult education. Sharing across generation lines about life's choices and challenges is valuable. However, if all learning settings are provided without regard to grouping that brings together adults of similar age and interest, churches may miss their best opportunities to focus Bible study on life's transitions.[6] Age-based grouping seems to hold the greatest potential for bringing together adults of similar circumstances, transition points, and needs. Interest grouping also offers a good alternative for adult Christian education. Under no circumstances can the most effective religious education be offered by ignoring the diversity that makes adulthood the fertile learning field that it is.

Adults Will Not Change

Perhaps one of the most devastating myths is the belief that adults will not change. Based on experience with some adults who have been reluctant to change and on the commonly held notion that aging always brings a conservative stance that discourages change, many staff and laypersons in church settings have concluded that adults are hopelessly set in their own ways. Holding to this myth squelches all incentive to provide stimulating learning experiences and to seek innovations that will offer a challenging adult ministry.

The tragedy is that those who adhere to this myth fail to recognize that adults are constantly dealing with change in their lives and in their world. That reality has great implications for adult Christian education. Aslanian and Brickell expressed the relationship between the reality of change and the need for learning.

> Adults never outgrow their need to learn. Change touches the life of every adult, although it touches life at some points more often than at others and it touches some lives more often than others. Whenever change comes, early or late, and to whomever it comes, rich or poor, learning is one way of dealing with it. There are no types of adults, black or white, educated or not, blue collar or white collar, who do not use learning to accommodate the changes in their lives.[7]

Adult survival requires coping with change. To say adults will not change is inaccurate. Perhaps it is true that some adults tend to resist change in the church because that is one area of life over which they still can exercise control and enjoy the stability associated with maintaining the status quo. However, even there they will change when they are convinced the change is desirable and worth the cost.

Elaine Dickson studied change and concluded that the elements associated with change may be expressed in this formula: $A+B+C>D$ = change.[8] The symbols in the formula may be translated as follows:

A—Significant level of dissatisfaction with things as they are

B—Awareness of a better condition

C—Knowledge of first steps toward the better alternative

> —Greater than

D—Cost of the change

Dickson suggests that when adults' significant dissatisfaction with their present condition is added to an awareness of a better condition plus the initial steps toward that improvement to produce a sum that is greater than the cost of the change, they will likely opt for the change.

Leaders in adult education who are willing to use educational experiences to heighten the dissatisfaction level and to increase awareness of a better condition will find adults amenable to change. Those who seek to impose change without proper preparation will discover that adults will resent and resist the change. Leading adults to desire and accept change requires time and patience. Haste makes waste and leads to the false conclusion that adults will not change.

Adults Are Poor Prospects for the Church

Adults are so hard to reach that they are unlikely prospects for the church. So goes another myth that is a barrier to aggressive outreach to adults. Because a show of hands in congregations at Christian conference centers or in revival services reveals that most Christians present were converted when they were older children, many observers have concluded that adults are so difficult to reach that evangelistic and other outreach efforts should be directed toward the younger generations. Moreover, adherents to the myth that adults will not change give added impetus to the false idea that adults are poor prospects for the church. In a day when four out of five prospects for most churches are adults and in a time when adults represent a greater proportion of the population of the United States than at any other time in her history, the facts that contradict this myth need to be brought to light.

The preponderance of persons converted at a young age who are present in most Christian audiences does magnify the receptivity of the young to the gospel. It highlights the need to seize every opportunity to share the good news in a manner that is appropriate for the age of the young recipients and that is not manipulative of their pliable wills. However, the small number of people who indicate conversion in the adult years does not bespeak an unwillingness of adults to receive the gospel so much as it serves to indicate the failure of the church to give high priority to adult outreach. Churches too often have yielded to the temptation to concentrate on younger, more responsive prospects while neglecting outreach to slow-to-respond adults. The poor adult response record is more a barometer of church concern for adults than of the level of adult interest in spiritual things.

Jesus' own approach to ministry is a testimony to the fact that adults are worthy prospects for a church's outreach efforts. He called adults as His apostles. He made them prime movers in the church He established. His strategy in outreach was adult focused. Adults like Nicodemus, Zacchaeus, and the woman of Sychar were a priority with Him. His conversations, illustrations, and messages were addressed clearly to the adult generation. The record of His ministry in the four Gospels reveals a concentration on adults. Jesus did not buy the myth that adults are poor prospects.

The 184,875 adults received by baptism into Southern Baptist churches in a recent year defy the myth that adults cannot be reached.[9] Moreover, contemporary churches that are reporting a good evangelistic harvest annually are usually congregations giving serious attention to unreached adults and reporting a high percentage of adults in the persons added to their membership. When churches are willing to act with compassion toward adults and to use a cultivative approach in reaching them, they discover that adults will drop their facade of indifference and become receptive to the gospel. Just as adults have a teachable moment with regard to learning in all other areas of life, they have a point of receptivity when their spiritual need intersects with an opportunity to hear the gospel. Leaders in adult ministry who care enough to create a climate in which points of receptivity to the gospel are likely to flourish and to use those opportunities prayerfully and sensitively will discover that the adult outreach field is white unto harvest.

Myths About Adults as Learners

We will now turn our attention to some myths about adults as learners. These false beliefs have created barriers to learning for adults and have fostered a complacency about adult education efforts in the church.

Aging Has a Negative Effect Upon Learning

The proponents of the myth that adults cannot learn are not so numerous as they were earlier in the century. But there are popular fallacies about adult learning that reveal reservation about adults' capacity for learning even in the enlightened final quarter of the twentieth century. According to popular perception, a decline in capacity to learn is anticipated as persons grow older. "You can't teach an old dog new tricks" is still a common reaction when adult learning is mentioned.

Popular notions notwithstanding, scientific research has revealed that aging per se is no deterrent to learning. Polly Cooper was right on target in reporting those research findings when she wrote:

> Current research offers evidence that any adult can learn anything he was ever capable of learning if he wants to strongly enough. Any deficit in learning that occurs as adults mature seems to be related to decline in speed of learning, not in the capacity to learn. This means that any adult can learn anything he was ever capable of learning, if given enough time.[10]

In fact, studies have shown that senior adults actually have an advantage over their younger counterparts in learning situations that require ability to grasp ideas and concepts, make judgments, and relate new insights to concepts previously held.[11] This knowledge is especially important for the Christian and for Christian educators because these are the abilities believers need most for continued growth in personal discipleship.

Speed in learning does decline with age. This is due partially to physiological changes and in part to psychological reasons.[12] The latter factor includes the reality that older persons may be more concerned about accuracy than younger subjects and thus inclined to take more time.[13] The assumption that decline in speed of learning was synonymous with decline in capacity for learning was based on timed intelligence tests. Once adults were no longer required to take tests measuring their speed, their capacity for learning was shown to have changed very little between ages twenty and sixty.[14] Irving Lorge attributed the decline in rate of learning to "losses in visual acuity, auditory acuity, and reaction time."[15] Such factors as increased fear of failure, desire to be accurate, retardation caused by unfamiliar stimuli or setting, and an altered attitude of adults to learning are among other factors cited by Lorge.[16]

Robert Proctor offered an accurate summary statement about the relationship between aging and the capacity to learn when he wrote, "Motivation, method, and opportunity are more important than the age factor."[17] He continued with these comments:

> The adult who thinks he cannot learn will not find much support for his belief in the findings of scientific studies done during the last half century. On the contrary, he will find evidence that he can learn anything he ever could have learned if he wants to badly enough.[18]

The challenge confronting churches is to address the interests and life needs that motivate adults to learn, to feature learning methodology appropriate for adult learners, and to offer opportunities for adults to learn in the midst of life's complex issues and pressured schedules. Given the motivation, method, and opportunity, adults will learn.

Adults Are Not Interested in Learning

Another myth closely associated with the belief that adults' ability to learn declines with age is the false notion that adults are not interested in learning. Leaders in adult religious education plagued with static or declining participation in the programs they seek to plan and maintain are likely to be victimized by this myth. But much evidence exists to prove that adults not only are interested in learning but also are engaged in learning activities.

Adults do not have an aversion to learning. A group of researchers in Toronto, Canada, discovered in a study of adults that "almost everyone undertakes at least one or two major learning efforts a year, and some individuals undertake as many as 15 or 20." They also found that it is

> common for a man or woman to spend 700 hours a year at learning projects. Some persons spend less than 100 hours, but others spend more than 2,000 hours in episodes in which the person's intent to learn or change is clearly his primary motivation.[19]

Informal learning is the pursuit of many adults as they read books, develop a new hobby, or accept the challenge of the do-it-yourself society. Formal educational programs for adults have led them to enroll in night classes that range from bookkeeping to real estate to aerobics. The number of older students enrolled in colleges and universities is steadily growing. In 1979 part-time students, most of them over twenty-five, accounted for 41 percent of the total enrollment in all colleges and universities in the United States. And they made up 64 percent of the enrollment in community and junior colleges.[20]

Adult interest and participation in learning may be viewed from still another perspective. Learning is change, and the process of life requires continuing change. This fact implies continuous learning. Adults are always learning, then, whether they are enrolled in a course or not. Pointing out that "we have become a society in which adults learn everywhere," Carol Aslanian and Henry Brickell wrote:

> This means that learning has become a characteristic of adult behavior, a pervasive and perhaps even a necessary aspect of adulthood in our society. It has become an activity without a fixed, predictable location—an

activity that can and does take place anywhere. This means, in turn, that social institutions other than schools are being redesigned to accomodate adult learning activities and, in many cases, to provide them.[21]

Adults *are* interested in learning. Churches can capture that interest when they offer learning opportunities that relate to adults' social roles and aid them in their quest for answers to life's perplexing questions.

Adults Learn Best by Listening

Still another myth that has determined the methodology of adult religious education endeavors is that adults learn best by listening. This false idea has given rise to teachers who teach solely or primarily by lecturing. Based on this myth, adults have conditioned themselves to be relatively passive in adult learning experiences in church. They often feel threatened by any effort to encourage a more active level of participation.

The myth has deep historical roots. Teaching as telling became common practice in pre-Gutenberg societies when printed materials were unavailable for individual study. That approach to teaching was reinforced in medieval universities when the teacher was perceived to be a content specialist who dictated a standard text such as the work of Peter Lombard and allowed students time to make copious notes. The lecture consisted of a series of glosses on the text. Even after books became available to students, teachers continued to follow the pattern of teaching as telling.

Kant received wide acclaim because he departed from the custom of "telling the text" to sharing his own thoughts. Civil authorities who wanted to keep a tight rein on independent thought and critical inquiry frowned upon Kant's approach.[22] To this day, his more creative approach to teaching is having difficulty catching on in institutions of higher learning and in adult education endeavors in the church.

Jesus offered insight into the error of the myth that listening is the primary avenue to learning when He said on more than one occasion, "Who hath ears to hear, let him hear" (Matt. 13:9). Even hearing requires concentrated listening. Participation of that quality occurs when the learner chooses to hear, and that choice is related to the learner's motivation. Listening is never enough. Understanding must also occur. The former never guarantees the latter, as Isaiah 6:9-10 clearly reveals. In Christian education efforts, some adults fail to understand because they have hardened their hearts. But others lack understanding while earnestly desiring to know. Understanding is enhanced when adult learners ask questions; interact with the teacher and fellow learners; and engage in learning activities that stimulate analysis, evaluation, and comprehension. These dimensions of learning are enhanced when learners are encouraged to verbalize their ideas.

Moreover, hearing and understanding are never the ultimate objective in adult Christian education. The Great Commission mandates that the church teach disciples to *practice* all that Jesus commanded (Matt. 28:-20). Jesus said that "everyone who listens to my words and practices their teaching" (Matt. 7:24, Williams) is prudent. James warned against the self-deception that is associated with listening to God's truth without obeying it (Jas. 1:22-23). Christian teaching must lead learners to go beyond listening. Teachers must utilize learning activities that stimulate commitment, include follow-through projects, and encourage assimilation into daily practice.

Adults Will Not Respond to a Variety of Learning Activities

Adults prefer to be listeners in learning situations. Introducing a variety of learning activities that require responses from the learners will pose a threat to most adult learners that will be a hindrance to their learning. Here is another myth about adults as learners.

The facts are that many adults have had limited experience with a variety of learning activities and will be reluctant to participate in them. However, when teachers are willing to meet learners where they are and to introduce new teaching methods gradually and patiently, most adults not only will cooperate but also will profit from the learning experiences.

Teaching as stimulation of inquiry should be preferred over teaching as telling in adult education if adults are to learn how to learn and to think independently. Skills in learning and thinking are essential for adults to be equipped adequately for the demands of lifelong learning. Moreover, if learning were only cognitive, perhaps the myth would be less damaging to adult education. But learning must affect the whole person. Learning that is most lasting has cognitive, affective, volitional, and behavioral aspects, and the effective leader will get adults involved at all those levels. Teaching-learning approaches are the tools used by the learning leader to achieve the learner activity that is relevant to the stated objective of a learning session.

Effective workers always rely upon a variety of tools. In learning, some of the tools will require primarily leader activity while others will depend upon learner activity.[23] The basic teaching-learning methods which the adult learning leader should master are lecture, questions-answers, group discussion, case studies (life situations), and brainstorming.[24] Learning to use these approaches effectively will assure learner involvement in the teaching-learning process and will give the teacher raw materials from which to develop more innovative approaches such as attitude scales, interviews, panel forum, current event analysis, listening teams, and problem-solving activities.

The use of a variety of teaching-learning methods will encourage adult learners to think, to do problem solving and self-evaluation, to express their feelings, and to deal with conflicting ideas that may be expressed by participants in the learning experience. Wise learning leaders will not try to introduce all these approaches overnight, but neither will they be misled by the myth that adults will not tolerate variety in learning activities so that they deprive learners of the best avenues to learning.

Adults Will Tolerate Poor Teaching

A final myth related to adults as learners is that adults will tolerate poor teaching. In many cases, teachers of adults in the church have been selected after the best teachers have been assigned to younger learners on the assumption that adult learners do not require as much creativity and preparation on the part of teachers as do their younger counterparts. To be sure, some of the more church-oriented adults will come faithfully no matter who the teachers are and what approaches are used. However, even they are learning at a minimal level and eventually may demonstrate their disapproval by an increasingly infrequent attendance pattern. The less church-minded adult will continue to be uninvolved in religious education until the quality of teaching improves.

Adult learners in the church are volunteer learners. Volunteers choose to participate in learning for a variety of reasons, but they usually fall into one or a combination of three sub-groups.[25] The *goal-oriented* learners use learning to gain specific objectives such as learning to deal with particular family problems. The second group, the *activity-oriented* learners, participates in learning primarily for the sake of the activity itself rather than to learn. The third group, the *learning-oriented,* pursues learning for its own sake. Perhaps the activity-oriented learners will continue to come to an adult learning experience in the church just to have somewhere to go or to enjoy the company of the group. But even they may look for greener pastures if the experience becomes too boring. Certainly the goal-oriented and learning-oriented learners will seek a more stimulating environment if their needs are not being met.

The quality of the teacher and the teaching do make a difference to adults. Educator Frank C. Pearce described the ideal teacher of adults as "people-oriented, more interested in people than things, more interested in individuality than conformity, more interested in finding solutions than in following rules. The teacher must have understanding, flexibility, patience, humor, practicality, creativity and preparation."[26] Florence Nelson said the teacher "must meet three requirements before being able to teach adults: a love for your subject, a desire to share it, and basic competence in the subject."[27] Commenting on the three requirements, William Draves noted that the problem students point to *least* in evaluating classes is the teacher's knowledge of the subject. Most complaints arise from the teacher's inability to share that knowledge effectively.[28]

Participation in adult education in the church will increase when more attention is given to the enlistment and training of teachers who love their subject, care about the learners, and guide the learning experiences skillfully.

Myths About Adult Organization and Ministry

A third cluster of myths relates to adult organization and ministry in the church. Adult work has been neglected in most churches because congregations have operated off assumptions related to several myths that will be discussed here.

Churches Must Reach Young Persons First to Assure Future Ministry

The younger generation is the church of tomorrow and therefore must have priority in a church's appropriation of its resources. Nothing must be spared in financing, staffing, and scheduling to assure that preschoolers, children, and youth have the very best. Since adults have had their day and are generally resistant to change, the more pliable and responsive age groups deserve center stage and priority. The beliefs set forth above comprise the myth that churches must assure their future ministry by giving priority to reaching the younger generation.

Lyle Schaller, a respected consultant in church administration and planning, is among those who have shown the fallacy of the myth. He pointed out that such thinking was more appropriate in 1790, when one half of the United States population was under seventeen years of age, but it is totally out of touch with reality in the closing decades of the twentieth century when the adult population is mushrooming. Schaller has appealed not only to the demographic picture to undercut the myth under discussion but also to his own research findings about congregational growth patterns. He wrote:

> Studies of hundreds of congregations have shown that it is rare for more than one-third of the eighteen-year-olds of one era to be active members of that same congregation a decade later. The usual proportion for city churches is between 10 and 20 percent. The most common characteristic of eighteen-year-olds is they move away and/or they soon "marry into" another congregation.[29]

The congregation that focuses attention upon ministering to younger persons in an effort to assure replacement of its aging members should not ignore Schaller's findings. Schaller has also provided evidence that growing congregations have revealed that the overwhelming majority of adult members are first-generation Christians; they did not grow up in that congregation.[30] These findings seem to indicate that growing churches are adult focused in outreach, evangelism, and ministry.

No one has articulated a better response to the myth presently under discussion than John T. Sisemore. He wrote:

> Churches have justified their neglect of adults by proclaiming that the children are the church of tomorrow. To be sure, this concept is true; but it is only a part of a larger truth. The full truth is this: The children are the hope of *the day after tomorrow,* the youth are the hope of *tomorrow,* but adults are the only hope for *today.* Lose the children, and the church will die in *two* generations; lose the youth, and the church will die in *one* generation; lose the adults, and the church may very well die in *this* generation[31]

The best way to assure quality ministry to the younger generation and to guarantee a church's future is to reach the present adult generation.

Quality Adult Religious Education Is Not a Priority in Building a Strong Church

A second myth akin to the one just discussed is that quality religious education for adults is not a priority in building a strong church. Proponents of this myth tend to place preaching, meaningful worship experiences, aggressive evangelism, and a strong outreach program above religious education in their priority system. Others who adhere to the myth recognize the value of religious education in developing a church, but they fail to appreciate the contribution made by adult religious education.

Religious education was a priority item with Jesus. He spent much of his earthly sojourn in a teaching ministry. He bade people to learn of Him (Matt. 11:29). His followers were referred to often as "disciples," meaning learners. When He gave His marching orders to the church, Jesus commanded her to make disciples and to keep on teaching His followers to obey all that He commanded (Matt. 28:19-20).

The New Testament church emphasized the teaching ministry (Acts 2:42). The apostle Paul placed a high priority on teaching in his personal ministry (see Acts 11:26 and Acts 19:8-10 for examples). Paul listed "apt to teach" as a qualification for pastors (1 Tim. 3:2) because he knew the value of an emphasis upon Christian education in the church.

There is a strong biblical base not only for a high priority on religious education in the church but also for an adult-focused emphasis in the teaching ministry. No evidence exists that the Christian education in the New Testament church was for anyone other than adults. A strong emphasis was placed upon teaching children, but the primary responsibility for instruction was in the hands of the parents, and the setting was in the home.

Contemporary churches that are growing and displaying vitality in other ways have strong adult religious education programs. Reaching and teaching adults are essential for every church, for adults set the pace, determine the tone and atmosphere of the congregation, provide the needed leadership and financial resources, and shape the quality of family life present in the homes of the membership. Quality religious education for adults will go a long way toward guaranteeing that a church is in the best position to do the best possible job with persons of all age groups.

Failure to reach and teach adults has short-circuited many efforts that churches have made with other age groups. A 1981 study was done by a Baton Rouge, Louisiana, church that became concerned about losing so many teenagers from active participation. Over the years they had lost 38 percent of their youth, and one year they had lost as many as 73 percent. The study revealed these interesting facts:

1. Where both parents were faithful and active, ninety-three percent of the youth remained faithful.
2. Where only one parent was faithful and active, seventy-four percent of the youth remained faithful.
3. Where parents were reasonably active, fifty-three percent of the youth remained faithful.
4. Where parents were very infrequent in Sunday School and worship attendance, only six percent of the youth remained faithful.[32]

Quality adult religious education must become a high priority in every church. Taking that approach will represent a proper response to the biblical mandate that the church teach. It will develop adult Christians who know what they believe, are willing to share their faith, and are committed to the church and her mission. Only then will they be in the best position to teach the younger generation in their families and in the church.

Young Adults Are Not Interested in Spiritual Things

A third myth related to adult organization and ministry is that young adults have little interest in the church and spiritual concerns. The myth seems to be fueled by the dropout pattern that afflicts churches as persons in the mid-teen years drop out of active participation and remain inactive until they are married and have children. This dropout rate has encouraged churches to expect that kind of performance and to offer fewer organizational options for younger adults.

The previously discussed relationship between degree of parental involvement and teenage attrition is seldom considered by many churches. What is blamed on decreasing interest in spiritual things may, in many cases, be attributed to a church strategy that set out to reach children and youth without a similar concern for reaching their parents. The loss of teen and young adult participation is then the fruit of misplaced priority in church outreach and ministry, not the manifestation of a declining interest inherent in the teen and young adult years.

The young adult years are stressful. Many pressing needs are clamoring for attention in each person's life. During the years of transition from adolescence into adulthood, about eighteen to twenty-two years of age, two primary tasks are demanding the expenditure of a great deal of energy; namely, achieving emotional and psychological distance from the family of childhood and achieving a beachhead in the adult world.[33] The early adult years are marked by eight developmental tasks, according to Robert Havighurst.[34] The first five of the tasks are directly related to family living. The other two have to do with occupational choice and finding a congenial social group. Working on all these issues can lead young adults to neglect the church. On the other hand, the need to address these issues can create in young adults a receptivity to the spiritual resources of a church that is in tune with today's young adult population and reaches out to them with sensitivity.

The time of transition from adolescence to young adulthood can be a time of restless uncertainty in the religious and moral life. "Renovation of the personal-belief system is the norm, not the exception, during the period [young adult transition]," according to Coleman. He continued:

> The values and beliefs inherited from parents must be traded for internalized values and beliefs based on the individual's growing identity as a self-directed adult. This does not mean that the religious beliefs and moral principles learned from parents will be rejected. It does mean that these will be retained, if at all, because they have been tested, subjected to critical examination, and reaffirmed by the young adult. And some leave the faith of their mothers and fathers behind.[35]

Once the transition into the adult world has been made, young adults continue to search for a faith that is really their own. With the coming of more responsibilities and the tests of life, they discover a need for something more secure than they may have found when in revolt against the faith of their parents, but they do not want to return to the faith of their fathers, so an intense searching goes on.

The apparent disinterest in spiritual things in young adults may really be their own attempt to deal with the issues mentioned in the previous paragraphs. Many churches may contribute to a sense of alienation in young adults. One study of young adults who felt that separation and expressed a great deal of dissatisfaction with the organized church revealed five factors which they identified as contributing to that distance. The five were: (1) the church's reluctance to allow young adults opportunity of full participation in its life; (2) the lack of meaning found in hymns that fail to speak to the contemporary world, in sermons that are boring, and in services so predictable and repetitive that they fail to provide a meaningful channel for worship; (3) the authoritative pronouncements by ministers and others that allow little room for differences of opinion and the possibility that gray areas exist on some ethical issues; (4) hypocrisy in the congregation; and (5) insistence upon a creedal belief system that leaves no room for a personal or experiential theology.[36]

Young adults are interested in spiritual resources to help them deal with the issues of their lives. Many of them will respond when churches offer units of organization that group young adults with their peers engaged in a similar pilgrimage. They will resist efforts to group them with older adults whom they perceive to be too far beyond their immediate concerns. Young adults *will* stay involved in churches that offer sound fellowship groups, guidance in achieving marriage or in making a wholesome adjustment to unmarried life, assistance in finding work that is compatible with God's call to serve Him and humanity, guidance in assuming responsibility as a Christian citizen, and help in establishing a faith in response to God's call and in daily reliance upon the Holy Spirit as a wise Counselor. Young adults will respond to leaders in whom they have confidence, to programs in which they have a voice, and to congregations in which they find a loving atmosphere that perceives each person to be of value and every contribution to be important.

Middle Adults Have Life in Tow and Do Not Need Special Attention as Do Young and Senior Adults

Another myth that is hindering adult ministry and organization is the belief that middle-aged adults have achieved a stability that has enabled them to get life under control, so they need less attention and fewer special programs than adults in other age brackets. The myth's existence can be proven if one studies church structures only casually. The burden of financial support and leadership responsibility rests upon adults in the middle years. However, seldom do church leaders plan any special retreats, seminars, or workshops specifically designed for median adult needs.

Nearly-wed and newlywed seminars are offered for young adults. Marriage-enrichment retreats are planned for younger couples. Senior adults have their own choir and their monthly get-togethers for fellowship, excursions, and inspirational programs. Median adults do much of the planning and financing of such ministries but are seldom recipients of similar opportunities. These facts are no plea to do less for young and senior adults but to remedy the neglect of middle adults rooted in the fallacy that they have life in tow.

The truth is that the middle adult years are marked by transitions, challenges, crises that are fraught with great potential for growth or disaster. The outcome is determined by the median adult's spiritual reserves and values. Someone has referred to median adults as the "pooped generation." The nomenclature may be quite accurate. The middle years are marked by tension as adults seeks to meet the needs of their younger children trying to achieve independence and their aging parents who are desperately holding on to an independence that is waning. The middle-aged couple is at a critical stage in marriage caused by the empty nest, the physiological changes in each spouse, and the career goals that may have set themselves against marital harmony. Preparation for retirement is also beginning to demand attention.

With all these challenges before them, middle adults do not have all the answers. Their lives are not safe and secure. They need to receive from the church, not just give for her support and maintenance. Contemporary churches who group middle adults for the best possible interaction with peers, who select leaders sensitive to median adult challenges, and who offer programs that address middlescent concerns in appealing formats not only will meet the needs of a growing segment of the population but also will assure the vital participation of middle adults in their life and ministry.

Summary

Churches are being hindered by myths about adults, about adults as learners, and about adult organization and ministry. So long as priorities are determined, programs are planned, and organizational patterns are set on the basis of these fallacies, the adult generation will go on unreached and spiritually underdeveloped. When churches can abandon these untruths and half-truths, they will be able to build a spirit and develop programs that will enable them to meet the challenges of the great adult frontier.

Notes

1. Daniel J. Levinson, *The Seasons of Man's Life* (New York: Alfred A. Knopf, Inc., 1978). See the discussion in chapter 2 of this book.

2. Mortimer Adler, "Why Only Adults Can Learn," *Invitation to Lifelong Learning,* ed. Ronald Gross (Chicago: Follett Publishing Co., 1982), pp. 88-102.

3. Leon McKenzie, *The Religious Education of Adults* (Birmingham, Ala.: Religious Education Press, 1982), p. 123.

4. The teachable moment concept is attributed to Robert Havighurst, *Developmental Tasks and Education* (New York: Longman, 3rd ed. 1979), u.p.u.

5. Carroll B. Freeman, *The Senior Adult Years* (Nashville: Broadman Press, 1979), p. 60.

6. Carol Aslanian and Henry Brickell concluded from research that "the learning a person undertakes is related to the transition he or she is undergoing. The transitions a person undergoes are related to his or her circumstances in life. . . . Every adult who learned because of a transition pointed to a specific event in his or her life that signaled, precipitated, or triggered the transition and thus the learning." See " 'Passages' of Adulthood and Triggers to Learning" in Gross, *Invitation to Lifelong Learning,* pp. 162, 164.

7. Gross, Ibid., p. 162.

8. Elaine Dickson, *Say No, Say Yes to Change* (Nashville: Broadman Press, 1982).

9. *The Quarterly Review,* XLIV, No. 4, July-Sept. 1984, p. 21.

10. Polly Cooper, *How to Guide Adults* (Nashville: Convention Press, 1982), p. 71.

11. Carroll B. Freeman, *The Senior Adult Years* (Nashville: Broadman Press, 1979), p. 49.

12. J. R. Kidd, *How Adults Learn* (Chicago: Association Press, 1973), p. 82.

13. Ibid.

14. Irving Lorge, articles in *Review of Educational Research:* XI (Dec. 1941); XIV (Dec. 1944); XVII (Dec. 1947); XX (June 1950).

15. Irving Lorge, cited by J. R. Kidd, *How Adults Learn,* p. 83.

16. Ibid.

17. Robert A. Proctor, *Too Old to Learn?* (Nashville: Broadman Press, 1967), p. 36.

18. Ibid., p. 37.

19. Allen Tough, *The Adult's Learning Projects,* 2nd ed. (Austin, Tex.: Learning Concepts, 1979), p. 1.

20. Bette Everett Hamilton, "Adult Part-time Students and the Higher Education Act," *Lifelong Learning: The Adult Years,* Oct. 1979, p. 10; reprinted with permission from *Change* magazine, Vol. II, No. 4 (May-June 1979). Copyrighted by the Council on Learning, NBW Tower, New Rochelle, NY 10801.

21. Carol Aslanian and Henry Bickell, " 'Passages' of Adulthood and Triggers to Learning" in Gross, *Invitation to Lifelong Learning,* p. 159.

22. For further information about this historical background, see Leon McKenzie, *The Religious Education of Adults* (Birmingham, Ala.: Religious Education Press, 1982), pp. 191-192.

23. The "teaching-learning method" and "tool" language are borrowed from Polly Cooper, *How to Guide Adults* (Nashville: Convention Press, 1982), p. 153.

24. These basic activities are well adapted to adult learning in the church. Group discussion, over-the-shoulder demonstration, show-and-do involvement, formal classroom instruction, and the project format are the primary learning formats for informal adult-oriented teaching suggested by William A. Draves, *How to Teach Adults* (Manhattan, Kans.: The Learning Resources Network, 1984), pp. 61-63. They, too, have potential for adult religious education.

25. C. O. Houle, *The Inquiring Mind* (Madison: University of Wisconsin Press, 1961). "Although Houle's sensitive study of the motivations for adult learning was done twenty years ago, his three-way typology remains the single most influential motivational study today," according to K. Patricia Cross, *Adults as Learners* (San Francisco: Jossey-Bass Publishers, 1981), p. 82.

26. Cited by William A. Draves, *How to Teach Adults,* p. 17.

27. Florence Nelson, *Yes, You Can Teach* (St. Paul, Minn.: Carma Press, 1977), p. 7, cited by Draves, *How to Teach Adults.*

28. Draves, *How to Teach Adults,* p. 17.

29. Lyle E. Schaller, "Proverbs of Church Planning," *Search,* Fall 1980, pp. 12-13, cited by Lucien E. Coleman, Jr., *Understanding Today's Adults* (Nashville: Convention Press, 1982), pp. 29-30.

30. Ibid.

31. John T. Sisemore, "The Challenge of Adult Christian Education," in Roy B. Zuck and Gene A. Getz, *Adult Education in the Church* (Chicago: Moody Press, 1970), pp. 14-15.

32. Research findings reported by Tal Bonham, "Growth-a-Gram" in *Ohio Baptist Messenger,* 3 Feb. 1983, p. 7 and quoted in *NSM News,* publication of National Student Ministries Department of the Baptist Sunday School Board, May, 1983.

33. For a more thorough statement of the early transition and the young adult years, consult Daniel J. Levinson, *Seasons of a Man's Life,* and Gail Sheehy, *Passages: Predictable Passages of Adult Life.*

34. Robert J. Havighurst, *Human Development and Education* (New York: David McKay Company, Inc., 1953).

35. Lucien E. Coleman, Jr. *Understanding Today's Adults,* p. 95.

36. Larry A. LeFeber, *Building a Young Adult Ministry* (Valley Forge, Pa.: Judson Press, pp. 20-21.

PART IV:

The Challenge and Future of Adult Christian Education

What's ahead in Adult Christian education? What are the challenges facing adult Christian education? These issues are addressed in Part IV.

Chapter 18 focuses on the importance of adults for Christian education. Adults provide the church with many opportunities for evangelism and outreach.

With the rapid advance of modern technologies, their potential use in adult Christian education needs to be explored. Chapter 19 identifies the new technologies and points out both advantages and disadvantages each has for adult Christian education.

Chapter 20 takes a futuristic look at adult Christian education—at innovative, creative approaches that can be used. This chapter suggests some ways adult Christian education can be effective in reaching and ministering to adults.

With the increase in the number of adults and the aging of the population, adults' needs must be considered in church staffing. Chapter 21 examines the need, opportunity, challenge, competency skills, training, and job description for a minister to adults.

18

Adults Are the Church Now

Lucien E. Coleman

From 1975 to 1985, the total population of the United States grew by 19.7 million. During the same decade, 23.7 million were added to the ranks of the adult population (18 and older). In other words, the adult population outgrew the general population by 4 million. At the same time, the number of children and youth (under 18) declined by 4 million.

Between now and the year 2000, nearly 21 million more men and women will be added to our escalating adult population. Adults presently make up 73 percent of the U. S. population, and they will account for 76 percent of the total population growth from now until the turn of the century.

Jesus reminded His early followers of the urgency of his mission when He said, "Do you now say, 'There are yet four months, then comes the harvest'? I tell you, lift up your eyes, and see how the fields are already white for harvest" (John 4:35, RSV). These words of our Lord could well apply to the vast throngs of adults populating our nation and our whole planet, today.

The Adult Imperative

Today's churches can ill afford to pursue strategies based on the archaic notion that children and youth must invariably be given top priority in programs of evangelism, education, recreation, and ministry. This is not to suggest that Christian concern for the young should diminish, but, rather, that churches ought to strike an appropriate balance in the allocation of resources. To put it simply, they should devote 73 percent of their resources to reaching, teaching, and making disciples of those who account for 73 percent of the population.

Speech makers often romanticize the young by calling them "our leaders of tomorrow" and "the hope of the future." But this point of view is more sentimental than factual. The truth is, today's adults will provide leadership for church and society today, tomorrow, and even the day

278

after tomorrow. And they will determine, in large measure, whether or not there will be any tomorrow. In this sense, adults are the hope of the present and the future as well.

A church glories in its children, but a church depends upon adults. Adults are the "prime movers" in the life of a congregation, just as they are in society as a whole. They provide the leadership, pay the bills, furnish wisdom and "know-how," make strategic decisions, and guide the younger generation, As parents, they profoundly influence the religious attitudes and practices of their children.

Sharing the Gospel with Today's Adults

In the late 1940s, the postwar "baby boom" created a tidal wave of humanity which has rolled through our population statistics in every succeeding decade. In the 1950s, churches experienced surges of enrollments in their elementary departments, and employed scores of children's workers. A decade later, the children of the baby boom were in their adolescence, and church youth programs came into their own. In the late 1960s and early 1970s, they became the "counterculture," crowding into rock concerts and staging demonstrations on college campuses. During these years, they commanded the attention of politicians, sociologists, and church leaders alike.

But, now, members of that generation are well into their adult years—some have turned forty. They are the parents of our teenagers. They occupy significant positions in the political arena, the educational system, the communications industry, the military establishment, and the business world. Their parents assumed that they would come back to church when they had settled down with families of their own. But many never did. Today, they present one of our greatest evangelistic challenges and constitute a vast source of potential power for carrying out the work of Christ on earth.

A few years ago, when church "bus ministries" were in vogue, it was widely assumed that adults could be reached for Christ through their children. If children could be enlisted, so the theory went, their parents and older relatives would eventually follow. Such a scheme stands in sharp contrast to the New Testament pattern. Jesus proclaimed the gospel to adults, and those who confessed faith in Him were adults. Children appear in the Gospel narratives from time to time. Jesus loved them, healed them, and used them as examples in His teaching. But the products of His evangelistic ministry were adult believers.

The early church followed their Lord's example. In the entire Book of Acts, there is no instance in which an adult became a believer as a result of the conversion of a child. Even in the accounts of "household conversions," in which an adult convert's family members (and servants) came to Christ (see Acts 16:15,31-33; 18:8), the sequence was always the same; adult converts led the way.

Evangelizing adults in contemporary society is made more difficult by the fact that most unchurched women and men have enough religion to satisfy them, but not enough to save them. Generally, they are not antagonistic toward religion. They tend to embrace religion as an ideal but reject it in its institutional forms. George Gallup, Jr., and David Poling wrote in 1980:

> Many Americans belong to the "not quite Christian" category: They believe, but without strong convictions. They want the fruits or reward of faith, but seem to dodge the responsibilities and obligations. They say that they are Christian but often without a visible connection to a congregation or religious fellowship.[1]

These authors cited a surprising series of findings from a major study of unchurched Americans. They found that 64 percent of these nonattenders, nonbelongers, and noncontributors said they believed that Jesus is God or the Son of God; 68 percent of them said they believed in the resurrection of Christ; no less than two out of five said that they had made a personal commitment to Jesus Christ; and 76 percent of them said they prayed to God.[2]

The same study uncovered disturbing evidence that many adults remain detached from the church because, from their perspective, churches are not what they profess to be. When asked for details, these unchurched adults mentioned the shallow and superficial stance of many church members, the inability of congregations to deal with the basics of faith, the absence of the feeling of excitement or warmth within the church's fellowship, and the self-serving attitude which focused more on raising money for buildings than on addressing the crying needs of humanity.[3]

It may be true, as Gallup and Poling point out, that such criticisms are often the result of distance from and ignorance about congregational life. But, whether or not these images of the church are erroneous, Christian congregations should find in them a reason for self-examination.

One of the great needs of the church today is to recapture the early church's basic evangelistic strategy. Long before the great preachers of Christendom came on the scene, the gospel had conquered the Roman Empire, a gospel passed on by countless witnesses—shopkeepers, traveling merchants, military men, slaves, and men of the sea. Adults introduced other adults to Christ, and authenticated what they said by the way in which they lived.

Adults and Christian Teaching

In a recent book, I shared an opinion that has grown into a fundamental conviction;

> Never before in American Christianity has there been a more urgent need for the church to develop informed, thinking men and women who know how to rightly divide the word of truth, discriminate between biblical revelation and popular folklore, and who have the holy audacity to live out an incarnational faith in a secularized society.[4]

Gallup and Poling believe that this isn't happening. They wrote:

> Earlier surveys have provided the evidence that many parents as well as their children are spiritual illiterates. Many professed Christians can articulate in only the most clumsy fashion the significance of the resurrection of Jesus Christ for the world. While most have Bibles in their home, many have been unable to channel the teaching of Scripture into their lives. Many are unable to even name the four Gospels.[5]

By and large, contemporary congregations have not lived up to the mandate of the Great Commission (Matt. 28:19-20), "teaching them to observe all that I have commanded you" (RSV), and are now reaping the harvest of that omission. Thousands of men and women occupy the pews of their churches weekly without having the most elemental knowledge of basic Christian beliefs. They regularly dole out contributions to sects whose representatives appear at their doors claiming vaguely to be "Christian missionaries." They give willing support to religious charlatans who invade their homes by way of electronic media. In multiplied instances, congregations have permitted winsome perpetrators of strange doctrines to capture their pulpits. Today, bizarre cults and offbeat religious sects flourish in a seedbed of spiritual naiveté. Approximately 27 million Americans report that they have been influenced by such groups.[6]

More subtle than these deviations, but just as insidious, is the tendency of many churchgoing Americans to incorporate the values of Capitol Hill, Wall Street, and Madison Avenue into their belief systems, never realizing that such values are often at odds with the teachings of Jesus.

One of the strongest arguments for adult education in the church is the obligation of Christian parents to instruct their children in the faith. This responsibility is spelled out with unusual clarity in Ephesians 6:4, "Fathers, do not provoke your children to anger, but bring them up in the discipline [*paideia*] and instruction of the Lord" (RSV). In secular usage, *paideia* was used to denote a broad kind of education which embraced the ideals of the whole Greek culture. For Christians, nurturing children in the *paideia* of the Lord meant schooling them in all the traditions of the Christian faith, including the gospel, interpretations of Scripture, and the ethical teachings of Christ. Obviously, Christian parents will carry out this educational role only if they themselves have grasped the meaning of the Christian faith. For one does not teach what one does not understand.

In addition to serving as spiritual mentors for their own children, the adult members of a congregation have a much broader educational task. For they make the decisions and carry out the actions that shape the church's life. What younger members of the community of faith think of the church will be largely determined by the congregational climate created by adults.

If, in its budgeting, the church gives boldly and liberally to mission enterprises at home and abroad that will speak convincingly of the worldwide scope of God's purpose on earth. If the church acts generously to alleviate human suffering, as Jesus Himself did, the lesson will not be lost on its younger members. But if the congregation habitually squanders its resources on itself, Sunday School lessons about self-denial will take on a hollow ring. For this reason, every aspect of a church's life— every committee meeting, every business session—should be firmly rooted in an understanding of biblical revelation. And this will happen only in congregations where adult education flourishes.

A Vision

Today, the status of adult education in the church can best be described as "marginal." For even the most committed, it often amounts to no more than a forty-five-minute Sunday School session each week.

And the majority of adult church members are not that involved in learning endeavors.

But picture what might happen were churches to begin to take the task of adult education with absolute seriousness. Envision a congregation where every member is expected to be a lifelong student of the Scriptures, where teaching is regarded as being an integral part of parenting, and where men and women are continually engaged in the task of reinterpreting the meaning of their faith in a constantly changing environment. The vision is not unrealistic. With a reorientation of priorities, and with a serious effort to implement the best principles of adult education, churches could turn this vision into reality before the end of the present century.

Notes

1. George Gallup, Jr., and David Poling, *The Search for America's Faith* (Nashville: Abingdon Press, 1980), p. 42.

2. Ibid., p. 90*f.*

3. Ibid., p. 18.

4. Lucien E. Coleman, Jr., *Why the Church Must Teach* (Nashville: Broadman Press, 1984), p. 167.

5. Gallup and Poling, p. 47 *ff.*

6. Ibid., p. 17.

19

Using Technologies of Instruction in Adult Christian Education

R. Michael Harton

Few educators need to be convinced of the capability of adults to learn or of the need to provide quality learning experiences for them. The frustration comes when educators are faced with the diversity of adult learning needs and preferred styles of learning. The complexities of those needs and styles have been the subject of much past research, yet they continue to pervade the literature on adult education.

Whitkin[1], Kolb[2], and Messick[3] among others have shown how some adults prefer to work alone and require little feedback and interaction. Others prefer much interaction and require almost constant reinforcement to maintain confidence in their ability. Knowles[4] has continued to emphasize the need of adults to become self-directing in their learning. As adult learners discover their own ability to take control of their learning and their learning needs, facilitators must provide resources and guidance. Since motivation, rate of learning, and ability vary so widely, self-paced approaches make good sense.

This chapter will attempt to show how the use of some new technologies of instruction can improve adult Christian education in several ways. Motivation can be heightened, needs can be more specifically addressed, self-direction can be enhanced and, in general, more learning opportunities can be provided through a variety of approaches.

The point has been made more than once in this book that the church now has many competitors for adults' attention in the education marketplace. Collectively, private concerns, business and industry, and even communities spend billions annually to attract adults to their adult education openings. Courses and approaches are widely varied. It is not unusual for community education enterprises in metropolitan areas to offer more than one hundred courses per year. Lest churches think their offerings are different because of the nature of the content, they need to know they no longer have a corner on the religious market.

Training is a particular area of need for churches and church leaders.

Most churches do not have the paid staff to single-handedly do all the training that is needed. There are teachers, committee members and chairpersons, activity leaders, department directors, and a host of other leaders in organizations to be trained. In addition, all adult church members need ongoing education to be "equipped for the work of ministry." New members need to be oriented (trained) to function effectively as good church members. Many ills of the church have been attributed to its failure to provide adequate training and education for its members. Increasingly, adults are volunteering their time elsewhere besides the church, and one reason is that many community organizations provide better training for persons' responsibilities in community volunteer service. Also, many new church members are not "conserved" due to lack of training.

There is no single panacea, no "dehydrated/packaged" plan to meet these diverse needs. However, instructional technology offers educators of adults a means by which they can multiply their educational and training ministries, broker their expertise, and often provide learning experiences without their physical presence! Because they allow for the importation of that expertise through mediation, technologies of instruction also reduce the burden of the staff for being specialists in all fields.

Technology of instruction, simply put, is the application of our scientific knowledge about human learning to the teaching/learning setting. A technology of instruction, therefore, is the particular, systematic design of teaching/learning episodes in such a way as to apply our knowledge of how people learn in a predictable, effective manner so that specific learning objectives are accomplished.[5] Four applications of technologies of instruction will be described here: *programmed approaches, video, simulations/games,* and *computers.*

Programmed Materials

Programmed learning can generally be defined as a self-paced instructional approach which includes not only the content for learning but also accompanying learning activities that provide immediate feedback on accuracy of response. It is not a new approach, actually having its roots in the late 1950s and early sixties. Recent applications have been a vast improvement over those early attempts, however, The primary rationale for utilizing programmed and programmed-type materials is the major advantage of *not* requiring the constant presence of a trainer. Further, they are learner centered, a primary consideration especially in good adult Christian education. All of the approaches have in common these characteristics:

1. Objectives are stated in advance.
2. There is a set sequence of activities.
3. They depend largely on discovery learning.
4. They enable the effective management of instruction.
5. They are individualized in approach.

Programmed tutoring has the major advantage of utilizing trained monitors where trained tutors or content specialists are not available. Thus most anyone can be trained to utilize the materials with the learner because all that is required is the ability to read the materials and monitor the pace of instruction. It can include branching, a process managed by the tutor. *Branching* simply refers to alternative paths a learner may follow depending upon specific needs or upon responses to programmed assessments. Programmed tutoring would be particularly appropriate for potential leader training, involving persons who are getting an introduction to leader development. It could also be used in in-service training for teachers, committee chairpersons, or even for new members.

As a minister of education in a setting which required training many persons at one time without the aid of outside "experts," I was challenged to develop materials for programmed tutoring. Over several weeks I wrote programmed materials for each set of age-group workers using content largely from Southern Baptist Convention program resources. Branching was used so that those with more advanced knowledge could move ahead faster while those needing additional information could follow an appropriate path. The material called at various points for reading part of a chapter, viewing a filmstrip, or listening to a tape. At each of three training sessions more than fifty leaders were assembled at tables in the fellowship hall, divided by age division, and physically separated by low partitions. There was no way I could help everyone, nor did I need to. Assistant "tutors" were present with each group to facilitate the use of materials and guide progress through the programmed materials.

Three additional self-paced components were used in conjunction with these training labs. At the conclusion of the first session, learners were given a collection of articles clipped from several leadership periodicals. During the week, at home, they were to read each article and make a brief notation in the back of the notebook drawing some implications of the article for their area of responsibility. At the conclusion of the second and third sessions, they were given a programmed workbook, *Developing Skills for Bible Interpretation* and *Teaching Tips* (secured from the Baptist Sunday School Board). They worked through these at home during the week. The three self-paced labs plus the individual activities at home brought the total training hours to approximately ten, with only three sessions held at church—and there were no lectures!

Audio tutorial has some useful unique aspects. It does not stem from the same programmed instruction roots but has certain characteristics in common with those mentioned above. It includes a personal learning component but also utilizes both larger assembly sessions and small groups. This approach would be very useful with new church members and could extend their orientation beyond the usual four-to-six weeks through use of large- and small-group meetings. Lectures on church worship, films and filmstrips on the ordinances, and so forth could include the entire group with subsequent discussions or individual presentation is small groups. It also could be used effectively for preservice teacher training.

Adult participants might be given introductory materials to read or a workbook for individual study at home. At assigned times adults could come together to discuss their reading or for supplemental lectures, films, and so forth. Sometimes we waste our time and that of our constituents by holding a meeting to tell them things they could learn on their own given the appropriate resources. I suspect we would get a positive response from adults if we affirmed their ability to learn on their own and held meetings only for discussion of unique needs or aspects of a task.

Video

Video offers one of the most exciting present possibilities for instruction, both because of its versatility and the fact that many churches already have the equipment for taping worship services. The Federal Communication Commission has reserved 615 channels for noncommercial educational use, like those associated with the Public Broadcasting Service and many colleges and universities. (Some schools already broadcast courses over their own channel. Students take a course in their own dorm or apartment. What are possibilities in local church education?) BTN already offers an array of educational programs via video.

Video can be used for *practice teaching,* taping a teacher at work, then critiquing performance with the trainer. Good and bad examples of teaching, or of leading small groups, could be taped for use in discussions. This technology of instruction also offers two major advantages: experts can be imported via tape, saving the rising expense of travel, lodging, and so forth. Further, with the expert's permission, taped sessions can be saved for repeated use, either for persons unable to attend or for future educational activities.

Video in combination with other modes also offers exciting possibilities. One example is something being done on a broader scale (the Southern Baptist Convention level) but which could be done in a local church or by a group of churches. The Seminary External Education Division (SEED) in Nashville has already developed a series of telecourses in specific "off-campus" settings. These include a videotape of a content expert (the teacher for the course), a written study guide, collection of readings, and periodic phone conferences with the teacher. An added component which may be included will be an actual "face-to-face" dialogue with the teacher via video.

Simulations and Games

Simulations and games are catching on slowly, but will continue to be a viable tool for instruction as more adult educators become versed in their use. Simulations offer the opportunity for dealing with scaled-down real life or hypothetical situations in a safe and managed setting. They are particularly useful for helping adults develop human relations skills. They lend themselves well to examining "people problems" with the safe use of trial-and-error problem solving. Games have the benefit of making learning fun, but the user should be certain that the game does offer practice in the skills to be developed. Also, competition may not be appropriate in some setting. Lucien Coleman's *Teaching Styles* is a good example of an educational game as is *Harvest,* a retirement-planning game.

Both simulations and games are useful for examining life dilemmas, in planning and problem solving. They are useful for training leaders as well. For example, committee chairpersons might be given details of a problem requiring use of relational, problem-solving, and conflict-management skills. Time might be allowed for participants to actually work through the problem to a suitable solution.

Computers

A current exciting application of technologies to instruction is the use of *computers*. Two factors contribute to the readiness of this application: (1) the low cost of micro/personal computers, and (2) the developed and broadening market for record-keeping applications. Already several computer service firms exist for servicing churches in financial management, record keeping, and file manipulation.

To this point the instructional possibilities have been almost totally overlooked. However, software is being developed on a small scale for limited training applications in the church. We can expect this market to develop rapidly as educators and programmers get together to develop Computer Assisted Instruction (CAI) modules in Christian education.

Educational Application of Computers

Reasons why computers have not been seriously considered for enhancing education range from fear to ignorance to unfortunate past bad experience. Some people remember the early and dull application of programmed instruction which merely elicited correct responses. The computer is an interactive tool, however, and can be used effectively in problem solving and other learning tasks. Heinich, Molenda, and Russell have outlined the advantages of using computers in education.[6] Motivation for learning may be raised. Color, music, and animation add realism to exercises. High speed, personalized feedback is highly reinforcing. And a positive affective climate can be provided through the patient, personal confirmations of responses.

Computer Assisted Instruction (CAI) provides not just one but a variety of instructional modes applying some of the afore mentioned approaches.

1. *Tutorial.* Today's tutorial programs are much more attractive to learners than the teaching machines of the sixties. The use of graphics, color, and sound now add much more creative feedback to the programmed instruction approach via computer. Branching makes it possible to send the user in any one of several alternative directions, depending upon responses to questions. The computer may patiently review material related to incorrect responses or plunge the user deeper into the content. Committee chairpersons, for example, might bone up on the tasks and responsibilities of their committees and, at the same

time, sharpen skills for chairing a committee by means of a tutorial program.

Envision this scenario: a new adult leader (or an old one for that matter) of the boys' missions education group sits down at the terminal in the church's media center to work through a preprogrammed assessment of his current knowledge and skill in leading boys this age in this organization. Based on his responses, a menu appears with several options for improving his leadership ability. Resources are listed along with instructions for finding them. The screen on the monitor might look like this:

Resources to Help You Become
a Better Teacher of Adults
1. A list of printed materials in our Media Center.
2. A list of Regional Training Conferences.
3. A computer-based training module right here!
    Press the number of the above item you wish to see.
    Then press *enter.*

Pressing *1* would elicit a display of printed resources available in the library. Menu item *2* would call up information on upcoming conferences with dates, times, and places. Pressing *3* would start the leader on an individualized training adventure based on his previous assessment. Why not? The illustration could have been a committee chairperson, any other program leader, or an adult who simply wants some self-enrichment! It's all within the realm of possibility. A church's computer holds tremendous potential for training and education.

2. *Drill and Practice.* Similar to the tutorial, this mode reinforces learning through repetition and varied examples. Bible students might practice memory drills, the definition of biblical terms, location of New Testament events, and so forth.

3. *Discovery Mode.* Heinrich described this as an approach to inductive learning, appropriate for training in problem solving.[7] It might be used for training church school or other program directors to analyze their organizational structures and leadership requirements for various positions in the organization.

4. *Simulation.* I feel this is the most exciting CAI mode. Simulations, as discussed earlier, provide vicarious experience in handling real-life situations. I once sat spellbound at a Plato terminal working through a

simulation designed for training public-school teachers. It led me through the interview process, through involvement in the social life of the faculty (and accompanying relational implications), discussions on grading scales, handling disciplinary problems, and dealing with problem parents. Depending on my responses, I could be awarded either "Outstanding Teacher" or "Fink of the Year," and granted or denied tenure. Why not help department directors learn how to deal with leadership problems or make decisions concerning the quality of Bible study in the department through computer-based simulations? Members of the leader search committee could learn how to make successful enlistment visits through vicarious experiences with simulations depicting various effective/ineffective interviews. Computer simulations could be an effective and interesting tool for marriage enrichment. Couples could work together through various conflict and communication situations, discussing them as they go. The possibilities are almost limitless.

5. *Games.* Computer games can not only be fun but can be effective learning tools. Instructional Bible games are among the few software items available now to religious educators. Games might also be developed for training teachers, marriage enrichment, or even making financial decisions for the finance committee.

Current and Future Possibilities for the Computer

Several exciting current applications of computers have implications for possible uses in religious education. Many of them reach far beyond our conventional ideas of the basic keyboard and television monitor.

1. *Peripherals.* Through the addition of peripherals, persons with special disorders are aided through synthesized music, speech, and prerecorded messages. Persons with limited mobility may operate computers by voice command. Light pens can be used to indicate answers to questions and to trace figures displayed on the monitor. Physically handicapped persons may use computers with oversized, touch-activated keyboards, knee switches, and joysticks.

The modem is a particularly useful peripheral which enables the user to access computers and software at other locations. A phone number is dialed, then a password, then the telephone receiver is placed in the modem. Direct-connect modems are available now which do all the above automatically. This enables educators to "plug in" to networks or computer systems such as those discussed below.

2. *Networks.* It is perfectly within the realm of possibility for denominational agencies and offices to have a centrally located mainframe to which terminals in local churches and associations are connected via telephone wires. A variety of programmed courses could be available and accessed from a menu displayed on the local church's terminal. Plato is such a network which is used extensively by educational institutions and businesses alike. Plato (Programmed Logic for Automated Teaching Operations) was developed by Control Data Corporation and is a "time-share" system with terminals scattered throughout the country, all linked to a central computer at the University of Illinois. Through a cooperative endeavor of the seminaries and denominational publishing houses, such a system could be developed for Christian education.

Linking Computers with Other Technologies of Instruction

Technology which combines the computer and television in new and creative ways is already available. One of the newest technologies is the videodisc, which has been linked to the computer to produce interactive, individualized educational programs. Pribble describes this new technology in terms of its capability:

> Fast random access currently lets one jump to any segment of a disc in less than a second—and the video disc holds up to 54,000 single video frames per side, or up to 30 minutes moving imagery. Controlling this access is a microcomputer, which also displays text or graphics, asks questions, evaluates responses, commands video segments and determines how the program will "branch."[8]

Consider the following scenario as an example of the application of such a linkage. Department directors view a video scenario depicting a confrontation or situation requiring intervention (for example, a "human relations" problem). They then take a computer quiz, with instant branching depending on individual responses. This branching might include a reviewing of the situation, or go on to slightly change the situation for a different approach and subsequent quiz.

One advantage of such an approach is that the adult educator is relieved from being primarily a content specialist in order to become a resource person. Thus the educator can be more observant of learner behavior and even spend more time building relationships!

Some Issues and Potential Problems

A major problem with many technologies of instruction is that systems for the application and development of software are few. As is often the case, the farther one moves away from the ideological inception of the idea, the less philosophical base one finds. With the development of technologies and the accompanying marketing strategies there comes an increasing product orientation. This violates the process understanding of instructional technologies and makes them ends in themselves.

For example, hardware and "concepts" are being set in place, but as yet there is little consideration being given to the systematic development of instructional strategies. Educators must work with the technicians so that the technology not only works correctly but is *sound educationally.* The field is currently ripe for the development of software for both video and computers. The saying "technology often gives rise to institutions" will be truer here than in many other fields.

We may be tempted, for example, to buy or promote some intriguing hardware without the needed software or savvy to service it. Parenthetically in this regard, the task of seminary educators is twofold. First, they must prepare church staff personnel to make wise choices and be able to apply these technologies. Second, they must be the "prophetic voice" to their denomination to keep the horse in front of the cart in the development of both the hardware and software. So often materials are developed to feed a hungry piece of hardware bought because it was "in vogue." Technologies developed and applied should always be developed in response to *need,* and in accordance with proven instructional development procedures.

Conclusion

Difficulties and potential perils should not keep us from advancing beyond the horse and buggy stage into the "space age." This is not so much an indictment as a plea to local church *and* denominational leaders. Having been a minister of education working primarily with adults, this writer knows the pressures to program and promote which keep us from giving adequate attention to improving teaching/learning.

To expand our horizons we should consider using a broader realm of technologies of instruction to provide alternatives to traditional classroom attendance, for example, computer-assisted instruction, teleconferencing, programmed tutoring, video courses. They also can help us "flex up" traditional teaching/learning schedules so as to include late afternoon, evening, weekend, holidays, lunch hours, and so forth. The individualized nature of most of these technologies means adults may be able to do their learning according to *their* schedules, not just those of the staff.

Furthermore, while we should heed Naisbitt's "high tech/high touch" warning, we should not be frightened away by it. Technologies of instruction will always supplement, never supplant, human instruction and group process-oriented approaches to learning.

Notes

1. H. Whitkin, "Cognitive Styles in Academic Performance and in Teacher-Student Relations," *Individuality in Learning,* ed. Samuel Messick (San Francisco: Jossey-Bass, 1976).

2. David Kolb, *The Learning Styles Inventory: Technical Manual* (Boston: McBer, 1976).

3. Samuel Messick and Associates, *Individuality in Learning: Implications for Cognitive Styles and Creative Human Development* (San Francisco: Jossey-Bass, 1976).

4. Malcolm S. Knowles and Associates, *Andragogy in Action* (San Francisco: Jossey-Bass, Inc., 1984), p. 1-24.

5. Robert Heinich, Michael Molenda, and James Russell, *Instructional Media and the New Technologies of Instruction* (New York: John Wiley and Sons, 1982), p. 22.

6. Ibid., p. 317.

7. Ibid., p. 320.

8. D. G. Gueulette, *Microcomputers for Adult Learning: Potentials and Perils* (New York: Cambridge, 1982), p. 33.

20

What's Ahead in Adult Christian Education
Lucien E. Coleman

Saint Augustine described time as a threefold present—the present as we experience it, the past as a present memory, and the future as a present expectation. As I think about the shape of adult Christian education in the years ahead, I am particularly mindful of Augustine's third observation, that the future is nothing more than a hypothetical construct, firmly rooted in the present. In a real sense, the future of adult Christian education has already begun, for the future will be determined to a great extent by present decisions.

To illustrate, consider today's cities, shaped by a network of radial interstate highways. Compare a current map of one of these cities to a map made fifty years ago, and it becomes obvious that these new highways have already changed the configuration of the city, and probably will continue to shape its pattern of growth for some years to come. The important point is that the present pattern was cut when those highways were planned two or three decades ago.

The building-planning committee of a three-thousand-member suburban church decided ten years ago to construct a honeycomb of class-sized cubicles, rather than departmental areas, for adults. During the years following that decision, the church could never departmentize its adult Bible study program because its committee had opted for an archaic class-centered model of Adult Sunday School work. That committee didn't just plan a building; they determined the shape of the church's adult program for the foreseeable future.

You see, we don't merely predict the future, by making calculated guesses about things to come. We actually *create* the future on the basis of today's biases and presuppositions. In this sense, the future becomes self-fulfilling prophecy. It conforms to what we expect because our expectations shape what we do to determine the future. Thus, today's dreams often do become tomorrow's realities.

The future of adult education in our churches will be shaped, in part,

by our responses to three crucial questions: (1) Will adult Christian
education seek to transform persons, or reinforce conformity to predetermined norms? (2) Will adult Christian education discover the relationship between learning and experience? (3) Will adult Christian education
become truly andragogical? These questions are unavoidable. They must
be answered in one way or another. If our answers do not grow out of
thoughtful reflection, they will spring from uninformed practice.

Transformation or Conformity?

There are those who regard Christianity as primarily a set of propositional truths to be accepted, who see religious education as a tool for
reinforcing adherence to approved beliefs, and who look upon the clergy
as custodians of the authentic Word. When adult education in the church
rests upon these assumptions, conformity to established modes of
thought is prized and rewarded while creative exploration of the meaning
of faith tends to be feared and penalized. This pressure toward conformity can relate to institutional forms (for example, grouping practices,
scheduling, methodology) as well as to doctrinal tenets.

This mentality not only contradicts the essential character of adult
education; it is also antithetical to the very nature of Christianity. For,
as Ross Snyder has aptly written:

> The *Christian* religion is a *change* religion, whose essence is transforma-
> tion. . . . Thus, Christianity is mocked by merely individualistic forms, by
> conventional Christians who do not intend to risk or change or deeply
> relate to their fellow man.[1]

The Gospels substantiate Snyder's assessment of the Christian religion
over and over again. Consider, for example, the revealing dialogue between Jesus and the Pharisees and scribes in Matthew 15:1-9. It opens
with an accusing "gotcha" sort of question, the kind traditionalists of
every age love to ask: "Why do Your disciples transgress the tradition
of the elders?" Verse 6 gives the gist of Jesus' response: "For the sake
of your tradition, you have made void the word of God." He then quoted
the prophet Isaiah: "This people honors me with their lips,/but their
heart is far from me;/in vain do they worship me,/teaching as doctrines
the precepts of men" (v. 8, RSV).

Jesus was not opposed to tradition, per se. He made this clear when
He said, "Think not that I am come to abolish the law and the prophets;
I have come not to abolish them but to fulfil them" (Matt. 5:17, RSV).

What He rejected was the Pharisaical habit of deifying traditional interpretations, so as to leave no room for fresh, new insights into the mind of God.

Adult Christian education at its best is something more than the tedious transmission of words, no matter how "correct" those words are thought to be. Because, as Snyder has pointed out, words do not *contain* meaning; they *evoke it in the hearer.* As adults meet together in Bible study, open to the Holy Spirit and to one another, the printed words should become a living and active word, "discerning the thoughts and intentions of the heart" (Heb. 4:12). It should also become a shared word, as friends in Christ become channels of new understandings for one another.

John Milton spoke to the same issue from a different perspective when he delivered his famed "Areopagitica" before Parliament in 1644:

> Truth is compared in Scripture to a streaming fountain; if her waters flow not in a perpetual progression, they sicken into a muddy pool of conformity and tradition. A man may be a heretic in the truth; and if he believe things only because his Pastor says so, or the Assembly so determines, without knowing other reason, though his belief be true, yet the very truth he holds becomes his heresy.[2]

Neither Snyder nor Milton intended to deny the importance of communicating the durable truths of our faith. Rather, they were speaking of the dynamic nature of a faith which must be appropriated anew by every individual, assimilated into personal experience, and shared with others in the give-and-take of Christian dialogue.

Learning and Experience

Will adult education discover the relationship between learning and experience? Let it be acknowledged that this question has its flaws: First, it might be argued that all learning *is* experience. But I have in mind that arena of experience we sometimes call "everyday life," that world of existence in which men and women work, love, play, hurt, and relate to the physical and social environment. Second, it might be inappropriate to suggest that Christian adult educators have not discovered the relationship between learning and experience, since, after all, we do try to "apply the lesson to life" each Sunday. But there is reason to believe that adult Christian education, as we currently know it, is experience centered more in theory than in actuality.

For instance, think about the discontinuity between the adult learner's life experience and the Sunday School lesson on a typical Sunday morning. I once sat in a men's Bible class with a friend whose wife had left him that very week. The lesson had to do with the exploits of some ancient king of Israel; I forget which one. And, I daresay, he forgot, too.

Adults come to church with their thoughts clouded by the dark suspicion that their teenagers are on drugs, or that last week's biopsy will reveal malignant tissue. And the teacher describes the relationship between Babylonian ziggurats and the tower of Babel.

They come preoccupied with the plight of aging parents who seem no longer able to go it alone. And the class hears an exposition of that earthshaking question: "Was that *real* wine at the wedding feast in Cana?"

In contrast, researchers in adult education tell us that the majority of adult learning is motivated by life-related events. Aslanian and Brickell, for example, reported in 1980 that "half of all Americans 25 years and older (over 60 million adults) learned one or more topics in the past year," and "83 percent of the learners surveyed described some past, present, or future change in their lives as reasons to learn."[3]

How can adult education in the church become more life-centered? The answer does not call for curtailing systematic Bible study. Christians must develop a working knowledge of the textbook of their faith. What is needed is a far greater diversity of learning opportunities, centered in a variety of life experiences and personal interests.

Picture a coordinated program of small-group learning experiences sponsored by a local congregation, a "seminary in miniature": study and support groups for single parents, families of teenage drug users, propective retirees, heart and cancer patients, people coping with addictions to alcohol, tobacco, or food; seminars for professional people who want to use their vocational skills for Christ in meaningful ministries; workshops for parents who want to become better teachers of the faith at home.

In addition to such group studies, modern instructional technology now makes it possible for a church to sponsor a diversified program of do-it-yourself studies for individuals via audio cassettes, printed materials, videotapes, cable television, and computer-based learning modules. Such programs will require the services of persons trained to help adults assess their learning needs and access suitable learning resources.

Life-centered adult education implies, also, that learning opportunities must break out of their present spatial and temporal boundaries. We must break away from the mind-set that confines Christian learning activities to the church building on Sunday morning. Problems like poverty, child abuse, mental retardation, and the plight of homebound older persons can best be understood in their natural habitats—hospitals, detention centers, unemployment offices, and inner-city ghettos. And, with today's ready availability of transportation, increasing numbers of adults will be able to deepen understanding of the worldwide mission enterprise by engaging in short-term service on mission fields at home and abroad.

Andragogy or Pedagogy?

Will adult Christian education become truly andragogical? The reference is, of course, to the concept of adult education called "andragogy" by Malcolm Knowles (see part III, chapter 15). Knowles contrasts andragogy (adult educational practice) with "pedagogy" (education of children).

Pedagogy is based on the assumption that learners are passive, dependent, and relatively uninformed. Andragogy assumes that learners are capable of participating actively in their own learning experiences.

Pedagogy casts the teacher in the role of an authoritative presenter of information who exercises exclusive control of the learning situation. Andragogy sees the teacher as a "facilitator" whose primary function is to help learners identify and achieve their own learning goals.

Simple observation of what goes on in the typical adult Sunday School classroom today will suggest to the unbiased observer that adult Christian education still relies heavily upon the pedagogical model. This is unfortunate for at least three reasons.

First, it encourages passivity in men and women who already are far too prone to take a spectator approach to religious experience. Sitting and listening to a sermon each Sunday morning has become their supreme expression of religious duty; so, naturally, they adopt the same attitude in educational settings.

Second, it tends to turn study sessions into sterile recitations of prosaic information and propositional abstractions, rather than tapping the rich resources of personal experience shared by groups of adult learners.

Third, placing responsibility exclusively upon teachers, the pedagogical model robs the adult educational experience of the motivational power of personal involvement. As my wise mentor Allen Graves used to say, "No man is lazy, except in pursuit of another man's goals."

To be perfectly realistic, andragogical principles are difficult to implement. Andragogy requires a great deal of the learners. And many men and women, steeped in the casual passivity fostered by pedagogical education, find it difficult to take responsibility for their own learning. To succeed in the practice of andragogy, we must give a great deal more attention to the development of adult learning skills, rather than focusing exclusively on content.

"What's ahead in adult education?" I would not have the temerity to make predictions at this juncture in our history. But, perhaps a few of the ideas set forth in this discussion will stimulate visions, and perhaps those visions will become part of an agenda for the future.

Notes

1. Ross Snyder, "Group Theory and Christian Education, *An Introduction to Christian Education,* ed. Marvin J. Taylor (Nashville: Abingdon Press, 1966), p. 278.

2. John Milton, "Areopagitica," *Great Books of the Western World,* Vol. 32 ed. Robert M. Hutchens (Chicago: Encyclopaedia Britannica, Inc., 1952), p. 204.

3. Carol B. Aslanian and Henry M. Brickell, *Americans in Transition: Life Changes as Reasons for Adult Learning* (New York: College Entrance Examination Board, 1980), pp. 43,49.

21

The Minister to Adults
Jim Walter

"A few churches are now employing directors of adult work."[1] So wrote W. L. Howse in his book *The Church Staff and Its Work* published in 1959. Prophet as he was, Howse saw clearly the needs of Southern Baptist churches to make staff provision for this large age group in churches.

At present, nearly one hundred Southern Baptist churches employ on full or part-time basis a minister to adults. Many of them are the first staff member to occupy that position. The field has virtually exploded in the last decade as churches, pastors, and ministers of education have sensed the need to provide specialized help in the rapidly growing adult area. Howse indicated four reasons why the adult minister is needed:

1. The scope and power of adult work
2. The expanding adult program
3. The changing psychology of adulthood
4. The importance of home-church relationships

This chapter delineates the unique roles and relationships of the adult minister. It also focuses on the work responsibilities, training, and opportunities of this staff member. I believe that the work of the minister to adults is dependent in large measure on the person's thoughtful understanding of his or her role. So role and work concerns interrelate throughout this chapter.

Role Expectations of the Minister to Adults

When a church considers calling a minister to adults, various role concepts emerge, some incomplete, some faulty. Church members in such instances may ask: How does the adult ministry differ from the general church program? If these programs are identical, why do we need another staff member? What is the uniqueness of this staff position

301

which calls for specialization? Is this another associate pastor? Is he or she just like a youth director, but for adults? Would this person's responsibilities relate to weektime activities and not Sunday? These and other questions should receive close attention as churches venture into this area.

In many instances the minister of education or equivalent has had responsibility for the adult ministry prior to the arrival of the minister to adults. For this reason it is important to establish the new adult minister as an age-group staff member, not as an assistant educational director. The minister of adults directs the adult program to the same extent that youth ministers lead the youth programs. As an example, the adult minister leads in planning for the adult component of Preparation Week, January Bible Study, Christian Home Week, revival preparation, and stewardship promotion.

Job titles also reflect role expectations. Churches describe this minister as minister to adults, adult minister, pastor with adults, single adults, or senior adults, minister to adults, minister of adult education. And, with additional specialization, they might have the title of minister of single or senior adults. Some churches have combined this staff responsibility with music or youth or activities.

Role Concepts of the Adult Educator

Several leaders in the field of adult education describe the role of the administrator or adult educator. Among them Malcolm Knowles describes the function of the adult educator.

1. Helping the learners diagnose their needs for particular learnings within the scope of the given situation (the diagnostic function)
2. Planning with the learners a sequence of experiences that will produce the desired learnings (the planning function)
3. Creating the conditions that will cause the learners to want to learn (the motivational function)
4. Selecting the most effective method and techniques for producing the desired learnings (the methodological function)
5. Providing the human and material resources necessary to produce the desired learnings (the resource function)
6. Helping the learners measure the outcomes of the learning experiences (the evaluative function)

The function of the adult education administrator follows in somewhat parallel fashion.

1. Assessing the individual, institutional, and societal needs for adult learning relevant to their organizational settings (the diagnostic function)
2. Establishing and managing an organizational structure for the effective development and operation of an adult education program (the organizational function)
3. Formulating objectives to meet the assessed needs and designing a program of activities to achieve these objectives (the planning function)
4. Instituting and supervising those procedures required for the effective operation of a program, including recruiting and training leaders and teachers, managing facilities and adminstrative processes, recruiting students, financing and interpreting (the administrative function)
5. Assessing the effectiveness of the program (the evaluative function)[2]

When should a church consider emphasizing or calling an adult minister? Hazel Rodgers lists five circumstances when churches should consider adding an adult division director. They apply to a minister to adults as well.

1. When a church does not have a minister of education.
2. When a church has a minister of education who carries heavy administrative responsibilities.
3. When the number of adult departments reaches six or more.
4. When the number of adult departments is less than six, but most department directors are inexperienced and untrained.
5. When a church needs to strengthen significantly its Bible teaching and outreach for a particular segment of adulthood.

The Work of the Minister of Adults

In 1978 John Sisemore compiled a book, *The Ministry of Religious Education.* In this book Alva Parks authored a chapter entitled "The Minister of Adult Education." This chapter is the most recent publication I know of on the work of the minister to adults.

According to Parks, the need for this position emerged from the realization that ministers of education were increasingly involved in administration and correlation of age-group work. He quoted a letter from Clois Smith, former minister to adults at the Tallowood Baptist Church in Houston, Texas:

Churches are saying to me that they are finally recognized; they should have moved to the adult "specialist" long ago (even before any other age group). . . . We are recognizing the need for dividing adult responsibilities re: singles, young adults, and senior adults. We now have a singles minister. We're moving toward the senior minister. With 80 percent of all prospects in this age group, we must concentrate on adults more than we have previously.[3]

It is crucial that both the church and the minister to adults understand the role of this staff member. The past two decades have witnessed a resurgence of lay participation coinciding with an emphasis on the equipping ministry of pastors and church staff members. Ministers to adults figure significantly in this New Testament mandate.

When churches routinely or casually enter into the calling of an adult minister, they may reap disastrous results by not examining the role and philosophy of the adult ministry.

The minister of adult education is not the program. He should be the catalyst. . . . The philosophy of adult education must include provision of educational opportunities for all ages of adults—both saved and unsaved, active and inactive, and adults with usual and unusual needs. For example, there are adults who have spent their lives in the church while rearing their children. After the children leave home, some parents are ready for a "rest" from responsibility in the church. The minister of adult education faces a challenge as he seeks to meet the needs of these adults before their loss of interest in the church is permanent.[4]

A key ingredient in developing the ministry with adults (note: not *for* adults) is conviction about the strategic importance of adults in accomplishing the church's mission. The minister to adults should be an adult advocate.

Parks lists nine special groups which constitute only a portion of his work: singles, internationals and language groups, young adults away, deaf adults, handicapped adults, homebound adults, Sunday workers and shift workers, in-service members, and senior adults.[5]

Other potential groups include newlyweds, mentally retarded persons, church vocational volunteers, and college students.

No other age group staff member has as many role relationships as the adult minister. Parks lists eight possibilities: pastor, church staff, church program organization leaders, volunteers, Church Council members, deacons, church committees, and denominational workers.[6] Enlarging on this already-complex listing, I suggest some additional relationships.

The minister to adults should cultivate professional relationships with his peers in community adult education enterprises. This enables him to develop in the field and provides valuable referral sources. In a sense he would function as an adult education broker with other community adult education resources.

The adult ministry is multidimensional. That is, adults who are parents deserve a cooperative ministry between the parent and children's programs. A fertile field for exploration is joint program planning of parenthood-enrichment activities between the adult minister and children's and youth workers. Outreach activities and even intergenerational Christian education programs are two other areas in which the adult minister can plan programs with children and youth leaders.

The adult minister has special relationships at certain times during the church year. These include stewardship promotion, enlistment of other age group workers and revival preparation.

Three metaphors are useful in describing functional relationships of the adult minister: *pilgrim, pioneer,* and *settler.*

All workers with adults readily admit that this age group is maturing rather than mature, growing rather than grown. Since this is a church ministry *with,* rather than *for* adults, this minister can feel comfortable walking alongside them, rather than in front or behind. The pilgrim metaphor describes the adult journey. It implies the destination of maturity. It dispels the notion of perpetual stagnation in the adult years. Ministers to adults must develop the capacity to see adults as persons in process of becoming. As strange as it may seem, many adults need someone to give them permission to grow. In word and deed adult leaders must say a positive yes to the question, Is there life after youth?

The pioneer metaphor also fits the adult minister. The 1980s are the first decade for vocational adult ministers. There is excitement in exploring virgin territory. In this spirit the work is experimental. The textbooks are being written in this decade. Churches are responding to the obvious demographic trends. The field is growing in depth and scope. New research data in adult religious education is promising. The adult minister is a pioneer.

In contrast to the pioneer, he or she is also one who assimilates gains, a settler. Some adult ministers describe themselves as vocationally committed to this ministry as a lifetime calling. The needs of Christian adults deserve a lifetime commitment. Unreached adults call for long-range plans for evangelism. Adults may move more slowly than other age groups, but they move ahead with measured steps. In contrast to the actual needs of adults, most church efforts on the whole have been largely cosmetic and organizational. Developing depth in discipleship is an awesome New Testament challenge. The adult minister is a settler.

The Minister to Adults as a Leader

The minister to adults is a leader among leaders. Perhaps the most demanding and rewarding leadership responsibility is with department directors in Sunday School. Ministers to adults should meet regularly with directors for planning. Sometimes this is prior to the weekly workers meeting. At other times, this is on Sunday morning during the class sessions. These ministers can exercise their equipping ministry most effectively when Sunday School leaders plan regularly not only for Bible study but for outreach activities as well. Regular unit preview studies offer an additional planning experience. Other possible planning opportunities include quarterly workshops and annual retreats. The agenda for those meetings may include goal setting, evaluation, examining of the Adult Sunday School Standard, and long-range planning. The minister to adults should also lead in developing and strengthening other Sunday School ministries such as week-time activities, homebound ministries, outreach Bible study, and Adult Vacation Bible School.

Class leader enlistment, training, and election is a constant feature of the work of an adult minister. Class leaders are not as obvious as department leaders and teachers. However, the development of their work may be the finest tribute to the long-range effectiveness of ministers of adults.

Another avenue for leadership training is the church library. Adult education books, pamphlets, audiovisuals, and other media provide a bonus leadership training resource. Further training experiences valuable for adult leaders include various denominational workshops.

The church looks to the minister to adults in organizing Sunday School units, discipleship training, and mission study and action groups. Much advanced planning is obviously needed in this effort. However, the long-range results of this are well worth the effort.

The minister to adults is a growth agent. Using a variety of tools he helps to focus leader's and member's attention on the priority of reaching unsaved and unreached adults. No other task supersedes this. The finest teaching method is a personal example. The minister to adults assumes personal responsibility for enlisting and winning adults. His work with volunteer leaders cannot substitute for personal witnessing. Leaders and members should receive regular invitations from the adult ministers to accompany him in visitation. These outreach efforts are ideally suited for training and motivating leaders in witnessing as well as in offering fellowship. "Our challenge is to win the world, not to re-sort the converts."[7]

Adults need to develop personal relationships through fellowship activities. Meeting these needs means more than scheduling socials and fellowships. It relates to the minister to adults' leadership style, as an open, caring, and responsive person. It means ensuring that genuine closeness occurs between persons during socials and fellowships. The minister to adults should be sensitive to this powerful adult need and seek to plan Christian fellowship activities and encourage other leaders to do as well.

If the church does not have a minister of recreation, the minister to adults assists in developing this ministry. Much can be accomplished in adult recreation even without an activity building. A recreational ministry with adults is multifaceted and deserves attention from the minister of adults.

Program correlation and coordination occupy considerable time for a minister to adults. Of course, this means more than calendar coordination. Sometimes adult leaders unintentionally compete with one another. Program correlation is more complex in the adult area because individual units make their own plans and each program organization also has its own goals. These factors mean the minister to adults must be the person who can make fair decisions and envision programming needs months and even years ahead.

There is enormous potential in churches for mission study, prayer support, and mission service. More than likely, adult ministers presently do not relate to the missions tasks through the adult missions programs. There are many ways in which the minister to adults can lend support to missions. For instance, in recent years, churches have sent adults on short-term mission trips and involved men and women in lay renewal activities.

Some churches sponsor prayer retreats and other church-wide mission projects. "Mission action is defined as *the organized effort of a church to minister and witness to persons of special need or circumstance who are not members of the church or its programs.*"[8] Mission action groups have great potential for harnessing adult aspirations to be involved with persons in need.

Churches should look to the minister to adults to plan and conduct family life programs. It is quite apparent that these programs demand astute vision and careful planning. Obviously, these programs should seek to meet crisis needs of adults, but they should also focus on growth avenues as well. As this field matures in the churches, adult ministers will be called on to devise a wide variety of family life education programs.

Job Descriptions of Adult Ministers

Church leaders should welcome carefully prepared job descriptions. They are mutually beneficial for the prospective adult minister as well as his supervisor and the church personnel committee.

First let's examine the work of the adult division director in Sunday School.

The leader of an Adult Division is the Adult Division director. This position is necessary when a Sunday School has multiple adult departments, and there is a need for administrative assistance in correlating the work of adults with other age divisions.

The Adult Division director is responsible to the Sunday School director for coordinating the work of the Adult Division. When there is a division director, he or she normally represents the Adult work on the Sunday School Council.

The specific duties of the Adult Division director are as follows:
Coordinate the total work of the Adult Division.
Represent adults on the Sunday School Council.
Plan training opportunities for Adult leaders.
Lead in the selection of curriculum materials and resources for adults.
Lead in setting up the appropriate organization for adults, being alert to the need for new classes and departments.
Assist the general outreach director, department and class outreach leaders in locating and assigning prospects.
Assist the church nominating committee in discovering and enlisting leaders for departments and classes.
Assist Adult department directors in conducting meaningful weekly workers' meetings.
Communicate information about the total Sunday School, the church, and the denomination to Adult department directors.[9]

Hazel Rodgers contributed significantly to this rapidly developing field. She lists eight responsibilities of the Adult division director.[10]

1. Guide adult department directors in preparing and maintaining adequate organization.
2. Assist in the selection and enlistment of leaders.
3. Consult with department officers and teachers and the director of teaching improvement and training for the Sunday School about the choice of curriculum.
4. Counsel with department directors concerning space and equipment.
5. Help department directors strengthen the department planning meetings.
6. Coordinate and/or initiate activities related to more than one adult department.
7. Serve as a resource person in offering suggestions for improvement in Adult Sunday School work.
8. Represent the Adult Division on the Sunday School Council.

Job Description:

Minister to Adult

I. Principle Function:

The minister to adults is responsible to the minister of education and ultimately to the pastor for planning, conducting, and evaluating the educational, outreach, and family ministries for and by adults.

II. Working Relationships

A. Responsible directly to the minister of education.
B. Work cooperatively with the minister of music in music activities of adults.
C. Work cooperatively with other age-group ministers in projects and activities related to their division.
D. Supervise any full- or part-time staff members selected to assist in the adult education program.
E. In the absence of the minister of education assume responsibilities as delegated.
F. Give such direction as necessary to secretaries.

III. Regular Responsibilities

A. Develop a growth mentality among all adult leaders.
B. Coordinate church program organizations for adults.
C. Enlist department leaders and assist them in planning thier work.

D. Develop and conduct publicity and promotion of adult activities.

E. Working with adult leaders, develop goals for the Adult Division.

F. Lead workers and members in consistant, effective evangelism.

G. Keep abreast of current developments in adult education and development.

H. Prepare annual budget for the Adult Division; maintain budget.

I. Encourage expansion of adult organization to reach more persons.

J. Coordinate activities of the Adult Division in special emphases such as stewardship, education and promotion, Vacation Bible School, training events, and Christian Home Week.

L. Develop new and varied programs of worship, ministry, witnessing study, and recreation that appeal to adults.

M. Recommend needs of space, materials, and policies to enhance the work of the division.

N. Coordinate use of facilities for adults.

O. Keep abreast of new materials, procedures, and educational methods.

P. Develop a program of leadership development.

Q. Encourage departments to reach the Adult Sunday School Standard.

R. Attend conferences and seminars to develop skills in adult Christian education.

S. Conduct personal counseling, weddings, hospital visitation, funerals as required.

Notes

1. W. L. Howse, *The Church Staff and Its Work* (Nashville: Broadman Press, 1959), p. 25.

2. Malcolm Knowles, *The Modern Practice of Adult Education* (Chicago: Association Press, 1980), pp. 26-27.

3. John T. Sisemore, *The Ministry of Religious Education* (Nashville: Broadman Press, 1978), p. 178.

4. Ibid., p. 179.

5. Ibid., pp. 180-181.

6. Ibid., pp. 182-184.

7. Robert E. Bingham and Ernest Loessner, *Serving With The Saints* (Nashville: Broadman Press, 1970).

8. John Sisemore, *The Ministry of Religious Education* (Nashville: Broadman Press, 1978), p. 103.

9. Larry Shotwell, *Basic Adult Sunday School Work* (Nashville: Convention Press, 1980), pp. 83-84.

10. Hazel Rodgers, *The Adult Division Director in the Sunday School* (Dallas: Sunday School Division, Baptist General Convention of Texas, n.d.) pp. 5-9.

Index